The Nature Company Guides

SHARKS & RAYS

The Nature Company Guides

SHARKS & RAYS

TIMOTHY C. TRICAS, KEVIN DEACON,
PETER LAST, JOHN E. MCCOSKER,
TERENCE I. WALKER, LEIGHTON TAYLOR

CONSULTANT EDITOR
LEIGHTON TAYLOR

THE
NATURE
COMPANY

TIME
LIFE
BOOKS

The Nature Company Guides are published by Time-Life Books

Conceived and produced by Weldon Owen Pty Limited
43 Victoria Street, McMahons Point, NSW, 2060, Australia
A member of the Weldon Owen Group of Companies
Sydney • San Francisco
Copyright 1997 © US Weldon Owen Inc.
Copyright 1997 © Weldon Owen Pty Limited

The Nature Company owes its vision to the world's great naturalists:
Charles Darwin, Henry David Thoreau, John Muir, David Brower,
Rachel Carson, Jacques Cousteau, and many others.
Through their inspiration, we are dedicated to providing products and
experiences which encourage the joyous observation, understanding, and
appreciation of nature. We do not advocate, and will not allow to be sold in
our stores, any products that result from the killing of wild animals for trophy
purposes. Seashells, butterflies, furs, and mounted animal specimens fall into
this category. Our goal is to provide you with products, insights, and
experiences which kindle your own sense of wonder and help you to feel
good about the world in which you live.
For a copy of The Nature Company mail-order catalog, or to learn the
location of the store nearest you, please call 1-800-227-1114.

THE NATURE COMPANY
Priscilla Wrubel, Ed Strobin, Steve Manning,
Georganne Papac, Tracy Fortini

TIME LIFE CUSTOM PUBLISHING
Time-Life Books is a division of Time Life Inc.
Time-Life is a trademark of Time Warner Inc. U.S.A.

VICE PRESIDENT AND PUBLISHER: Terry Newell
EDITORIAL DIRECTOR: Donia A. Steele
DIRECTOR OF NEW PRODUCT DEVELOPMENT: Quentin McAndrew
VICE PRESIDENT OF SALES AND MARKETING: Neil Levin
DIRECTOR OF FINANCIAL OPERATIONS: J. Brian Birky

THE NATURE COMPANY GUIDES
PUBLISHER: Sheena Coupe
ASSOCIATE PUBLISHER: Lynn Humphries
PROJECT EDITORS: Helen Bateman, Bronwyn Sweeney
COPY EDITOR: Lynn Cole
EDITORIAL ASSISTANTS: Edan Corkill, Miriam Coupe,
Vesna Radojcic, Shona Ritchie
DESIGNERS: Clive Collins, Kylie Mulquin, Mark Thacker
JACKET DESIGN: John Bull
PICTURE RESEARCH: Annette Crueger
ILLUSTRATIONS: Martin Camm, Gino Hasler, Ngaire Sales,
Roger Swainston, Genevieve Wallace
PRODUCTION MANAGER: Caroline Webber
PRODUCTION ASSISTANT: Kylie Lawson
VICE PRESIDENT INTERNATIONAL SALES: Stuart Laurence
COEDITIONS DIRECTOR: Derek Barton

Library of Congress Cataloging–in–Publication Data
Sharks and rays/Leighton Robert Taylor, Jr. ... [et al.],
p. cm. — (Nature Company guides)
Includes index.
ISBN 0–7835–4940–7
1. Sharks. 2. Rays (Fishes) 3. Sharks—Identification.
4. Rays (Fishes)—Identification.
I. Taylor, L. R. (Leighton R.) II. Series: Nature Company guide.
QL638.9.S47 1997   97–10718
597.3—dc21   CIP

Color Reproduction by Mandarin Offset, Hong Kong
Printed by Leefung-Asco Printers
Printed in China

A Weldon Owen Production

If there is magic on this planet, it is contained in water …
Its substance reaches everywhere; it touches the past and
prepares the future; it moves under the poles and wanders
thinly in the heights of air. It can assume forms of
exquisite perfection in a snowflake, or strip the living to a
single shining bone cast upon the sea.

The Immense Journey,
LOREN EISELEY (1907–77), American anthropologist and writer

CONTENTS

FOREWORD

The Nature Company began in 1973, practically in the Dark Ages of our understandings of the complexity and infinite beauty of life in the oceans of our planet. It was a time when environmental groups around the world were called to action to save the whales.

Jacques Cousteau was bringing underwater photography into our living rooms, stressing the beauty and fragility of this water world. We've grown up together with the TV documentaries and the explosion of information about the creatures who live in the deep.

As we learn to understand and appreciate this intricate web of life, it's my hope that we can turn the same volume of energy that went into protecting the great sea mammals, into a profound stewardship of preserving the complex web of life in the oceans of the world.

Over the past 25 years we have been able to change peoples' perceptions of whales from monsters of the deep that wreaked havoc on whaling ships into intelligent, multifaceted creatures with complex songs, age-old migratory patterns and family structures. Now is our chance to elevate and expand our vision of sharks from demon-like characters in movies and cartoons to interesting and powerful creatures who have survived from Earth's earliest history to dominate a most vital niche in the oceans of our "Water Planet."

PRISCILLA WRUBEL
Founder, The Nature Company

INTRODUCTION

When asked in 1979 by underwater cinematographer Al Giddings "what is the most exciting dive yet to be made by a marine biologist?", I replied without hesitation, "to be in the water with great white sharks." Little did I realize what soon would follow. Scientists Tim Tricas and Leighton Taylor joined me in a number of early dives with great whites. Nowadays, a growing coterie of amateur and professional shark watchers comb the globe for adventures with cartilaginous fishes.

Those cage-rattling and awe-inspiring experiences are now rivaled by seeing hand-sized deep-sea sharks aglow in the gloom from the window of a submersible and coming face to face with a huge manta ray or whale shark.

In my lifetime, a sea change has occurred in peoples' attitudes about our selachian cousins, namely that they are no longer to be feared, but rather to be respected, appreciated, and marveled at. Our kind now understands the insignificant risk but significant benefit that their kind provides to us, to ocean ecosystems, and the other species that depend on them. Even potentially dangerous species, such as great whites and tigers, are more valuable to us alive than dead because of their role as top-level carnivores. The senseless shark slaughters and wasteful finning that would have been applauded in the past are now deplored by an enlightened public. It is my hope that this guide will inspire all of its users to better understand, respect, and enjoy their cartilaginous relatives.

JOHN E. MCCOSKER
Senior Scientist, California Academy of Sciences

... *A dark*

Illimitable ocean without bound,

Without dimension, where length, breadth, and highth

And time and place are lost.

Paradise Lost,
MILTON (1608–74), English poet

CHAPTER ONE

UNDERSTANDING SHARKS *and* RAYS

THE FASCINATING WORLD *of* SHARKS *and* RAYS

Sharks and rays touch the lives of nearly all organisms that live in their seemingly inhospitable marine environment.

From the perspective of a land-dwelling human, the world's oceans represent an intimidating, hostile, enigmatic environment. Our terrestrial habitats are dwarfed by the oceans, which cover more than three times as much surface area.

The seas are a diverse three-dimensional environment, ranging from the warm, sunlit shallows of tropical reefs to near-freezing waters of abyssal trenches. Laden with salty minerals that sting our eyes and make the water undrinkable, the oceans are quite unlike our clear, gaseous atmosphere. They are often clouded by silt or microscopic plankton, which can reduce visibility to only a few feet. So it is not surprising that humans find it an inhospitable habitat.

WATERY WORLD

Suspended in this alien world are the fishes, the most successful group of vertebrates in Earth's history. Estimates put their numbers at more than 25,000 living species, and for many, there is a rich fossil record from which we can trace their evolution.

Within the group is a wide array of relatively recently evolved bony fishes that inhabit nearly every aquatic environment on Earth. For example, herbivorous parrotfishes and surgeonfishes harvest microscopic algae on tropical coral reefs, while large tunas and billfishes cruise the open oceans where they feed on small fishes and squid.

But the lives of each of these species are touched by a unique group of boneless fishes known as the sharks and rays, which can compete directly with them for food resources, or in many cases prey directly upon them.

The elasmobranch fishes consist of about 800 species of living shark, ray, and skate. Unlike the skeletons of their bony cousins, the body frames of elasmobranchs are composed primarily of cartilage, a light and flexible support material. Most of their fossil

LITTLE CHANGED *A fossil ray (above) (Cyclobatis longicaudatus) from the Cretaceous, and an early Permian shark fossil (left) (Orthacanthus senckenbergianus), share features with descendants such as the whale shark (below left).*

record comes from a few calcified body parts, such as teeth, spines, or vertebrae. Occasionally, whole fossilized skeletons, formed under fortuitous geological conditions, provide a glimpse of their evolution between ancestor and modern form. Today, paleontologists believe the direct descendants of modern sharks date back more than 400 million years.

DESIGN ELEGANCE

Their long evolutionary history and lack of bone can give the false impression that sharks and rays are primitive animals. On the contrary, the elasmobranch fishes, thought to have descended from bony ancestors, show remarkable adaptations for a successful life in nearly all marine communities. Most living species have a protrusible upper jaw and specialized dentition that make them very proficient predators. The sensory system is extremely well developed, and the brain is large.

The reproductive system and behaviors are often highly specialized, and in many ways

are more similar to birds and mammals than to the other fishes. These characteristics have made the sharks and rays successful organisms in a diversity of marine habitats.

THE RAYS

Closely related to sharks, rays (also known as batoids) fill many ecological niches. They are thought to be a sister group of the sawsharks, and

are represented by more than 450 species. Some batoids, such as guitarfishes, skates, and electric rays, have well-developed dorsal and caudal fins, and strong tails. Others, such as the stingrays, eagle rays, and devilrays, have greatly reduced tails that usually have only a rudimentary caudal fin, if any. These fishes range in size from small bottom-dwelling stingarees that may be only the size of a human hand, to the massive manta rays that swim in the open ocean and are more than 20 feet (6 m) in wingspan.

They are found in nearly all marine habitats and are also common in many estuaries, freshwater rivers, and lakes. While most skates and rays eat invertebrates that live in soft sediments, some butterfly rays feed only on small fishes, and many mantas feed primarily on plankton. Much remains to be learned about the behavior and biology of these most remarkable fishes.

SHARKS AND HUMANS

Even in today's world most people are under the impression that sharks live in a secretive environment far removed from our daily lives. In reality, humans and sharks have major interactions with sometimes dire consequences for these fishes. In the early part of this century, sharks and rays supported small regional fisheries in many parts of the world. However, the recent human population explosion and improved fishing technologies have resulted in the massive harvesting of sharks and rays around the world. In addition to their food value, there is now a major international market for fins, especially those of the shortfin mako shark pictured above, which are used to make shark fin soup. There is a smaller market for cartilaginous shark skeletons used in health-food remedies. While many shark stocks have recently suffered a serious decline in numbers, some countries are starting to regulate shark harvests in the hope of maintaining a sustainable shark fishery. Individual, national, and international cooperation are necessary to ensure the shark's survival.

THE OCEANS—THEIR HABITAT

The lives of the sharks and rays are shaped by the nature of the diverse habitats in which they occur.

In many ways, the ocean world of sharks and rays is stable, predictable, and forgiving. The fluctuation in daily temperature is low in most habitats, mainly because there is so much water. Mass movement is usually caused by slow wind-driven currents or coastal upwellings, which make relatively minor change.

Atmospheric storms cause destructive physical disturbances, but these are usually limited to the upper few yards of the water column, and can be avoided by short vertical migrations. The photoperiod of shallow-water species is set by the movements of the Sun and phases of the Moon. Many deep-dwelling species live in constant darkness while others are surrounded periodically by low levels of light.

Despite the ocean's many amenable features, it also imposes some unique challenges. Unlike the Earth's gaseous atmosphere, water presents a very dense environment and calls for an efficient power engine and hydrodynamic design to produce rapid movements during swimming. The high salt content of the oceans constantly removes water from the soft body tissues, and requires efficient water barriers and physiological mechanisms to replace it.

Compared to air, the oceans have a relatively low oxygen content, so ingenious oxygen-extraction factories have evolved in the gills. Relatively low visibility in the marine environment has resulted in many specializations of the eye, and the evolution of specialized sensory organs.

DIFFERENT HABITATS

Many habitats are recognized in the world's oceans, with distinct boundaries for the different species of shark and ray. On a horizontal scale, habitats can be distinguished as coastal and open water. In the higher latitudes, intertidal and coastal-reef habitats are composed largely of rock and rubble substrates, on which grow vast beds of macroalgae that present habitats for small fish prey and invertebrates.

Vast stands of kelp forests stretch along the shores of many temperate coastlines, where they provide a good habitat for food items and shelter. In tropical regions, living corals and coraline algae build calcium carbonate reefs that support a high density of invertebrate and fish organisms. Between these reef areas of most seas are found stretches of beaches that support a rich variety of sand-dwelling

HOME GROUNDS *The megamouth shark (above) inhabits the mesopelagic zone to great depths and is rarely seen. The whitetip reef shark (right), on the other hand, is easily sighted in the coral environment that suits its way of life.*

worms, mollusks, crustaceans, and small fishes.

Also adjacent to many temperate and tropical reef areas are sea-grass beds, which may cover the sandy bottom. These harbor a rich diversity of organisms. The productive waters of back bays and inland estuaries provide rich food resources for sharks and rays, and also important habitats for mating, pupping, and nursery grounds for their young.

CONTINENTAL SHELVES

The coastal regions of major landmasses and islands are usually surrounded by a shallow submarine shelf made primarily of sediments and rocky outcroppings. These can extend many miles seaward and hundreds of feet deep. These regions are usually inhabited by large populations of numerous species of shark, ray, and skate. At its most seaward extent, the shelf usually breaks to a descending slope, which on the upper reaches attracts large elasmobranch populations that decline in numbers with increasing depth.

Pelagic waters differ from other marine habitats by being separate from the bottom and therefore have little habitat diversity. The epipelagic zone, which begins near shore and extends out to the open oceans, ranges from the surface to about 330 feet (100 m) deep.

This zone receives abundant sunlight, which in near-shore areas with nutrient upwellings supports a rich supply of phytoplankton, zooplankton, and small

TAKING COVER *A juvenile lemon shark (above) is a common sight in shallow mangrove swamps, especially those near tropical reefs. The Pacific electric ray (below) seeks the cover of a kelp forest for its foraging expeditions.*

planktivorous fishes. Many species of shark and ray take advantage of these highly productive waters for their food resources. In the nutrient-poor epipelagic waters far out to sea, only a few species of shark and perhaps only one ray are found.

GOING DEEPER

Below the productive surface waters is the mesopelagic zone, where daytime light levels fade into darkness and cannot support phytoplankton populations. This extends down to about 3,300 feet (1,000 m) and is characterized by a decline in oxygen and nutrient levels, and water

temperature, which makes this a relatively inhospitable environment. As a result, many of the invertebrates and small fishes that inhabit this region make daily migrations (usually at night) up into the epipelagic zone to feed. This includes many species of small sharks and a few pelagic rays that prey on small fishes, crustaceans, and cephalopods near the surface.

AND DEEPER

The bathypelagic zone extends from below the mesopelagic to the ocean floor. This habitat is populated by relatively few organisms adapted for a slow, dark, cold life. Although many species of shark are collected at depths below 3,300 feet (1,000 m), few could live exclusively in this area because of lack of food. More deep-water sharks and skates are found near the bottom, especially below the mesopelagic zone. Here sharks feed on bottom dwellers and mesopelagic fishes that venture close to the bottom. There is also a considerable invertebrate community, which provides food for many species of skate.

MYTHS *and* LEGENDS

For many years humans have viewed sharks and rays as mysterious villains;

only today are we able to begin to dispel such myths.

For thousands of years, the natural behavior and nature of sharks and rays were shrouded in mystery by their inaccessible environment. Until recently, most information came from untrained observers who provided only brief glimpses and often biased interpretations. With the advent of scuba and other technologies, humans are now able to observe these animals directly for prolonged periods in their natural environment.

Today's sharks have inherited an unflattering and unjustified reputation that crosses many human cultures. Records of aggressive interactions between sharks and humans

in the Western world can be traced back to the ancient Greeks, but they are conspicuously absent in Egyptian history. Many descriptions record the shark's fearsome nature. Herodotus recorded attacks by sharks on shipwrecked Persian sailors in about 500 BC. Around AD 50, Pliny the Elder wrote about the shark hazard to Mediterranean sponge divers. Today, many scholars believe that the word "shark" is derived from the German word *schurke*, meaning villain or scoundrel.

Sharks and rays usually appear in cultures that have strong ties to the ocean. Some beliefs are more superstition than fact, while others are integral to cultural mores or religion. In eastern Africa, boat builders anoint a new hull with oil extracted from hammerhead sharks, which is thought to bring good fortune to its seafaring crew. Many fishers in the Mediterranean believe that if a thresher shark crosses the bow of a boat, bad luck will follow. A similar belief is held by many Japanese fishers. Chinese myths tell of a god that takes the form of a shark to scare its believers. Chinese pearl divers respected and avoided the shark as the vicious guardian of the pearls.

Perhaps the best recorded shark legends come from the Pacific cultures of Polynesia.

SEA MONSTERS *The "wonderful fish" (above) captured off Maine, USA, in 1836, was really a basking shark. The illustrator interpreted the claspers as webbed feet. A sixteenth-century French woodcut of a sea monster (right).*

The Hawaiians recognized individual species of shark, collectively called *mano*, by giving them specific names, such as *kihikihi* for the hammerhead sharks, and *niuhi* for those that killed humans, such as the tiger shark. There was a great reverence for sharks among these people. A deceased member of a family could return in the form of a shark.

The reincarnated person became a guardian, or *aumakua*, of its relatives and protected them and their resources on the reef. Sharks were believed to be capable of emerging from the sea as "shark men," or *mano kanaka*, and tricking swimmers or fishers by asking their destination so that they could later devour them.

THE LORE OF RAYS

The sting of the rays also holds a prominent place in Greek and Roman myths. To kill his father, Odysseus (Ulysses), Telegonus tipped his spear with a large stingray spine. Pliny tells of the sting's remarkable ability to kill trees, and also to pierce armor with the strength of steel.

Contrary to some tales, the stingray cannot shoot the spine from its tail into its victims; the spine is thrust in during direct contact. Stings are almost always the result of stepping on an unseen animal, or of handling a threatened or wounded ray. But the stingray spine was used by natives in many Pacific islands, Australia, and Central America as part of their weaponry.

CONTROVERSY

Even today, it is easy to find examples of honest misinterpretations of the truth.

CULTURAL MORES

In Hawaiian belief, all sharks (even the human-eating tiger shark [left]) are accorded respect in legend, religion, and daily life. The spines of southern stingrays (below) were believed to be able to kill plants and trees. They were often used to make weapons.

In the fall of 1808, a large sea monster was washed up on the Isle of Stronsa in the northernmost British Isles. It was measured and described by a number of quite reputable individuals as a sea snake that was 55 feet (17 m) long and about 4 feet (1.2 m) thick. It had a mane like a horse and six separate feet.

The possibility of it being a whale was quickly discounted because it had a long thin neck and tail. A detailed analysis of its skull, neck, shoulders, paws, and toes was made. After considerable inquisition by the local authorities, it was decided that the Stronsa beast was not a hoax, and in 1811 a paper was published on the find, and a new genus *Halsydrus* (sea-water snake) was noted.

The following year, the paper was noticed by Everard Home, a London physician and naturalist. Home had studied the local sharks and realized from the description that the Stronsa beast was really the carcass of a large basking shark (*Cetorhinus maximus*, then known as *Squalus maximus*). He thought that the "mane" was probably the fibers of the fins, and that the third pair of "feet" were probably the claspers.

For more than a century, scientists disagreed on the nature of the beast. The controversy was finally put to rest in 1933, when Professor James Ritchie, of the Royal Scottish Museum, published a paper supporting Home's conclusion and showing that the vertebral centrum exactly matched that of the basking shark.

WHAT IS *a* SHARK?

Sharks share most of the general features of the other fishes,

but are distinguished by some unique characteristics.

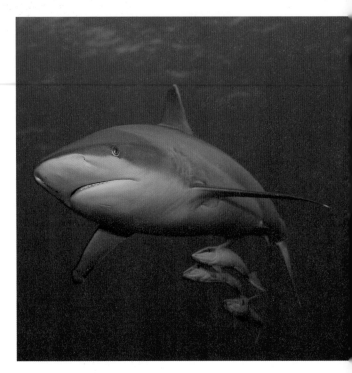

Sharks comprise only about 1 percent of all living fishes, and share nearly all the major features of their finned relatives. Like all fishes, sharks use gills to extract oxygen from the water in which they live. The body of most species is designed for hydrodynamic efficiency and usually has three types of unpaired fins (dorsal, anal and caudal) and two sets of paired fins (pelvic and pectoral).

Swimming is achieved by side-to-side undulations of the tail, which creates forward propulsion. The vertebral column, or backbone, is composed of a series of individual vertebrae held together by connective tissue, cartilage and surrounding tissues. Sharks also share with other fishes nearly all the same general features of their internal anatomy, including circulatory, digestive, reproductive and nervous systems.

But there are a number of features that separate the elasmobranchs from the other fishes. Externally, all of the shark's five to seven gill slits are visible, while the gills of most other fishes are protected by a bony plate known as a gill cover or operculum. The shark's fins are thick and relatively stiff, and lack the delicate bony spines that are found in the fins of most bony fishes. The shark's skin has a layer of tiny, but tough, dermal denticles, as opposed to the much larger flattened scales in most other fishes.

THE SKELETON

Internally, the body is supported by a cartilaginous skeletal frame, complete with a protective cartilage skull, while most other fishes have a hard, more dense skeleton made of true bone. Sharks do not have an internal swim bladder to help achieve neutral buoyancy but instead rely upon their low-density cartilage, liver oils, and hydrodynamic planing to keep from sinking.

Some of the most notable

ALL RELATED

While the silvertip shark (above) in Papua New Guinea looks very different from the Pacific angelshark (left) in California, and the hammerhead shark (top of opposite page), they all share many distinctive characteristics.

O MISTAKE *A great ammerhead shark is one f the easiest to identify.*

ifferences in the natomy of sharks nd most bony fishes re found in the con- truction of the jaw, he method of its uspension from the ead, and the organ- zation of the teeth.

The upper jaw of the hark bears a full set of teeth, nd is derived directly from he palatoquadrate cartilages hat form during development rom the upper mandibular rch. In the more recently erived bony fishes, this struc- ure also supports the upper aw, but the major tooth- earing elements develop rom special bones derived rom the skin.

Similarly, the lower jaw in harks, known as Meckel's cartilage, is formed from the lower portion of the mandibular arch during development and also bears a full set of teeth in the adult. This structure is greatly re- duced in bony fishes, and forms the joint in the corner of the jaw. The teeth develop from other specialized dermal bones.

In most living sharks and rays, the upper jaw is seated on the underside of the skull where it is loosely attached by ligaments and connective tissue. It is suspended from the skull by the hyoid cartilage, which attaches near the back corner of the jaw. This arrangement permits the upper jaw to be thrust out from the skull during feeding, and this is an important means by which many sharks are able to take large, powerful bites from relatively large prey.

GROUPINGS

Like all living organisms, sharks are classified by the characteristics they share— sharks with more shared characteristics are thought to be more closely related. The differences that can separate major groups of sharks are usually apparent to casual observers. For example, hammerhead sharks are easily distinguished from all other sharks by the broad lateral extensions of the head that give them their name. However, among the different species of hammerheads, characteristics as subtle as the number of lobes on the leading edge, or the presence of a central notch on the head may be a key feature. Other detailed differences of their internal anatomy or their skeleton are usually used by scientists to identify species.

ARISTOTLE'S EARLY OBSERVATIONS OF SHARKS AND RAYS

The first critical look at shark biology in the Western world was by Aristotle (right) in his work entitled *Historia Animalium*, which appeared in 350 BC. Aristotle was a great observer and logician, and made many insightful observations on their anatomy, reproduction and behavior. For example, he recognized that sharks differed from other fishes in the construction of their uncovered and exposed gill slits. He wrote: "And of those fish that are provided with gills, some have coverings for this organ, whereas all the selachians [sharks and rays] have the organ unprotected by a cover."

He also understood the differences in the swimming mode of the sharks and rays: "Of the shark-kind some have no fins, such as those that are flat and long-tailed, as the ray and the stingray, but these fishes swim actually by the undulatory motion of their flat bodies."

And he formally recognized the sexual difference between male and female sharks: "Again, in cartilaginous fishes the male, in some species, differs from the female in the fact that he is furnished with two appendages hanging down from about the exit of the residuum, and that the female is not so furnished; and this distinction between the sexes is observed in all the species of the sharks and dogfish."

21

WHAT IS *a* RAY?

The ray lives in an almost two-dimensional body yet continues
to thrive in a three-dimensional world.

Rays and skates, known collectively as batoid elasmobranchs, are closely allied with the sharks. This remarkable group is represented globally by nearly 500 species and accounts for more than half of all living elasmobranch fishes. They are widespread in almost all bottom-dwelling communities of the oceans, inhabit offshore pelagic environments, and also extend into many inland freshwater habitats.

Batoids made a relatively recent appearance in evolutionary history, appearing some 200 million years after the first sharks. The first rays, relatives of present-day guitar-fishes, are thought to have been derived from flattened sharks around the time of the dinosaurs.

Living rays and skates have some important features that separate them from the sharks. The main body is highly flattened, both on the top and bottom. Unlike most sharks, which have short and stout pectoral fins that extend from the body below and behind the head, the pectoral fins of the batoids are attached at the back of the skull, and are greatly enlarged to form a body disc. The tail of most rays is usually reduced in size and not used for swimming. Instead, locomotion comes from the undulation of the tips of the pectoral fins.

The majority of species either lack dorsal and caudal fins on the tail, or have small ones. The eyes, positioned on the top of the body rather than on the sides, provide a good view of the bottom around the animal, the distant horizon, and the waters above but batoids are blind to their lower surface. Objects, such as prey items, under the animal are detected and located by a well-developed olfactory system in front of the mouth, and lateral line and electro-receptor systems that span much of the body's underside.

BREATHING EQUIPMENT

Another major difference is the positioning of the gill slits. In batoids they are located on the bottom surface of the body, whereas in sharks they are found along the sides. Like several bottom-dwelling sharks, the batoids have well-developed spiracles behind the eyes, and these serve to take in water for breathing when

SOCIABLE ANIMALS *The spotted eagle ray (right) and the thornback skate (above) both belong to groups that engage in complex social behaviors. The whole family has a well-developed sensory system.*

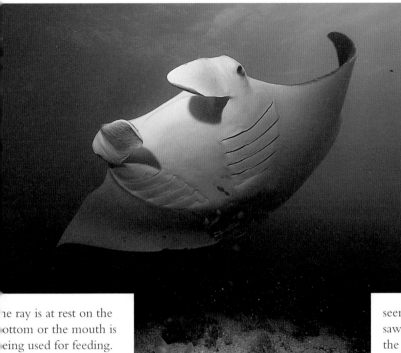

muscular shark-like tail with well-developed dorsal and tail fins. A remarkable convergence can be seen between the batoid sawfishes (Pristidae) and the sawsharks (Pristiophoridae) in which the body shape is much like that of the guitarfishes, with the addition of an elongated rostrum in the shape of a toothed sword that is used to capture prey.

…e ray is at rest on the …ottom or the mouth is …eing used for feeding.

Many batoids, such …s whiptail stingrays, …ingarees, eagle rays, …me devilrays, and …thers, have sharp spines …n the tail. These …enomous weapons are …sed defensively against …rge shark predators and …lso during social interactions …mong their own species.

Rays and skates show a …ide range of body forms and …zes. Skates are characterized …y a round or diamond-…aped body with a small …uscular tail that bears two …mall dorsal fins, and a tiny …audal fin. They are common …habitants of deep waters …round the world but also …ccur in near-shore areas.

Skates have weak electro-…enic organs along both sides …f the tail, that may be used in …ocial interactions in the wild. …lectric rays usually have a …ounded disc, well-developed …orsal and tail fins, and modi-…ed muscles in the pectoral …ns that in some species can …roduce electric discharges of …undreds of volts for capture …f prey and defense. Whiptail …ingrays and stingarees …re common inhabitants

of inshore reef areas, and are major predators of small invertebrates in the soft bottom sediments, and also small fishes. Eagle and cow-nose rays actively swim near the bottom or up in the water column around reefs or open coastal waters, and have broad dental plates used to crush hard-shelled mollusks, such as snails and bivalves.

The large pelagic mantas and other devilrays inhabit waters of the open ocean and are distinguished by the presence of cephalic fins on either side of the mouth, which are used to channel water into the mouth while the manta feeds on plankton or small fishes.

The body shape of some batoids seems to be midway between that of a shark and ray. A good example is the guitarfishes, which have a flattened ray-like head and a

SIZABLE BRAINS

The rays have the largest of the elasmobranch brains, and are highly complex animals that use their exquisite sensory systems for intricate social behaviors. For example, researchers have recently shown that male stingrays in wild populations use their electroreception system to find buried mates.

Other species form large schools that can be seen making long migrations along the coastline. Divers often encounter large aggregations of rays or skates engaged in social interaction or mating activity near the bottom. These animals are easy to watch and can usually be followed for an extended period of time. From simple observations, much can be learned about the behavior of these remarkable creatures.

RELATIVES *of* SHARKS *and* RAYS

The closest living relatives of the sharks and rays are the chimaeras,

thought to be descended from the same direct evolutionary lineage.

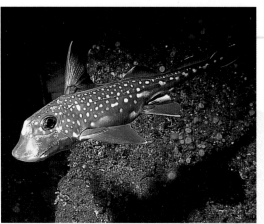

CLOSE RELATIVES *Ratfish (above) occur mainly in deep offshore waters. They have compressed, cartilaginous bodies and rodent-like teeth.*

Sharks and rays are members of the taxonomic class known as Chondrichthyes, and are separated from most other living fishes by having a cartilaginous skeleton. They have a long evolutionary history dating back more than 400 million years. During this long time period, they have coexisted with many different forms of fishes, many of which are still living today.

Also within the class Chondrichthyes are the chimaeras, sometimes referred to as ratfish, elephantfish, or ghostsharks, which are the closest living relatives of the sharks and rays. There are approximately 35 species of chimaera worldwide and all are marine creatures. Recent work by paleontologists has shown that the chimaeras first appeared about 340 million years ago during the Devonian, when they are thought to have split off from the early sharks. Some of the extinct species that lived during this time looked much like their living descendants, reinforcing the long history of these fishes.

The body plan of living chimaeras is quite different from that of the sharks or rays. The head is large, with prominent eyes, and the mouth is located on the ventral surface. The skin of the body is smooth and without scales, and a network of electrosensory pores and lateral line canals is evident on the head and body. Most species have elongate bodies that taper to a small and sometimes whip-like tail.

The first dorsal fin is movable and positioned above the pectoral fins, while the second dorsal is smaller and fixed. There is a long, sharp spine on the leading edge of the first dorsal fin that often bears a venom gland for defense. These fishes swim either by rapid movements of their pectoral fins, or by slow lateral movements of their tails. They are found in cold-water habitats on deep continental shelves and slopes but some species frequent cold shallow waters in the higher latitudes.

THE BASIC DIFFERENCES

Like sharks and rays, the chimaera skeleton is formed of cartilage with only slight calcification in some parts. They have a spiral valve intestine and possess no swim bladder. The palatoquadrate cartilage that forms the upper jaw is fused to the bottom of the skull, and does not move during feeding as in most sharks and rays. This type of jaw suspension, termed "holocephaly" or "holostyly," is a major reason for their separation from the elasmo-branch fishes, and the source for their scientific name "holocephalans."

In addition, the four gill arches on each side of the head are shielded by a gill cover with a single opening behind it. The ratfish gill apparatus is located below the skull, as opposed to behind and to the side in the sharks, and there is no spiracle. Water for breathing is taken in through the large nostrils rather than the mouth. The teeth are usually arranged into grinding plates that are beak-like or knobby, compared to the numerous, small, cutting teeth found in many sharks.

LONGNOSE CHIMAERAS *The snout of the spookfish (left) is used for sensory perception. The two elephantfishes (below) belong to the same genus. Note the mucus canals and sensory pores on the head (top picture) and the distinctive plownose (lower picture).*

These are used by most species of ratfish for feeding on small fishes, hard-shelled invertebrates, or cephalopods.

Like the elasmobranchs, all male chimaeras have pelvic claspers, which are used during mating for sperm transfer from the male to the female. However, male holocephalans also have a secondary clasper located on the head known as a frontal or head clasper. This auxiliary structure is used by males to grasp the rear portion of the female's pectoral fin while the pelvic clasper is inserted into her cloaca. This sexual difference may explain why most male chimaeras are smaller than the females. A set of prepelvic claspers is also found in the male chimaera, but its function is still enigmatic. Female chimaeras lay large, tough, flask- or tadpole-shaped egg cases on the ocean bottom where the young later hatch.

THE LIVING CHIMAERAS

There are three families of living chimaeras distributed in tropical and temperate areas of the world. The shortnose chimaeras, also called ratfishes or ghostsharks, (family Chimaeridae) consist of the two genera *Hydrolagus* and *Chimaera*, and about 21 species distributed widely across the Pacific and Atlantic oceans. These have a large head, a short, usually round snout, and a body that tapers to a thin, pointed tail, often with a filament extending beyond. The ratfishes occur in deep offshore waters but sometimes move into shallow waters along the coastline.

The plownose chimaeras, also known as elephantfishes, (family Callorhynchidae) occur in the southern hemisphere, mainly off the coasts of Africa, South America, New Zealand, and Australia. This family has one genus (*Callorhynchus*) and four species, which occur in shallow to deep waters. The plownose chimaeras are easily recognized by their elongate snout, which is down-turned directly in front of the mouth. They have a small tail with an elongate upper lobe, like that seen in many sharks.

The longnose chimaeras, also known as the spookfishes (family Rhinochimaeridae), are named for the long, straight, and pointed extension of the snout. There are three genera (*Rhinochimaera*, *Harriotta*, and *Neoharriotta*) and about six species. They occur in deep waters of continental slopes and the bottom of most oceans of the world.

WHERE *in the* WORLD?

Sharks and rays are found in nearly all geographic regions of the world,
and there are few boundaries that can restrict their movements.

A human's view of the Earth differs considerably from that of a shark or ray. Marine organisms are free to roam at will, restricted only by the availability of resources, such as food, shelter, mating grounds, and nursery habitats.

The polar regions of the world are characterized by cold waters, relatively long annual periods of darkness, and seasonal productivity. The ice-capped Arctic regions are further limited by weak surface currents that do not promote high biological productivity. As a result of seasonal productivity, year-round food chains that can support sharks and their prey are meager.

Only a few species of shark are found in polar waters, and usually this represents an extreme of their range. Best known examples of polar sharks are the sleeper sharks of the genus *Somniosus*. The Greenland shark, *S. microcephalus*, extends its range into shallow Arctic waters to about 80 degrees north in the cold winter months, but retreats to deeper waters in the summer.

Similarly, the Pacific sleeper, *S. pacificus*, extends its northerly range into the Bering Sea. The primary batoid elasmobranchs that occur in polar regions of the world are the skates, which are usually found on the outer region of continental shelves down to abyssal depths.

FOOD ABUNDANCE

As one moves away from the polar regions of the Earth, there is a dramatic increase in primary productivity and complexity of the marine food webs. The subpolar and temperate coastal regions of the Earth are rich in inorganic nutrients where spring and summer light levels produce large phytoplankton blooms. This extra light triggers a seasonal explosion of zooplankton and the small bony fishes that feed upon them.

Basking sharks take direct advantage of this seasonal productivity and make migrations into higher latitudes near almost all large

CHOICE OF HABITAT *Pacific cownose rays (above) schooling in a quiet lagoon on the Galapagos Islands. A southern stingray (right) prefers tropical shallows, such as around the Cayman Islands.*

islands and continents during summer months. Here, a basking shark may filter a half million gallons (2 million L) of water per hour to collect large numbers of the abundant zooplankton, such as larval crustaceans, small copepods, and fishes and fish eggs.

Blue and mako sharks make seasonal migrations to higher latitudes to feed upon small zooplanktivores and large species, such as mackerel and small tuna. Other species, such as the porbeagle and thresher sharks, may also leave their normal epipelagic habitat to come to inshore waters during the summer to feed on the abundance of small fishes.

Similar trophic links to the distribution of sharks and rays are seen in coastal areas of

REEF DWELLERS *Hornsharks (left) dwell in temperate, rocky, reef habitats, such as those of California's islands and the Galapagos. An ornate wobbegong (below), Great Barrier Reef, Australia.*

temperate seas. In coastal temperate habitats, a high amount of photosynthetic energy is captured during the summer by both populations of phytoplankton and also by large expanses of macroalgae that grow on the bottom.

Numerous species of hornsharks, catsharks, houndsharks, and small requiem sharks are prominent members of temperate rocky reef habitats around the world, where they feed heavily upon herbivorous invertebrates and smaller fishes. Because of their relatively small size, most of these species do not make long seasonal migrations to other areas, and can be observed year-round.

TEMPERATE ZONES

Many species of stingray and bat ray are found in shallow temperate regions where they feed mainly on large bottom-dwelling mollusks and crustaceans. Larger shark species, such as many requiem sharks, are regular inhabitants of these areas and feed upon larger predatory fishes including other small sharks and rays.

The distribution of sharks and rays in the warm waters of the tropics is often related to the features of a particular region. For example, many large sharks, such as the whitetip reef, gray reef, and blacktip reef sharks, live

almost exclusively on coral reefs of the Indo-Pacific. Among these sharks one may see eagle rays swimming up in the water column, or whiptail stingrays feeding on invertebrates on the sandy bottom.

Usually found on the coral bottom are wobbegongs, catsharks, or nurse sharks, which coexist with round stingrays, torpedo rays, or guitarfishes. Up off the bottom are the whale sharks and mantas, which feed upon plankton and small fishes in nearshore waters or lagoons. Other species, such as many hound and weasel sharks, bat rays, and some whiptail stingrays, congregate near river mouths and on continental shelves in tropical regions.

Unlike many species that are associated with a particular area, most pelagic sharks and rays are circumglobal in distribution. This includes the epipelagic blue, oceanic whitetip, thresher, and mako sharks; the mesopelagic crocodile sharks; and the bathypelagic cookiecutter and pygmy sharks. Similarly, pelagic rays, such as the manta ray, are also widely distributed in oceanic waters of the world.

THE DANGERS *of* OBSERVATION

Sharks and rays have few ways with which to express their intentions,
so patience and common sense can be a diver's most valuable protection.

To generalize about the behavior of all sharks and rays would be an impossible task. Each species lives in a particular habitat, feeds on slightly different prey and responds to a different set of conditions in its respective environment. So it is easy to understand why their behavior is hard to predict.

BODY LANGUAGE

The mental state of a dog can be predicted reliably by observing the position of the ears, the exposure of the teeth, and the wagging of the tail. We are less familiar with the body language and movements of most sharks and rays. Rather than to advertise their presence or give conspicuous signals about their motivational state, shark bodies are designed for hydro-dynamic efficiency and to be as unobtrusive as possible. To understand the behavior of a particular shark or ray species,

one must spend hours observing their natural movements and interactions with other organisms.

Small bottom-dwelling sharks and rays in coastal temperate waters or on tropical coral reefs are the easiest to observe. Many sharks, such as catsharks and hornsharks, spend much of their time at rest or probing in crevices and cracks on the reef for food. Other small coastal sharks, such as houndsharks, swim over the sandy bottom where their feeding or social behaviors can be observed by a snorkeler. When watching the behavior of small shallow-water species, it is important to stay well clear. Moving in close to a small shark will usually upset the animal and it will swim rapidly away. The observer must avoid inadvertently in-fluencing its behavior.

THE BOTTOM DWELLE[R]

Most bottom-dwelling spec[ies] of ray make excellent subjec[ts] for observation. Unlike mos[t] species of shark, which are constantly on the move, ma[ny] whiptail and round stingray[s] will forage in the sandy bottom or probe the reef bottom for hours within a small area. Often divers will encounter small groups of ra[ys] inspecting one another or interacting in some interesti[ng] way. These ray behaviors ca[n] be watched for hours from the surface while snorkeling or up close using scuba gear. Rays can often be closely approached by prone divers.

KEEP YOUR DISTANCE

A great white shark (left) goes after tuna bait set to attract it. Observing a southern stingray (above), Grand Cayman Island.

Many of the larger sharks and rays are rather shy of the scuba diver, and require special attention in order to get close enough to watch. Most are fast swimmers and afford only a brief glimpse or snapshot from the camera as they swim by on their regular daily rounds.

If the diver is suspended in the water column, many sharks, such as the tiger shark, will often circle the diver just at the limit of visibility, and occasionally approach for a closer look. One technique in watching large sharks within an area is to sit quietly on the reef bottom hidden from view, and use slow, controlled breathing. The noise from the diver's regulator is noisy and distracting to the shark.

Larger requiem sharks, such as the Galapagos or gray reef sharks, can be unnerving to the novice as they approach to inspect the diver. In these cases, experienced divers stress that it is essential to stay calm.

One prominent exception to the general lack of known behaviors in large sharks, is the well-documented agonistic display of the gray reef shark of the Indo-Pacific.

Gray reef sharks will exhibit this behavior (see p. 108) when they are threatened by an approaching diver, and will often attack if further pressed. However, the risk can be greatly reduced by understanding the nature and meaning of the agonistic display, and also by making allowance for a path by which to exit, if necessary.

SENSIBLE PRECAUTIONS

Although sharks are clearly not the ravenous killers of the oceans so often portrayed in films and stories, they must be respected and not provoked. Many divers directly provoke resting nurse sharks by pulling them by the tail, and end up with serious bites.

In other cases, provocation may be something as simple as one's presence in the personal space of a gray reef shark. Some divers are bitten when sharks are artificially baited. In these circumstances, the diver has set the sharks in a feeding situation and their excitement increases. This can only heighten the chance of a diver being bitten, whether by accident or intent. Common sense is the diver's best tool.

VIEWING SHARKS IN BAITED SITUATIONS

With increased interest in sharks by the public, and more people taking up diving, tours that view sharks underwater in the wild are becoming popular. Many of these operations put out bait, as in the picture above, to attract sharks into the area of a reef and also to keep them around for viewing. In some areas, this practice is highly controversial. Some feel that chumming is unnatural and potentially unhealthy for the sharks, and that it may make them dependent on humans for food. Such baiting activity may also increase the number of sharks in areas used for other water sports, putting people at risk. Others argue that the sharks will stop feeding on natural prey, and this will ultimately affect the health of the local reef. Much remains to be learned about the interactions between humans and sharks, and how best to arrange our meetings.

FAMILY VIEWING *Neal Watson with his two sons (left), watching a Caribbean reef shark in the Bahamas. Observation of the behavior of various species adds to our overall knowledge and helps us to understand how all organisms interact.*

... all at last returns to the sea—to Oceanus, the ocean river, like the ever-flowing stream of time, the beginning and the end.

The Sea Around Us,
RACHEL CARSON (1907–64), American writer and biologist

CHAPTER TWO

OUR RELATIONSHIP
with SHARKS *and* RAYS

SHARKS *and* RAYS *in* HISTORY

Historically and geographically, not everyone has the same perception of sharks and rays.

The better we know a place and the animals that inhabit it, the richer and more complex are our relationships with them. These associations are often reflected in the legends and historical accounts that make up our cultural fabrics.

VARYING VIEWS OF SHARKS AND RAYS

The cultures, ancient and modern, of peoples who rely on the sea for their livelihood and recreation are rich in lore and knowledge about the animals that live within it. The Haida and Klingit people of Pacific Northwest America,

for example, featured dogfish sharks (as well as killer whales, salmon and other creatures) in their art. Clan hats, screens, and tall, carved wooden poles sometimes include dogfish sharks, with their typical spines before the dorsal fins being clearly visible.

Polynesian cultures viewed diverse kinds of sharks in a variety of ways, from utility to

reverence. On the other hand, continental cultures have had starker perspectives of sharks and a shallow tradition about marine creatures. A well-known story in the Judeo-Christian tradition involves the prophet Jonah, thrown overboard by fearful sailors and swallowed by an ocean monster. Biblical scholars and biologists still speculate whether it was a great white shark, a baleen whale or some other species.

CULTURAL ICONS *The Haida screen (above) features dogfish faces. The early sixteenth-century painting (below) depicts the story of Jonah and the whale*

SHOCK TACTICS *Aristotle knew that the ray* Torpedo torpedo *(right) could deliver a severe shock.*

For the most part, the cultural histories of western industrialized nations, such as the United States, have been dominated by cultures not familiar with the diversity of life in the ocean. European mythology is more keyed to terrestrial animals. The fearsome predator is likely to be a bear or a wolf, certainly not a shark. But in oceanic cultures, legendary animals are more often sea creatures. The werewolves of European tales have their shark counterparts in the legends of Polynesia.

EARLY RECORDINGS

Aristotle (384–322 BC) spent several years on the island of Lesbos, where he observed sea life and talked to sponge divers, fishermen and sailors. He wrote in detail on the biology, anatomy, and behavior of sharks and rays. In *Historia Animalium*, he recognized the relationship of the group and the cartilaginous nature of their skeletons. He noted the differences from fishes in gill anatomy, and recognized their universally carnivorous habits.

Aristotle also noted the startling behavior of what modern divers and fishermen call the electric ray (*Torpedo torpedo*): "The torpedo narcotizes the creatures it wants to catch, overpowering them by the power of shock that is resident in the body; and feeds upon them; it also hides in the sand and mud and catches all the creatures that swim its way and come under its narcotizing influence. This phenomenon has actually been observed in operation ... the torpedo is known to cause a numbness even in human beings."

Despite his interest and keen reporting about sharks and rays, Aristotle's accounts contain very little about shark threats to humans. Perhaps the Mediterranean of ancient times offered few encounters between humans and sharks, or perhaps such were taken for granted as part of making a living in the sea.

HAWAIIAN LEGEND

In contrast, the oral tradition of ancient Hawaii features many particulars about interactions with sharks, including species implicated in human attack in modern times. Various interpreters of Hawaiian legends have called the large dangerous sharks of Hawaii *niuhi*. However, it is seldom clear which of the larger species is intended. It is likely to be the tiger shark, but it is also possible that the name refers to the great white. Based on the behavioral and anatomical differences in the two animals, however, we can make some educated guesses about which species is involved in a particular legend. Kapa'aheo, the Kohala shark god, seems almost certain to be a great white shark. In this legend, Kapa'aheo is transformed into a stone—a long, shark-sized reclining lava column (seen above)—which has been transported from its original site to rest in a secluded garden in the Bishop Museum in Honolulu.

THE LEGEND OF KAPA'AHEO

Long ago, young local girls enjoyed swimming in a lovely cove in Kohala on the Big Island (Hawaii). Often a swimmer would disappear and never be seen again. The people were very afraid and wanted to learn what had happened to the girls. A fisherman noticed that when a swimmer disappeared, a mysterious stranger named Kapa'aheo could be seen sitting on the shore nearby. This fisherman then gathered all of the fishermen together so that they were on hand when the girls went swimming again.

As before, the stranger was sitting on the rocks overlooking the cove. When he vanished, the leader of the fishermen ordered them all to dive into the water and form a protective circle around the girls. A shark swam toward the group and a huge fight began. Many times the shark was wounded by the spears of the fishermen. Finally the shark swam away. When the men swam back to shore, they found the stranger dying from many wounds that looked as if they had been made by fishing spears. When the man died from the wounds, he was transformed into the stone found near the edge of the cliff by the ocean.

SHARK FISHING

Although some traditional cultures have shown respect and even reverence for sharks and rays, humans have, for the most part, considered them as creatures to be at the least exploited, or at the most exterminated.

Even cultures with great respect for sharks have fished for them. It is likely that humans have caught sharks since pre-historic times. Ancient graves of the Chumash people of what is now the coastal area of Santa Barbara County in California contain nasal cartilages of mako sharks.

The purpose for which these cartilages were used is unknown, but they were probably associated with rituals of some sort.

Cultures of Melanesia, Micronesia, and Polynesia have long traditions of shark fishing. The hooks they crafted especially for shark fishing can be large and elaborate. They used shark skin in drum heads, shark teeth in weapons and tools, and shark flesh for food as well as for ritual purposes.

WHO IS THE MORE FEARSOME PREDATOR?

From 1990 through 1996, sharks attacked 344 people worldwide and killed 44, an average "take" of about 6 humans per year. Although there are remote areas of the world where a shark attack might go unreported, death by shark is sensational enough to come to wide attention, so we have some confidence in this estimate.

According to the United Nations Fishery and Agriculture Organization (UN/FAO), humans landed at least 633,600 metric tonnes of sharks in a single year, 1991. Most fishery biologists believe that this is only a fraction of the real catch. Many countries do not report their catch to UN/FAO, and unlanded bycatch is not included. In any case, even if this number is low, humans catch many sharks every year. If the average shark caught is estimated to weigh 110 pounds (50 kg), the UN/FAO figure indicates that humans killed at least 12 million sharks in 1991 alone. And we have every reason to believe that shark fishing has increased in the past five years.

For every human killed by a shark, two million sharks are killed by humans. In other words, 12,000,000 sharks are killed by humans per year compared to 6 humans killed by sharks. If we express these statistics as the score of a sports competition, it is obvious that sharks are losing disastrously. And so, in fact, are we humans, because by fishing at this rate we are jeopardizing world populations of apex predators that are essential to the health of marine communities.

THERE'S ALWAYS A CATCH

A wooden hook with rope attached (above left), used by islanders in the South Pacific to catch sharks. Shark teeth are embedded in these swords (right) from Wuvulu Island, Bismarck Archipelago. The pile of shark carcasses (below) was discarded after a sportfishing tournament.

COSTLY DELICACY *Sharks are often taken by the unscrupulous for their fins (right) alone, which command high prices for shark fin soup. But the cost to the shark is its life. How can society tolerate such greed and waste?*

EXPLOITATION

Modern fisheries continue to exploit a wide diversity of sharks, from small (spiny dogfish) to large (giant whale sharks), from coastal to pelagic, and from tropical to temperate seas. There is strong evidence that all shark fisheries are over-exploiting their resources. Because of their small litter size and slow rate of reproduction, sharks are particularly vulnerable to overfishing.

A wide selection of shark products (see pp. 36–7) is sold in modern marketplaces. These include fins and flesh for food, liver oil as a source for pharmaceuticals and vitamins, hides for leather, skin for abrasive sheets and for surgical skin implants, teeth and skeletal parts for jewelry, and blood components and cartilage for health-food supplements (reputed to diminish the risk of cancer). Demand for these products has varied over time, in part because of technological and cultural changes.

FISHERIES

Since the mid-1980s, demand for shark products has greatly increased. As swordfish and tuna catches have fallen, fishers have, increasingly, turned to sharks. Because of demand for shark meat and for the fins used in shark fin soup, many species of sharks have come under heavy harvesting pressure in North American waters. Historically, with a few regional exceptions, there have been few commercial shark fisheries in these waters.

A significant harpoon fishery for whale sharks is now underway in the western Pacific. Scientists have plans to see whether the whale sharks of Ningaloo Reef, Western Australia, may travel to the area of this extensive fishery.

Information on the international shark trade is limited, but it is estimated that world trade of shark products exceeds $240 million. True numbers are unknown because many foreign markets do not reveal catch or trade statistics.

PROTECTING SPECIES

Recently, the United States published plans to protect 39 species of shark. This Fishery Management Plan aims to reduce commercial and recreational fishing of sharks through quotas and licensing requirements. The plan also bans the practice of stripping the fins from sharks and dumping the maimed sharks back into the ocean.

Major environmental groups are also becoming increasingly concerned about overfishing of sharks and other species. In the United States, the Ocean Wildlife Campaign was launched recently as a collaborative effort involving the National Audubon Society, the National Coalition for Marine Conservation, the World Wildlife Fund, and other interested organizations. The effort is intended to increase public understanding of giant ocean fishes (sharks, tunas, and billfish) and to facilitate management measures that are appropriate.

Conservation of sharks is gaining support in many quarters. Some species, including great white sharks (*Carcharodon carcharias*), are protected in California and in Australia. Perhaps in the twenty-first century, the exploitation of the twentieth century will turn toward the reverence held for sharks by coastal cultures of long ago.

THE USE
of SHARKS *and* RAYS

Sharks and rays are a valuable resource, but their harvesting will have to be carefully monitored and regulated if they are to be used and yet conserved.

The use of sharks and rays for meat and other products predates recorded history. Every part of these creatures has been used by humans for some purpose. As a result, their conservation is a serious problem (see pp. 44–5). In a traditional fishery in northern Australia, Aborigines continue to catch sharks and rays to prepare *buunhdhaarr*, in which the liver and flesh are boiled separately, then minced and mixed for food. They also use the stinging spines of stingrays as tips for spears.

ARTIFACTS
Shark teeth have traditionally been used in many cultures for making functional and ceremonial objects. The Maoris of New Zealand used the teeth of the broadnose sevengill shark (*Notorynchus cepedianus*) to make war weapons, and prized the teeth of the mako shark (*Isurus oxyrinchus*) as ear ornaments. Inuit people made knives from the teeth of the Greenland sleeper shark (*Somniosus microcephalus*). Today, the teeth and jaws of this shark are widely used in local curio trades, and are eagerly sought after by trophy hunters.

When Europeans first settled Australia in 1788, as well as eating shark meat, they began to extract oil from shark livers for lighting and medicinal purposes. This practice continued through the first half of the nineteenth century. Later, between 1875 and the early 1920s, sharks were used as fertilizer for Tasmanian orchards. Today, in other regions, sharks and rays are still processed into fertilizer and fishmeal to

CURIOS *The shagreen-covered box c. 1932 (above) was probably used for cigarettes. Scrimshaw of a sailing galleon on the tooth of a great white shark (left Shark fins for sale (below) in Hong Kon*

eed domestic animals.

During the 1930s and 1940s, shark liver was in demand as a source of vitamin A, but this market collapsed during the 1950s when synthetic vitamin A became available. Recently, there has been a demand for squalene oil, extracted from the livers of several species of shark, particularly deep-sea dogfishes. Rapid development of fisheries was triggered by demand for the soupfin shark (*Galeorhinus galeus*) in several parts of the world. Considered an aphrodisiac in parts of Asia, shark fin soup has been regarded as a delicacy by the Chinese for more than 2,000 years—it became an essential part of formal banquets during the Ming Dynasty (1368–1644). The fins of many species of shark and ray are currently among the world's most expensive fishery products, with Hong Kong the acknowledged world capital for shark fin cuisine.

VARIED USES

Because it is embedded with enamel-tipped scales, the skin of sharks and rays is quite rough. Dried but untanned skin, called shagreen, is often used like fine sandpaper for polishing wood. In Sumatra, the stretched shagreen of the cowtail stingray (*Pastinachus sephen*) is used for the skins of drums and tambourines, and in Japan, it was used to bind the hilts of swords to provide a non-slip grip. During the seventeenth century, European artisans began imitating the Oriental practice of binding books with shagreen and also used it to cover personal articles, such as jewelry

LIVER OIL

The oil (or lipid) content of shark liver varies from nil to more than 90 percent, depending on the species and the maturity of the shark. The lipid contains vitamin A and squalene. Vitamin A is essential for the formation of visual pigments within the retinal cells of the eye; people lacking this vitamin are likely to suffer from night blindness. Squalene, which is synthesized by sharks, has many commercial applications. It is used as a fine, high-grade machine oil in high-technology industries; as a skin rejuvenator in the cosmetics industry; and for pharmaceutical products requiring a non-oily base. Oils rich in squalene are low in cholesterol. They may also be rich in the polyunsaturated fatty acids that act as anticoagulants and keep the blood moving freely.

boxes, spectacle cases and silverware cases.

Today, boroso leather, made from the shagreen of small sharks by lightly polishing the scales to a high gloss, is expensive and in demand in specialty markets. Shark leather, made by chemically removing the enamel tips, has higher tensile strength than leather made from cattle hides.

Although it is traditionally consumed dried, salted, and smoked by coastal communities around the world, shark meat today forms a significant part of the fresh fish trade. Marketing campaigns have been introduced to overcome consumer resistance to shark meat for human consumption, and shark has often been sold under market names designed to disguise its true identity. For example, piked dogfish (*Squalus acanthias*) has been marketed in the United States as grayfish. Various shark organs are eaten in some areas, too. In the Solomon Islands, for example, all tissue other than the intestine is consumed. Elsewhere, consumption of intestine, stomach, heart, and even the skin is common. The rough

scales are first removed, then the skin is prepared for the table by bleaching.

Interest in sharks and rays for medicinal purposes is also growing rapidly. In the United States, shark corneas have been transplanted to humans. Many scientists believe that extracts from shark cartilage suppress the development of tumors and now use these extracts in the treatment of cancer. Chondroiten, derived from cartilage, is used as artificial skin for burn victims, and extracts of shark bile have been found effective for treating acne. Anticoagulant bloodclotting agents have also been extracted and may be beneficial in the treatment of some cases of cardiac arrest.

THE EYE OF THE SHARK *In the US, shark corneas are proving successful as transplants for human eyes.*

DECLINE *in* SHARK *and* RAY POPULATIONS

Fishing practices, habitat modification, and programs designed to reduce the risk of shark attack to bathers have all contributed to the decline in shark and ray populations.

All around the world, shark and ray populations are falling as harvesting continues by traditional, artisanal (which includes small-scale commercial and subsistence fishers), and industrial fishing. Game fishers, divers, and other recreational fishers also play a significant part in the harvesting process. This raises serious ethical questions about the conservation of sharks and rays (see pp. 44–5).

INDUSTRIAL FISHERIES
Reported landings of cartilaginous fishes currently exceeds 700,000 tons a year. A small part of this consists of chimaeras, with the rest fairly evenly divided between sharks in one category and skates and rays in another. Although cartilaginous fishes comprise less than 1 percent of the

RAYS *Spotted eagle rays (above) with their white markings and whip-like tails. A large manta ray (below) caught in the Sea of Cortez, Mexico.*

world's fish catch, commercial fishing is having a major impact on shark and ray populations.

The catch has been rising steadily since the 1920s, but several fisheries began much earlier than that. One fishery off the west coast of Ireland caught basking sharks (*Cetorhinus maximus*) for some 60 years from 1770 until the species became scarce. As stocks subsequently became re-established, the fishery renewed its activities during the 1940s, but the catch had peaked and then declined to a low level again by the end of the 1950s.

A similar pattern occurred in the Norwegian fishery for porbeagle sharks (*Lamna nasus*), where

the catch peaked in the 1940s and 1960s but declined to a low level by the mid-1980s.

Demand for shark liver oil during the 1930s and 1940s stimulated rapid growth of fisheries for the soupfin shark (*Galeorhinus galeus*) on the continental shelves off California, New Zealand, southern Australia, South Africa, the east coast of South America in southern Brazil, Uruguay, and northern Argentina. While profits fell during the 1950s because of a drop in demand for liver oil, the fishery had already collapsed in California during the 1940s because of a decline in the population of mature females.

In southern Australia and New Zealand, where this species was persistently targeted for the production of shark meat, catches have fallen steadily. More recently, similar trends have occurred for the piked dogfish (*Squalus acanthias*) taken in trawl fisheries off North America and in the eastern Atlantic, and for some of the larger species of shark taken off the east coast of the United States.

In addition to such specialized fisheries, trawl and tuna fisheries operating over wide areas take significant numbers of cartilaginous fishes as

HUNTERS AND HUNTED *A diver inspects the carcass of a scalloped hammerhead shark (left) caught in an illegally set net. Anglers A. Dean and B. Rogers with a great white shark (below) caught in Australian waters. One-time attack victims Rod Fox and Henri Bource look on.*

bycatch. Much of this accidental catch from bottom trawling on the continental shelves and continental slopes of the world is not adequately reported, or is discarded dead at sea. The widespread practice of removing the fins (finning) and discarding the rest of the carcasses, often while the animal is still alive, raises huge ethical questions.

INSHORE FISHERIES
Many of the world's unregulated artisanal and recreational fisheries for bottom-living sharks and pelagic sharks have large numbers of small fishing boats in coastal waters. This results in the overfishing of many species of shark and ray in these waters. The effects of this vary considerably among species, because many of the species harvested are distributed widely inshore and offshore, and the boats are restricted to a much smaller range, generally only a few miles from shore. The falling catch rates in these areas probably reflect falling numbers of sharks in the local area rather than a major decline in overall population.

Traditional fisheries are wide and varied but, like the artisanal and recreational fisheries, have been confined to inshore and coastal waters. Catches have been small compared with those from the industrial and artisanal fisheries and for most species have had negligible impact on populations of sharks and rays.

HABITAT MODIFICATION
The stock of juvenile soupfin sharks in Port Phillip Bay, Australia, has been depleted over the years, probably permanently. As a result of intensive fishing of juveniles, the catch from the bay increased threefold between 1942 and 1944, and then fell rapidly until the early 1950s, when small sharks of the species became protected by the introduction of a legal minimum length. At this time, the western region of Port Phillip Bay, known as the Geelong Arm, was identified as an important nursery area for the soupfin shark. Given the high movement rates of adult sharks, it is surprising that this inshore area has not been replenished. It now seems likely that the reduced use of this formerly important nursery by soupfin sharks is a result of habitat modification in the now highly industrialized area of the Geelong Arm.

SHARK-ATTACK STRATEGY
The trend of initial decline in catch rates followed by stable numbers is a common one for most species detected in shark-fishing programs designed to reduce the risk of attack. These are in place at such centers as KwaZulu-Natal, South Africa, and in Queensland and New South Wales, Australia. Some of the trends seem to be caused by a fall in local numbers rather than by stock depletion. This theory is supported by the general pattern where catch rates are higher when fishing begins at a new site than at neighboring sites that have been fished for long periods.

CHANGING HABITATS

The close links between sharks and rays and their habitat mean that any disturbance to that habitat has the potential to change their distribution and abundance.

Changes to a habitat can be natural or induced by humans. Cyclones and typhoons are natural events that can damage reef and inshore habitats. Large swells can cause structural change to shorelines, and storm tides can flood inshore areas and upset the balance in areas not accustomed to heavy wave action. Large, sudden influxes of abnormally warm, cold, fresh, or saline water into an area have been known to cause fish kills, and may even affect the survival of sharks and rays, particularly if the area is a nursery for newborn or young animals. But in general, sharks and rays have been living with these natural cycles of habitat change for millions of years, and are well adapted to cope.

They are not well adapted to cope with more permanent habitat changes induced by human activity. This sort of modification is most conspicuous in freshwater habitats with the construction of physical barriers, such as dam walls, and the collection of water for heavy industry and agricultural irrigation. Land clearing and poor land-use practices in a river catchment can affect shark habitat within the river, the estuary, and offshore. Sediment carried down rivers will muddy the water and may smother reefs and sea grass. Such changes can lead to infestations of noxious plants and animals that disturb a species' habitat.

Fishing activities also impact on fish habitat. Methods such as deep-sea trawling and scallop dredging can modify the seabed and affect the plants and animals living on it. While occasionally a change to habitat might be beneficial to a species, it is more likely that it will not.

FISHING

The habitats and behavior of sharks and rays can be affected by various fishing practices. Fishers in the industrial shark fishery off southern Australia who target the soupfin sharks (*Galeorhinus galeus*) and

HUMAN INTRUSIONS *Satellite map (left) shows the hole in the ozone layer over Antarctica. A highway across the Florida Keys (above). Sign (below) on a California beach warns of contamination*

gummy sharks (*Mustelus antarcticus*) believe that the presence of sharks captured in bottom-set gill nets repels free-swimming sharks temporarily from an area. The noise and disturbance to the habitat caused by trawl fishing also seems to have the effect of keeping sharks away.

Fish and other wildlife can become entangled in lost or discarded fish netting and plastic bait wrapping that often pollute their habitat. New laws and codes of practice in various parts of the world are being implemented to discourage people from discarding unwanted plastic and fishing gear at sea.

Gill nets can continue fishing ("ghostfishing") after being lost, until eventually they roll up into a ball. This is not such a problem in areas of strong tidal flow where they roll up fairly quickly. Gill nets are rarely lost by experienced fishers equipped with modern position-fixing instruments and reliable equipment for retrieving the gill nets.

ECOTOURISM

Growing interest in viewing and filming sharks, particularly white sharks (*Carcharodon carcharias*), from boats on the surface and from underwater cages is giving rise to a new form of ecotourism. Development of ecotourism based on sharks, however, depends on attracting the sharks to an area by spreading chum (a type of bait) made up of mammal or fish blood and oil. With the development of such an industry, there is an urgent need to answer such questions as: What are the effects of chumming sharks to an area? Does chumming impact on seals and other marine life, either directly by fouling an area, or indirectly by

concentrating sharks in that area? What do sharks do after chumming ceases? Does chumming in an area increase the risk of shark attack on humans in nearby areas?

OZONE DEPLETION

Ozone thinning, through its effect on whole ecosystems, has the potential to alter shark habitat. An increase in the ultraviolet radiation that penetrates surface waters has the potential to alter phyto-plankton which, through the process of photosynthesis, provide the primary source of food in marine waters. Any changes at this primary level of the food chain have flow-on effects farther up the chain.

GLOBAL WARMING

At the global level, climate change also has the potential to alter shark habitats in the future. Long-term effects of climate change could include alterations in sea level, water temperatures, tidal and current patterns, coastal erosion, and storm patterns.

INSIDIOUS DAMAGE *Sand is eroded relentlessly by wave action in the Maldives (above); and a coastal settlement in Cairns, northern Australia, (below) inevitably causes pollution.*

Ecologists do not wholly understand what controls the distribution of species. Many factors, including climate, food supply, and the ability to compete with other species, are involved, and all of these factors affect the others in a complex web of interactions. Changes in climate can affect interactions between species within an ecosystem. A species that is successful in today's climate might be ousted by invaders better suited to a new climate.

Most important, global warming will vary from place to place. For example, changes are likely to be much greater at the poles than at the equator. Changing patterns in climate could impact first on migratory species of shark where migration is timed to fit in with food supplies along the route, or to take advantage of conditions suitable for the survival of large numbers of offspring. If events get out of phase, the effects on the migratory species could be catastrophic.

OCEANS *under* THREAT

Pollution of the oceans occurs worldwide, and whether deliberate or not, it has devastating and far-reaching effects on the marine environment.

Dumping chemical, animal, and plant waste products into the oceans must be closely monitored. The shipping and oil industries must be tightly controlled to minimize their impact on marine ecosystems. And rapidly developing aquaculture practices—the cultivation of marine plants and animals for human consumption—must be regulated.

POLLUTION

Physical disturbances and pollutants can affect whole ecosystems. Some of the more obvious pollutants are sewage effluent, plastics, chemicals, and pesticides. Extra amounts of the nutrients nitrogen, phosphorus, and silicon can find their way into the marine environment, causing an increase in phytoplankton and other plant growth. An abundance of nutrients often promotes or contributes to

algal blooms (some of which are toxic), leading to clogged rivers, channels and bays, or overgrowth of corals and reefs.

Some pollutants, such as heavy metals and organic chemicals—for example, PCBs (polychlorinated biphenyls)—take a long time to break down. When these materials persist in the environment, they can adversely affect aquatic organisms and ecosystems in general. Some are absorbed from the sea water into the tissues of organisms that feed on polluted materials. Individual organisms can accumulate

some of these pollutants to concentrations much higher than background levels ("bioaccumulation"). When these organisms are in turn eaten, the concentration of pollutants increases again, and so on, up the food chain ("bioamplification").

The heavy metal mercury is one pollutant that reaches high levels in sharks and rays. Mercury accumulates naturally in these organisms in the course of feeding, but when its background levels are further elevated from human sources, concentrations can become markedly increased. Very low levels of some organic pollutants ("environmental estrogens") can suppress the number of male fish produced.

OIL AND SHIPPING

More than two million tons of oil escape into the marine environment each year, and only about 15 percent of this comes from natural seepage. The remainder comes from discharges by tankers and other shipping, discharges from storage facilities and refineries, and accidental events

POLLUTION *Underwater sewer outlets (above) and industries, such as this paper mill (left) in New Brunswick, Canada, pollute the oceans mercilessly.*

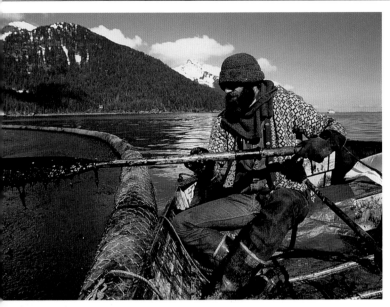

CLEAN-UP *An oil spill in Prince William Sound, Alaska, is a nightmare to rectify.*

proliferate to levels that swamp the new site and replace indigenous species.

Many of the inshore and coastal waters receiving ballast water are already disturbed by the effects of urbanization around ports. This makes them particularly vulnerable to invasions that further alter community structure and function. Invasion by exotic species is a very serious threat to marine habitats, and the ecological impacts cannot be fully predicted by knowing the biology of the introduced organisms and ecology in their original habitat. Inshore areas used by sharks and rays as nurseries are particularly sensitive.

ch as oil spills and ruptured pelines. Recent wars sulted in major oil contami-tion in the Middle East.

Although less of a problem open waters, hydrocarbons d other toxicants in oil can ntaminate fish flesh either rough direct contact or via e food chain. Impact from l spills is most likely through mage to vulnerable coastal a grass, mangrove, salt arsh, coral reef, rocky reef, d polar habitats. Nurseries d shallow waters where arks and rays gather are one to harm from oil spills.

Dredging harbors and ipping channels can stir up ud and silt that may settle in nsitive coastal ecosystems. eplenishing sand on beaches r recreational purposes can ve similar localized effects.

PREAD OF MARINE RGANISMS

iological invasion of marine eas by foreign organisms is major threat to the natural mmunities of plants and imals. Organisms that come attached to the hulls ships and to oil rigs are nsported with them. Ships aw sea water into ballast nks and floodable holds for bility. This water is later

discharged while the ship is underway or in various ports. Water taken aboard may contain planktonic organisms and sediments. In this way, plankton groups are spread over long distances. Surveys show that all major taxonomic groups are being introduced to new areas in this way.

These transported organisms occur at all levels of the food chain, but some of the species that keep the system in balance may be missing. Without these natural controls, certain species may

FARMING COASTAL WATERS

As catches from wild fishery stocks decline, one way to supply an increasing demand for fish is by aquaculture. But such operations have many drawbacks. Aquaculture requires pollution-free waters but its practice alters and pollutes mangroves, marshlands, and other inshore habitats. Some species, such as shrimp, are farmed in such huge numbers that disease is a constant threat. When a site becomes contaminated, the industry tends to move on to a fresh location, devastating whole stretches of mangrove coastline. Escape of cultured exotic species and genetically altered strains is another worrying factor.

The most rewarding targets for aquaculture are high-value species such as prawns, shrimp, scallops, abalone, oysters, pearl oysters, salmon and tuna. So far, there is no interest in farming sharks and rays. Their relatively low value and the small number of young produced by individuals make them poor prospects.

SHOULD *the* FISHING *be* REDUCED?

Sharks are valued as a food resource and for other products by many communities, but there are signs that current usage levels are not sustainable.

Declining catch rates from many of the world's fisheries indicate that if we continue to harvest the oceans as we are now doing, populations of many species will continue to collapse. Sharks and rays tend to be longer-lived than other types of fish, and produce fewer offspring.

After the early stages of life, when all animals are most vulnerable, sharks and rays tend to have low natural mortality. Harvesting populations of such long-lived animals that produce only small numbers of young requires special care. It is usually safer to harvest

THREATENED SPECIES *The sand tiger shark (above) and the great white shark (below) now have protected status in certain parts of the world.*

short-lived animals that produce large numbers of young.

SUSTAINABILITY

Only a small proportion of the shark and ray populations can be taken sustainably each year. In southern Australia, it is estimated that with gummy sharks (*Mustelus antarcticus*), about 5 to 6 percent of the population can be taken each year without threat to the population. That means no more than 5 to 6 percent of the combined weight of all the gummy sharks in the population before fishing began. This species has a maximum lifespan of about 16 years.

For the soupfin shark (*Galeorhinus galeus*), which is known to have individuals

older than 50 years, no more than about 2 to 3 percent of the population can be taken sustainably. Continued harvesting of these species at greater than the above rates will inevitably lead to collaps of their stocks. Abundant species, such as the gummy shark, can continue to be harvested sustainably at present levels of fishing. But for some other species, fishin must be stopped, or markedl reduced. For example, populations of the great white

WHAT IS SUSTAINABLE FISHING?

The low natural mortality rate and well-developed young of sharks and rays provide for remarkably stable populations compared with many short-lived bony fishes where the populations can vary greatly from year to year. In a fishery where the population size and the catch remain fairly constant over time, the population is said to be in equilibrium and harvested sustainably. Here, there is a rough balance between the number of fish recruited to the population from reproduction each year, and the number dying from natural causes and from fishing.

Mullet (left) netted by professional fishermen.

Fishing can be sustainable at many levels. Low levels result in small sustainable catches, and the population remains large. High levels can result in a similarly small sustainable catch, but the population becomes smaller, and the fishers have to work much harder to take the catch. The highest sustainable catches are obtained somewhere in between low and high levels of fishing. If the level of fishing is very high, such that total mortality is too high for recruitment to keep up, the population will continue to decline until it is either uneconomic to continue fishing, or the population collapses.

amount of fresh water in rivers and lakes is small compared with the amount of sea water on Earth. Second, tropical rivers and lakes where freshwater species occur are mostly in developing countries with large and expanding human populations. Such areas are much more vulnerable to exploitation than marine waters.

At least three species of "river shark" are now extremely rare. The Ganges shark (*Glyphis gangeticus*) is known only from the Ganges-Hooghly River system of the Indian subcontinent, although it is possible that more than one species of *Glyphis* occurs in the region of New Guinea, northern Australia and Borneo. The giant freshwater whipray (*Himantura chaophraya*) is considered endangered throughout its range and, as a result of fishing and river-habitat changes, it is critically endangered in Thailand. Sawfishes (family Pristidae), which to varying degrees occur in fresh and estuarine waters, seem to be much less common today than they were 50 to 60 years ago.

Carcharodon carcharias) have been severely reduced in most regions where it occurs. As a relatively long-lived, top-level predator, producing very few young in a lifetime, it cannot replace losses quickly. In most areas, fishing for this species needs to cease immediately if the populations are to be allowed to build up again.

THREATENED SPECIES

Several species of shark that gather in coastal waters to feed or breed are regarded as vulnerable. Notably, large, maturing or mature great whites are easily caught when feeding around seal-breeding colonies. The decline in abundance of the great white has led to its being protected in South Africa and several states of the United States and Australia. The sand tiger shark (*Carcharias taurus*), vulnerable to spearfishing, is protected in New South Wales, Australia.

Dogfishes and chimaeras inhabiting the continental slopes are taken as bycatch in several bottom trawl fisheries. Much of the catch of these species is either discarded dead, or not recorded. Like many of the bony fishes studied from these deeper and colder waters, the dogfishes are likely to be particularly long-lived and to have relatively few young. Given the limited areas occupied by these species, and the intensity of fishing, some of the species of dogfish and chimaera are at risk of severe depletion in some regions.

Some of the most "at risk" species of shark and ray are those occurring in freshwater habitats. These species are more vulnerable than those inhabiting marine waters, first because the

VANISHING ACT The sawfish (right), a type of ray, is now becoming much less common.

MYTHS *and* FACTS

Knowledge of their biology, lifestyle and environment is the key to understanding and demystifying the behavior of sharks and rays.

The more we know, the better equipped we are to deal with rays and sharks rationally and responsibly. Reliable information is reaching more people through books, films, magazines, and aquariums, but myths still abound.

There are two kinds of myth about sharks and rays in contemporary lore. First, those stories that are grand representations of conflicts between good and evil, with the shark or ray always embodying the face of evil rather than good. Some of these, such as those from Hawaii related on page 33, come to us from other cultures.

Others have very recent origins in our modern folkways. Peter Benchley's novel *Jaws* and the resulting films, for example, created a substantial mythology about great white sharks (*Carcharodon carcharias*). Ian Fleming, in his novella *The Hildebrand Rarity*, tells of master spy James Bond's stalking and spearing a large stingray while skin-diving in the Seychelles Islands. The stingray had done nothing to Agent 007 other than reveal its evil nature as a relative of those useless devils, the sharks. Bond kills it as a good deed.

SWITCHTAIL *The southern stingray (Dasyatis americana) of the Cayman Islands is found in the offshore shallow*

MISCONCEPTIONS

While sensational accounts make exciting reading, we can recognize them as exaggerations. More insidious effects on our thinking are rooted in the second kind of myth—those of misconception. These once appeared widely in older books, but even now we can find such statements as: "the shark is a swimming nose;" "sharks are color blind;" "the shark is a living fossil;" "sharks have a rigid upper jaw and must turn on their backs to bite."

Although some of these misconceptions have a basis in fact, they are at best misleading, and at worst completely wrong. "The shark is a swimming nose" implies that all sharks rely principally on their sense of smell. It is true that all sharks that have been studied have well-developed olfactory organs in their paired nostrils the size and location of which vary with the species. But sharks use a variety of sensory systems to find prey and to survive in their world.

Most sharks have a well-developed sense of vision. Sharks active in low-light environments (such as the deep sea or the nocturnal ree have special structures in thei eyes called tapeta. These reflective layers under the retina reflect light back to the light receptors to boost the low signal. Some species, suc as the great white shark, have been shown to have color vision. Although they did no have the instrumentation to confirm color vision, ancient

SCARE TACTICS
The pointed teeth of the sand tiger (right) fit the image of predator; the rounded crushing teeth of the Port Jackson (below) do not.

waiians recognized the arp eyesight of sharks. waiian legend recounts that ring her pregnancy, the other of Kamehameha, the ture Great King of the waiian Islands, was struck an intense longing to the eye of the *niuhi* eaning tiger shark or eat white shark). obably at some convenience to others, e rare dish was pro- ded for her. It was er said that the shark's rit influenced the en vision of Kame- meha's leadership.

ISLEADING LABELS e statement that sharks are ing fossils implies that all cies are of ancient lineage. hile it is true that there are 0 million years of fossil ord through which shark eages can be traced, only a v living types extend well ck into the geological ord. One example is the lhead, or hornshark, ily, Heterodontidae. ornsharks are now mmon along the tem- rate coasts of Japan, thern California, the lapagos Islands, South rica, and Australia. e fossil record of this ily extends back 160 lion years to the ographic limestone of Jurassic Period. To e a perspective, this is same fossil stratum in ich the early ancestor birds, *Archaeopteryx*, s found. Thus the lhead family has nained relatively changed (at least in its etal structure) for the e period in which ds have undergone

substantial changes. By comparison more highly evolved sharks, such as great whites, sand tigers, and makos, are believed to date only to the Eocene, about 50 million years ago, the same as many coral reef fishes.

Another, now faded, myth about sharks purports that their upper jaws are rigidly fixed to the skull (or neuro-cranium, as biologists prefer to call it). This old tale made its way into semi-serious writings about sharks as early as Aristotle's time (384–322 BC). It was supposed that, because of the rigidity of the upper jaw attachment, sharks needed to swim upside down to take a proper bite. This miscon-ception began to wane when people began to observe sharks in their environment.

A conclusive demonstration of the marked flexibility of the upper jaw in the biggest biter, the great white shark, has been provided by shark biologists Dr. Timothy Tricas and Dr. John McCosker. They analyzed slow-motion films taken by noted cinematographer Al Giddings of great white sharks feeding, and showed that while a great white is biting, the upper jaw protrudes a substantial distance.

Skepticism is one defense against being misled by myths. Far more fun, however, is the first-hand obser-vation of these beautiful animals living free in all their splendor.

The terrifying motion picture from the terrifying No.1 best seller.

JAWS

ROBERT SHAW
ROY SCHEIDER
RICHARD DREYFUSS

JAWS

Co-starring LORRAINE GARY · MURRAY HAMILTON · A ZANUCK/BROWN PRODUCTION
eenplay by PETER BENCHLEY and CARL GOTTLIEB · Based on the novel by PETER BENCHLEY · Music by JOHN WILLIAM
Directed by STEVEN SPIELBERG · Produced by RICHARD D. ZANUCK and DAVID BROWN · A UNIVERSAL PICTURE ·
TECHNICOLOR® PANAVISION®

FALSE TEETH *Although the monster in Jaws is well known to be a great white shark, the artist for this poster provided the more dramatic-looking teeth of a mako.*

47

CHANGING ATTITUDES

Our attitudes toward sharks have always been—and probably always will be—colored by the fact that some species kill humans.

The primal fear of being devoured by a predator is deeply rooted in our psyche. But too often that fear has been used, at least in part, to justify our wasteful killing and overfishing of such creatures, especially sharks.

Yet as each of us has learned more about the complexities of sharks and their behavior, our collective attitude is becoming far more enlightened. Certainly mixed into every personal point of view is a healthy respect and fundamental fear, but it can be ventured that our feelings toward sharks today are very different from the attitudes prevailing among the generations of the past.

STUNNING IMAGES

Less than 40 years ago, there were few opportunities for general readers (or, for that matter, even scientists) to see even mediocre photographs of living sharks and rays. Today, books, magazines, and television afford a treasure house of sharp color images of an abundance of marine animals. Almost every reader of this book will probably have seen breathtaking images of even some of the largest species, whale sharks and manta rays. Many readers have seen or plan to see and photograph them firsthand.

A generation ago, to swim with sharks was to engage in the pursuits of a lunatic, or at least of a bold adventurer whose accounts were the stuff of sensational tales. But our current

LEGENDARY ADVENTURER
Using a bathyscaphe, naturalist William Beebe (above) stirred imaginations with investigations of the deep. Photographer Hans Hass (left), an early pioneer of underwater photo techniques, lifted the veil on ocean mysteries.

attention and enlightening interest is based on the foundation of such mad adventures. It is useful to review some of these accounts and realize the changes in our perspective and to appreciate the wealth of opportunity now available to us.

One of the earliest adventurers to look living sharks in the eye and to popularize his exploits was the American naturalist William Beebe. In addition to traveling to great depths in a

bathyscaphe in the 1930s, a swim-suited Beebe made shallower dives on coral reefs in the Caribbean and the Pacific with compressed air supplied through a brass helmet. He viewed sharks firsthand, with the perspective of a biologist. Still, his account of harpooning a whale shark near Cabo San Lucas, Baja California, Mexico, in 1938, strikes us today as particularly brutal. But we must remember that at the time he thought he was collecting a rare species.

Many a present-day marine biologist was brought up on the adventuring tales of diving photographer Hans Hass, who

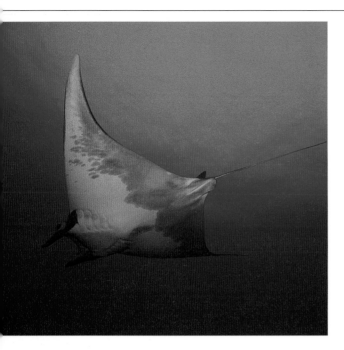

ed a modified military re-
eather air-supply to explore
e Caribbean in the late
930s and the Red Sea in the
te 1940s. His classic
*IANTA, Under the Red Sea
ith Spear and Camera*, was for
any readers an introduction
> the phlegmatic and graceful
ankton feeders we still hold
high esteem. In Hass's day
owever, these unfamiliar
ant "devil-fish", as they
ere called, were considered
ninous creatures—a percep-
on reflected in his writings.

REATER ACCESS
/hen Jacques Cousteau's
>-invention of the scuba
gulator made it easier for
ore people to swim with
arks and rays, and to share
eir views with others,
aders gained a wider
nowledge of the sea. Interest
creased with books such as
achel Carson's *The Sea
round Us*, Cousteau and
umas' *Silent World* (1953),
d Eugenie Clark's *Lady and
e Sharks* (1969).

As a result of these and
any other vivid descriptions
d filmed adventures and
oservations, we have come
have a better understanding

of the sea and its creatures,
including its predators.

Despite these changes in
attitudes, the world is still
hungry for fish and profit.
Many fisheries are unregulated
or regulations go unenforced.
Fisheries management has
been reactive rather than
planned. New fisheries are
outpacing the managers and
their rules. In central Indonesia, observers report that
whales, manta rays, billfish,
and sharks are newly
jeopardized. In the Lembeh
Straits, migrating sea
mammals and large fishes
enter the strait to feed and
take a shorter passage
around the island of
Lembeh. Here, a Taiwan
fishing company has set up a
huge, permanent fish trap
with an opening almost half
a mile (0.8 km) wide. Set
strategically in the middle of
the migration path, it can
catch everything that comes
down the North Sulawesi
coast, including dozens of
giant manta rays.

Changed attitudes have
coalesced into advocacy. In
1995, to help alleviate a
recognized global crisis in
overfishing, the World

Wildlife Fund (WWF)
launched a three-year effort
known as the Endangered
Seas Campaign to promote
the conservation and
sustainable use of marine
fisheries worldwide. WWF
will invest millions of dollars
to reverse the effects of
unsustainable fishing on sharks
and other marine creatures,
and the ocean ecosystems on
which they depend.

The campaign will work all
around the world to build the
political will to end chronic
overfishing, restore devastated
fisheries, improve management schemes, and reduce
the use of destructive fishing
practices. WWF knows that it
won't be easy: "fish neither
'sing' like whales nor look
like pandas." Yet anyone who
has seen a free-swimming
shark or ray can attest that
they have value beyond flesh,
and beauty beyond danger.

HUNTER AND PREY *Setting a modern
bottom-fishing net in Indonesian waters
(above), a very efficient catch-all method
of fishing. The huge manta ray (top)
once seemed more terrible than it is.*

THE NATURE *of* SHARK ATTACK

Sharks are beautiful; they are graceful; their biology and behavior are complex and fascinating. But the fact remains: some of them have bitten and killed people.

From a statistical point of view, shark attack is a very rare event. On average between 1990–6, 50 attacks per year were recorded worldwide, and fewer than 15 percent of these were fatal. To a victim, however, small statistical probability becomes total certainty. Interestingly, some survivors of even severe attacks have expressed philosophical attitudes. At least one Australian survivor, Rodney Fox, has made a career of helping people appreciate and understand the value of living sharks. Other survivors have continued their enjoyment of ocean sports and activities, declaring themselves guests in the sea, and assigning no hint of blame to the sharks.

Knowledge and good judgment are the best protection against shark attack. Good judgment means understanding the behavior of the kind of large shark that has been implicated in attack. In some cases, judgment may dictate that one avoid swimming or diving in an area known to abound with sharks.

NATURAL BEHAVIOR *Tiger sharks in Hawaiian waters often take the green sea turtle (above) for food and may attack humans by mistake. Since surviving a shark attack in 1963, Australian Rodney Fox (right) has made it his mission to work for their welfare.*

WHY DO SHARKS ATTACK HUMANS?

Most shark attacks on humans are prompted by two basic situations. First, there are those attacks related to threat and aggression. This kind of attack has been likened to a watchdog biting a mail carrier who enters a yard the dog is protecting. Second, there are attacks related to feeding, in which the shark approaches the victim as a meal.

Attacks in the first group can be subdivided into provoked attacks and unprovoked attacks. Provoked attacks involve the very poor judgment of divers who may for example, pull the tail of a whitetip reef shark as it rests in an underwater cave, or attempt to hand-feed it. In the same way, any fisher who is bitten by a landed shark is considered to have provoked the "attack."

Unprovoked attacks are those in which victims blunder into the behavioral sphere of a shark and seem to threaten it with harm. For example, a surfer or windsurfer may speed into an area where a reef shark is swimming. If the surfer falls from the board near the shark, the shark will lash out to meet the perceived "threat."

Attacks motivated by feeding are most frequently

ssociated with large species, uch as the tropical tiger hark and the temperate great vhite shark. It is these attacks hat can result in fatalities. Tropical tiger sharks have a liverse diet but are known to eed on large sea turtles. It is robably good judgment to void swimming in areas vhere sea turtles abound. Tiger sharks are also known o feed on floating carcasses of vhales. Off Maui, Hawaii, in 995, the body of a male umpback whale killed in ourtship activities attracted at east five large tiger sharks. This would have been an rea to avoid!

At smaller sizes, great white harks feed on fishes. As they nature to a larger size they hange their diet to seals and ea lions. It would be dvisable to avoid swimming n areas of seal rookeries.

Even smaller species of hark may be confused by timuli that are associated with rey behavior, for example, ashing of shiny surfaces such s jewelry, bleeding, and istressed swimming motions.

HARK BITE

ny injury from a shark hould be considered a signifi- ant medical problem. Such njuries can range from slight brasions to deep punctures, ssue damage or loss, and evere bleeding. In many oastal areas influenced by uman activity, puncture or brasion of the skin can result n severe infection. In some ropical areas, serious bacterial nvasions are almost certain.

Abrasions from rough shark kin can result in many tiny uts caused by the sharp treamlining edges of the enticles on the skin of the hark. Tissue damage from

RARITY OF ATTACK

Risk of human death by shark attack is far down the list compared to other causes of death. Below are selected statistics for Hawaii, an area where shark attack is likely to be higher than many other places, yet where disease and accident rates are "near-normal." In Hawaii, millions of people engage in ocean activity, fatal shark attacks have occurred, and both great white sharks and tiger sharks (shown above) have been implicated in attacks.

Selected Causes of Death in Hawaii, 1996

Total deaths, all causes	7,206
Heart disease	2,178
Cancer	1,713
HIV	145
Motor vehicles	124
Falls	58
Homicide and legal intervention	44
Poisoning	40
Drowning	40
Shark attack	0

(Two non-fatal attacks were recorded in Hawaii in 1996)

shark teeth is a far more serious matter, and medical attention should always be sought. First-aid measures in- clude staunching the bleeding by pressure and covering the wound with cloth or rubber.

Medical treatment of shark bites involves treatment for shock; careful cleaning, debriding, and closure of the injury; treatment of broken bones crushed by the shark's jaws; removal of any tooth fragments; antibiotic regimens

to fight infection; and the restoration of fluids.

Some people have survived very serious shark attacks because of the initial control of blood loss. When Rodney Fox was severely bitten by a great white shark in Australia, his rubber wetsuit undoubt- edly helped control the loss of blood. Joe Thompson, a surfer attacked in Hawaii by a tiger shark, lost one hand in the attack but managed to control blood loss with the other.

FIRST AID

The Natal Sharks Board of South Africa reports a decrease in fatal injuries through the development of a treatment procedure and the widespread availability of a specially designed first-aid kit, known as the Shark Attack Pack. The key to treatment lies in stabilizing the victim before transfer to hospital.

LUCKY ESCAPE *Surfer Rick Grunzinski shows the chunk bitten from his board during a shark attack off Hawaii.*

THE REALITY *of* SHARK ATTACK

Although the chance of being attacked by a shark is statistically small,

to each observer entering their watery world, it is a very real possibility.

For peace of mind when diving, it helps to have an intellectual understanding of shark behavior and the low probability of attack. It also helps to appreciate that you are entering a world that is wild, natural, and not totally predictable. Knowing that sharks share the same waters with you yet, one hopes, keep their distance, adds to the thrill of any ocean experience.

IN TROUBLE *Snorkelers (left) should swim in groups so they have less chance of being attacked by a shark. A hammerhead (below right) hopelessly entangled in a mesh beach net in Queensland, Australia*

KNOWING THE ODDS

Any gambler, whether card player or swimmer, likes to know the odds. To estimate the chance of an event, a statistician needs to know at least two numbers: the observed number of "hits" (in this case, shark attacks) and the number of opportunities,

that is, how many people were in the water where dangerous sharks occur. Thanks to the International Shark Attack File and the biologists who maintain it, there is fairly good information on the first figure, although the estimate might be slightly low because not all attacks are reported.

Estimating total human exposure is more difficult. It is less than the world population

because not everyone enters the ocean. One thing is certain: as human populations continue to increase, and as more people enter the sea for their livelihood and recreation, more people are exposed to attack.

There is also a third important figure to estimate: how many sharks of the kind implicated in human attack are there in the sea? We don't know but, given increased fishing catches, there is little doubt that there are fewer than there were a decade ago

In the panel at left are statistics for the seven-year period 1990–6 for selected coastal areas with significant human activity in the sea. Note that death from a great white shark and a nip on the hand from a small reef shark are both considered to be shark attacks in this summary

BETTER CHANCES

Regardless of the estimated chances of shark attack in an area, humans can attempt to influence them, individually and collectively. Of course, individuals can greatly change the odds in their favor by staying out of the water—but

SHARK ATTACK NUMBERS

Area	average number attacks/year	average number fatal attacks/year
World	50	6
Australia	6	1
New Zealand	1	0
Brazil	5	<1
South Africa	4	<0.5
Hong Kong	1	1
Japan	1	<0.5
Florida, USA	15	0
California, USA	3	<0.2
Hawaii, USA	3	<0.5
Other Areas	10	<3

MISTAKEN IDENTITY *From a shark's viewpoint, a surfer on a board looks like a turtle or a seal.*

that's no fun. In the panel at the right, there are some suggestions for swimming safely with sharks and rays.

GROUP ACTION

Groups of people have acted collectively to reduce the likelihood of shark attack. The best known of these measures is the netting of beaches to separate the activities of people and sharks, and in many cases to catch and remove sharks from the entire area. Netting of beaches is practiced most notably in Australia and South Africa.

In South Africa, as early as 1904, the Durban City Council ordered the installation of a semicircular enclosure, about 320 feet (100 m) in diameter, to protect swimmers. By 1928, the successful barrier had deteriorated and was removed. Few attacks were recorded in the next 20 years, but between 1945 and 1951, Durban recorded 21 attacks, 7 of them fatal. Desperate city authorities adopted an Australian system first used in 1937 when large-meshed gill nets were anchored seaward

of the breaker zone at many Sydney beaches. The nets trapped large sharks and greatly reduced the incidence of shark attack. In 1952, 7 gill nets, each 400 feet (130 m) long, were stretched along the Durban beachfront. In the first year, 552 sharks were caught in these nets and they were judged successful in reducing serious injuries from shark attack on local beaches.

CLUSTER OF ATTACKS

A series of shark attacks at seaside resorts without nets south of Durban between December 1957 (since known as Black December) and Easter 1958 claimed the lives of 5 people in 107 days. After trying such ad hoc methods as depth-charging and the hasty construction of temporary barriers, authorities decided to expand Durban's netting operations. Soon after, the government established the Natal Anti-Shark Measures Board, now called the Natal Sharks Board, and charged it with "the duty of approving, controlling and initiating measures for safeguarding bathers against shark attacks." By March 1966, 15 beaches had protective nets, maintained either by commercial fishers or municipal employees. In 1974, the Sharks Board assumed the servicing and maintenance of net installations, and since 1982, it is solely responsible for all shark netting in the province.

Barrier netting has not been used in the United States because the practice also catches and kills significant numbers of sharks. Changed attitudes now argue against such wholesale "fishing."

53

LIVING SAFELY *with* SHARKS *and* RAYS

It seems that people's attitudes toward sharks are changing. Twenty years ago, sharks were widely feared and assigned little value.

Today, people may still be apprehensive, but they are beginning to view sharks as interesting, even beautiful creatures, that deserve their place in the ocean. More than one shark attack survivor has said, in essence, "I regret the attack, but it wasn't the shark's fault. The sea is the shark's home, and I am only a visitor there."

KEEPING SHARKS AWAY FROM PEOPLE

Around the world, people have attempted to lessen the chance of shark attack by controlling sharks in two ways: physically excluding them from places of human activity, and killing and removing them from such areas. Both methods have their own sets of problems. Physically excluding sharks usually involves stretching long nets across the mouths of bays with swimming beaches. This is the method of choice in Australia and South Africa, but netting is labor intensive, nets need repair and even reinstallation after storms, and sharks that become entangled in them must be removed.

In South Africa, the Natal Sharks Board provides protection against shark attack at some 60 beaches. It services more than 25 miles (40 km) of netting, spread at intervals along 200 miles (325 km) of coastline in KwaZulu-Natal.

Beach-netting is also maintained in Australia. There, as in South Africa, nets occasionally entrap other kinds of marine animals, including whales. Recently, authorities in Queensland have begun trials with acoustic

DEVICES *The US Navy Shark Chasers (above) were widely used during WWII. In an anti-shark bag (below) the navy diver is safe from the nearby tiger shark*

signals to warn away baleen whales that may become entangled in shark nets.

Fishing programs to reduce shark numbers, in attempts to reduce the threat of shark attack, were in notable use in Hawaii in the 1950s, '60s and early '70s. Such fishing programs are ecologically questionable, expensive, and probably doomed to failure. Extermination of any species, especially a top predator, is inadvisable at best, and probably not practically possible

PROTECTING AND REPELLING

The best kind of repellent against shark attack is to avoid attracting or confusing sharks. Always avoid murky water, areas

lled with prey, waters
olluted by a dead or
leeding animal, and waters
ver drop-offs.

Choice of activity can
ake a difference, too. An
nalysis of shark attacks
ndicates that scuba divers are
ttacked more rarely than
vimmers and
norkelers on the
urface. In the few
ecorded attacks, the
cuba divers have
ther been at the
urface rather than at
epth, or have been
ssociated with
nusual activity that
nay have excited the
hark. For example, in
n attack on a scuba
iver in July 1995, off
1onterey, California,
a midwater depth
f 40 feet (12 m), the

COSTLY SECURITY
*Swimmers frolic safely
in the surf (right) at a
net-enclosed inner-
harbor Australian
beach. A great white
(below) strikes at the
motorized cage of
an abalone diver.*

ver was driving a submarine
cooter with a battery-
owered electric motor. It has
een suggested that the elec-
ical activity of the motor
ay have confused or even
tracted the shark.

The quest for a chemical
pellent was ambitiously
ursued by the United States
lavy and cooperating
ologists during and after
Vorld War II in order to
rotect downed fliers and
ip-accident victims awaiting
scue from the sea. Various
bstances were tested. A
nemical preparation named
Shark Chaser" was routinely
tached to life jackets. It
onsisted of a copper-based
emical packaged in
ombination with a brightly
olored dye. Behavioral tests
ith sharks indicated that the
pellent was ineffective, but
may have comforted many a
rvivor by its visual effect.

A physical barrier was also

developed by the United
States Navy to protect crash
survivors from sharks. The
Johnson Shark Bag was
essentially a surface flotation
device with a long, closed
tube extending downward.
The survivor filled the
sleeping-bag-sized tube with
water and climbed into it.
The tube retained any blood
or other olfactory cues.
Studies showed that the bag
was effective, except that
sharks would still approach
and investigate if stimulated
by bait in the water around it.

SAFETY FIRST

Although scuba divers are
rarely attacked, some divers
wear protective suits or
carry protective devices
(see p. 76) if they are exposed
to sharks in the course of their
work. Steel mesh suits and
gloves are worn by divers
filming sharks in feeding
situations, and by guide-divers

who feed sharks for
diving shark-
watchers.

Photographers
and researchers also
use stainless-steel and
aluminum cages to
protect themselves
from large species.
Australian abalone
divers have adapted
cages into mobile bottom-
vehicles for protection from
sharks while prying abalone
from the bottom. Pole spears
with explosive heads have
been used to kill sharks as
they approach divers. But
interest in repellents and
defensive devices seemed to
be higher in the past decade
than now.

Recently, the Natal Sharks
Board of South Africa has
developed a battery-powered
electrical repellent called a
POD (Protective Oceanic
Device) (see p. 77). This is
intended to protect against
attack from the three species
considered "most dangerous"
in the Natal region, the great
white, tiger, and bull sharks.

Most scientific divers and
scientists are cynical about the
promise of repellents. As one
diving scientist has said, "The
best repellent for shark attack
is dry desert sand. Lie down
in it and you will be safe."

UNVEILING *the* MYSTERIES *of the* OCEANS

Aquariums allow everyone a glimpse of this fascinating realm and a chance to see sharks and rays that most divers would never encounter.

Sharks and rays have always had the ability to inspire our imaginations, but we are only beginning to understand the role they play in our environment. They are often feared as vicious predators, or revered as powerful adversaries to the human race. With the advances made in scientific research and education, however, these attitudes are starting to change.

Much of this recent change in attitude can be attributed to the direct access people now have to sharks and rays through scuba diving. Researchers, cinematographers, conservationists, and many others, now have incredible access to sharks and rays and can observe them in their natural environment.

Unfortunately, not everyone has the opportunity to scuba dive. For those people who feel a need to get close to sea creatures, the public aquarium is the next-best alternative. In fact, it is the only place you can get close to animals such as sharks and rays in absolute safety.

HANDLED WITH CAR[E]
Capturing a shark or ray in the wild is a delicate operation. A lasso (left) inflicts little damage; the animal is constrained in [a] sling (below), and sedate[d] for transporting (bottom)

AQUARIUMS

There are many public aquariums throughout the world, and the number is growing rapidly. This is due to an increased interest in our aquatic environments. One of the major displays in most aquariums is often the shark and ray enclosure—it seems that most people are fascinated by these large predators. The Aquarium of the Americas and the Monterey Bay Aquarium, both in the United States, and Osaka Aquarium in Japan all have outstanding shark exhibits. These aquariums excel because of the care and attention to detail taken in creating natural environments for the animals.

On a global scale, there are approximately 100 species of shark and more than 50 species of ray on display. There are several species of shark that are arguably the

best for display in aquariums. They are the sand tiger (*Carcharias taurus*), bull shark (*Carcharhinus leucas*), sandbar shark (*Carcharhinus plumbeus*), blacktip reef shark (*Carcharhinus melanopterus*) and the

hitetip shark (*Triaenodon
esus*), all of which adapt to
aptivity very well. With
he greatly increased size
f modern aquarium
nks, better husbandry
chniques, and greater
nowledge of shark
iology, aquarists have
egun to display many
ecies not previously kept.
Most notable among these
ew attractions are whale
harks (*Rhincodon typus*). So
r, they have only been dis-
layed in Japanese aquariums.

These types of shark tend
o be the drawcard animals for
he institutions that display
hem. Surprisingly, they make
p only a very small percen-
ge of the sharks that are
oused in public aquariums.
Many of the sharks in public
quariums are small—less than
feet (1 m) in length—or
ottom-dwelling species, and
re often viewed as oddities or
urios, as they exhibit rather
range and unusual biology
r behaviors. Horn sharks
Heterodontidae), for
xample, are widely displayed
n aquariums because their
ody shape is prehistoric and
ecause the cases in which
hey lay their eggs are threaded
ke a carpenter's screw.

TOCKING AQUARIUMS

ublic aquariums have several
nethods for acquiring their
harks and rays—by donation,
y breeding, and by collecting.
Donation and breeding are
he most common means with
he smaller sharks, which
neans that their population
n aquariums is stable and
ven increasing. The larger
harks tend to be more
ifficult to breed and harder
o acquire through donation,
o they are usually collected
om the wild.

A WINDOW ON THE BAY

Financed by the family foundation of philanthropist David Packard,
a group of dedicated marine biologists, divers, and enthusiasts is
busy creating an aquarium that fires the imaginations of some two
million visitors a year from all around the world. In the former
Hovden fish cannery beside Monterey Bay, California, people can
now experience the world that divers visit, including getting close to
sharks, in absolute comfort and safety. There's a great kelp forest
(above) that sways in an artificially created tidal surge and teems
with nutrients for the creatures that hide among its branches, as well
as habitat exhibits for all manner of aquatic animals.

The aquarium focuses on the creatures and rich ecosystems of
Monterey Bay, including its beaches, estuaries, offshore waters, and
its deep, natural canyon that drops eventually to an incredible
12,000 feet (3,700 m). The opening of the aquarium in 1984 was
soon followed by the establishment of MBARI (the Monterey Bay
Aquarium Research Institute) in 1987. Staff from both institutions
work together to develop new collection and husbandry techniques
in order to display and keep animals never before seen by most
people. They also generously share their success with other
aquariums so that a wide public can learn about the ocean world.

When a public aquarium
needs to collect a large shark,
there is one rule that must
always be adhered to—the
shark must be kept in the best
condition possible. This has
led to the development of
several different ways of
catching the animal.

The most popular method
is to use a barbless hook and
line, either with a diver hand-
feeding the shark or by fishing
directly from a boat. Another
often-used method is to have

a diver lasso the shark and
have the boat crew haul the
animal to the side of the boat.
With both of these methods,
the shark is then maneuvered
into a sling, brought on board
the boat, and lowered into a
transport container where it
may be sedated for the trip to
the aquarium.

Rays are treated with
the same amount of respect
and are generally carefully
caught in nets or with barbless
hooks on a line.

SHARKS *and* RAYS
behind GLASS

Zoos and aquariums in the past were often categorized

as simple menageries, merely catering to the curious observer.

If you satisfy people's curiosity, you have the opportunity to educate them about the animals they are viewing. Millions of school children around the world visit public zoos and aquariums annually. Most of these children are simply curious. Their exposure to live, display animals, such as sharks and rays, will help them to develop not only a better understanding of wild animals but also, with supporting educational programs, a strong conservation ethic.

ANIMALS IN CAPTIVITY

Most zoos and aquariums now have education, conservation, and research programs. In fact, much of what we know about sharks and rays

VICARIOUS DANGER *Part of the aquarium experience in many places is to see divers actually feeding sharks.*

has come directly from public aquariums. They also assist indirectly, by allowing fisheries and other research organizations the use of their facilities and space to house their research animals.

The downside to keeping animals in captivity is often their lack of ability to adjust to the artificial environment. This can be due to inadequate or inappropriate management, or poor selection of the species to be kept. Great white sharks (*Carcharodon carcharias*), for example, have been displayed at several

aquariums around the world with little success. A great deal of research is needed on the quality of the food provided for great whites and the design of a facility that can house them successfully. Fortunately, inappropriate management is becoming less of a problem as we become more aware of the needs of captive animals, and because of government regulation of zoological institutions.

When sharks and rays are kept in aquariums, it is always a balancing act to keep the animals at a healthy weight. Most sharks and rays, when well maintained in a low-stress environment, grow larger than their wild counterparts. In most species of animal, one finds a physical difference between the wild and the captive creature. In captivity, the problem is often trying to keep an animal's weight down, whereas in the wild it is quite often the opposite. This is because in captivity an animal has more food available, and needs to expend less energy to catch its prey. After a few weeks in captivity, the sand tiger (*Carcharias taurus*), for example, which is often collected in a very lean state, can dramatically increase in weight. Most sand tigers will

ed the day they are brought
to a captive environment,
which is a good indicator of
their ability to adapt.

SHARKS IN AQUARIUMS

Most species of shark can be
kept in aquariums, and with
adequate husbandry they will
prosper, reproducing as
regularly as they would in the
wild. In fact, with a few
notable exceptions, sharks and
rays in aquariums live longer
than those in the wild. Whale
sharks (*Rhincodon typus*) and
basking sharks (*Cetorhinus
maximus*) both feed on large
quantities of plankton and are
difficult to hold for any period
of time because this food is
difficult and expensive to
supply. Being very large, these
animals also require gigantic
aquariums to give them
adequate space for a healthy
lifestyle. The king of sea
beasts, the great white shark,
is also difficult to display for
reasons of size. Some smaller
sharks, such as angelsharks
(Squatinidae), need a deep,
sandy or muddy bottom so
that they can bury themselves.

Most sharks in aquariums
are housed in multi-species
exhibits, so they need to be
able to survive within a mixed
community. There may be as
many as 20 different species of
shark within one communal
exhibit, as well as an
assortment of rays and bony
fish. If the correct species are
housed together, the end
result can be a spectacular
exhibit with little or no
aggression among its
inhabitants. The ability of
most sharks to live together
makes them one of the most
suitable large aquatic animals
for display. Their ferocious
reputation adds to the mys-
tique surrounding
them, and makes
them the most
popular of all the
aquarium animals.

RAYS IN AQUARIUMS

Rays are one of the
most intriguing of
all the animals that
aquariums display.
They do not usually
have obvious fins, their mouth
generally faces the ground,
and they have a reputation of
being dangerous to humans.
They are also one of the
hardiest marine creatures kept
in aquariums. All of which
makes them particularly desir-
able as display animals.

Of all the rays, there are
only a few that present any
problems in captivity. Devilrays (Mobulidae) are by far

TUNNEL VISION *Displays are often
set up so that sharks pass within a few
feet of viewers walking through a tunnel,
as at Sydney Aquarium (above); divers
in the tank at feeding time (below).*

the most difficult to display.
They need a constant supply
of plankton and a very large
aquarium because of their size.
Torpedo rays (Torpedinidae)
and shorttailed electric rays
(Hypnidae) can be a handful
for aquarium keepers, as they

can deliver an electric shock
capable of stunning a human.
These animals are not often
kept in aquariums for that
reason. The main environ-
mental requirement for most
rays is a soft, deep substrate in
which to bury themselves.

As with sharks, rays that are
given the right conditions in
aquariums will reproduce and
prosper just as well as they
would in the wild.

WHAT'S HAPPENING TODAY

Research on sharks and rays is being conducted in centers all over the world. In just about every country with a coastline, biologists are investigating sharks and rays.

Much of what we know about shark and ray biology has been learned from dead specimens, caught by fishermen or in active research-fishery programs. Scientists once felt that the way to learn was by "sacrificing" animals.

CHANGING PERSPECTIVE

We can still learn from dead specimens and in experimental situations, but refreshingly, more and more researchers are studying living animals in the wild. The scientific museums of the world are well stocked with specimens of sharks and rays that are available for study.

Scientists around the world are studying living sharks and rays. For example, at the Department of Biological Sciences, Florida Institute of Technology, Dr. Timothy C. Tricas and his students are studying the neurobiology and behavior of stingrays.

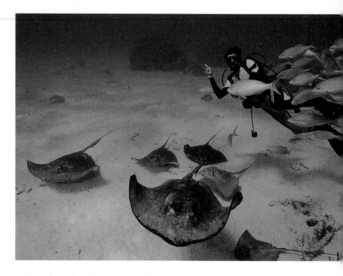

Tricas has also investigated the biting mechanics of the jaws of great white sharks and the wanderings of tiger sharks in Hawaii.

Current research focuses on how information from biological sources is processed by the brain, and especially how rays use their electrosensory system. This work combines watching stingrays in their native haunts, studying natural bioelectrical stimuli encountered by rays and skates in the wild, and studying the neural responses of the electrosensory system to these natural stimuli.

Florida's Mote Marine Laboratory Center for Shark Research (MML/CSR) was established in 1992 as an outgrowth of the

ON SHOW *A diver with rays (above) at Stingray City in the Cayman Islands. A shark encounter exhibit (below) at Sea World, San Diego, California.*

Laboratory's Shark Biology Program. It is now an international center for scientific cooperation, research, education, and public information on sharks and the related skates and ray

CSR research includes basic and applied studies of shark biology, from anatomy and physiology to ecology and fisheries science. In contrast to the MML Biomedica Research Program, which concentrates on sharks and skates as laboratory models fc studies of disease-resistance, the CSR research program has a broader focus on field and laboratory studies of thes animals. CSR scientists

RISKY BUSINESS *Diver Gary Adkison tags Carcharhinus perezi, a Caribbean reef shark, at Walker's Cay, Bahamas.*

investigate various biological adaptations that sharks have made to their marine environment, with an emphasis on the role of sharks as an important marine resource.

STUDYING WILD SHARKS

Watching a wide-ranging shark or ray go about its life day after day, 24 hours a day, would be enlightening, but it is not practicable. However, intrepid field biologists do spend many sunny hours and dark nights watching and following sharks. Some researchers have developed ways to tag sharks with battery-powered transmitters that can record or transmit selected information about the tagged animal. Tags can relay location, depth, compass heading, temperature of the water, temperature of the muscle tissue, and so forth.

At the Hawaii Institute of Marine Biology, University of Hawaii, Kaneohe Bay, Dr. Kim Holland and his students are tagging and studying scalloped hammerhead sharks and tiger sharks. Dr. Samuel Gruber, University of Miami, Florida, continues his research program and tagging studies of lemon sharks in the vast sand flats and shoals of Bimini, in the Bahamas. He and his students are building on more than 20 years of data collected from living lemon sharks. Gruber's program admits volunteers and seasonal students to help in the research.

Scientists from Scripps Institution of Oceanography and Hubbs-Sea World Institute in San Diego are designing programs to tag western Pacific whale sharks with radio tags. These transmitters will send signals via satellites, and help us to learn whether these largest of all fish migrate, and if so, to where.

ANGLERS CAN HELP

The need for shark fishery management and depletion of shark populations worldwide are changing attitudes toward sharks by sports anglers. Mote Marine Laboratory, Florida, has organized an annual fishing tournament since 1988. Not a single shark is needlessly killed. Instead, all sharks caught are identified and measured, tagged when possible, and released. The collected data are used to track local shark populations, to gauge catch-and-release mortality, and to provide migratory and age/growth information. Fishers compete for prizes, and the event publicizes the state of the sharks and the importance of management measures.

CLUBS, SOCIETIES, AND WEBSITES

The Resources Directory (page 272) provides a list of some of the larger clubs, societies and websites that are involved in the research and conservation of sharks and rays. It also lists universities and museums that curate excellent collections for study.

ACCIDENTAL CATCH

In 1976, some United States Navy acoustic researchers off Oahu, Hawaii, made an unusual discovery. Entangled in their equipment was a large, adult male shark. Unfortunately, the shark could not be saved, but the researchers realized that it was unusual and invited scientists to inspect it. Preliminary inspection by Leighton Taylor and other scientists confirmed that it represented a very distinct, undescribed species. The so-called megamouth shark (*Megachasma pelagios*), pictured above, is now known from less than a dozen specimens. Who knows how many earlier megamouth specimens were discarded by accident?

GETTING INVOLVED *in* SHARK CONSERVATION

The oceans of the world need our help. The human race is harming the habitats of marine creatures and it is up to us to stop the damage.

Knowledge and awareness are the keys to living in harmony with the diversity of life on Earth. As we learn more about sharks, we begin to appreciate their important ecological roles and to understand the consequences of our predation on them and of our disturbance, and destruction of their habitats.

Faced with drastically changed environments or catastrophically reduced population sizes, many species may change and evolve, become rare, or even go extinct. The changes humans continue to make, through the effects of our technology and our sheer numbers, gravely affect many habitats and species, including most sharks and rays.

Overfishing of sharks, especially those caught as bycatch, is of growing international concern. Few shark fisheries have any kind of enforced management controls in place. Combined with the longevity and low reproductive rates of sharks, overfishing is certain to result in rapid declines in populations.

Biologists and conservation groups recommend immediate measures to reduce fishing to sustainable levels, to stop wasteful fishing practices, and to protect fragile habitats, such as inshore breeding grounds.

PEOPLE POWER

Humans have the power to change the world. Of course, so do many other species. Birds transport seeds to newly created islands and forests are born. Corals and algae build reefs and islands. But the power humans possess is in many ways unique. We can make changes by accident or by design. We can try to understand the consequences of our acts or we can act in ignorance and carelessness.

Like every species, Homo sapiens interacts with and depends upon the multitude of other species with which we share the land and ocean. But unlike other species, our power to change is greatly magnified by our technology and by our overwhelming

GOOD AND BAD MANAGEMENT

Responsible control of Australia's Great Barrier Reef Marine Park (above) mea[n] that it will survive in good order for futu[re] generations to enjoy. Poor local government practices result in rubbish on beaches (below). Cleaning up after oil spills (below right) is a recurring probler[m]

umbers. Many of the changes we have made and continue to make are careless or heedless of consequences, motivated by greed and selfishness. Every environmental change we make, oil spills, silting of reefs, forest clear-cutting, even flushing a toilet, eventually affects the seas.

Each of us can choose to act in ways that do not harm the ocean. We can act in ways that cause the least disturbance to the species around us, realizing that every action will still have some effect. We can ensure that, for example, the flushed toilet goes to an environmentally sound treatment plant; that land-grading for our house lots does not send mud into coastal waters.

One of the best ways to help is to see that our children and our fellows recognize the power we have to change the environment, but we risk our credibility if we oversimplify or preach stridently. Sharks and rays and all other creatures are in jeopardy unless we truly understand how nature works and modify our acts to have minimal consequences.

THE PUBLIC FORUM

We can act individually, and in concert. Consider joining one of the societies or conservation groups

GREENPEACE: A FORCE TO BE RECKONED WITH

An international action group, Greenpeace has been a visible force for change in the way we treat our environment for the past 25 years. Formed by a group of Americans and Canadians, it has since attracted a growing band of activists and supporters worldwide. It accepts no government or corporate funding, financing its campaigns solely from donations and member support. Some of its abiding concerns are the ecology of the oceans, and how to prevent them from becoming a barren dumping ground for waste. It is often Greenpeace that blows the whistle on dubious activities taking place unobserved far out to sea.

Greenpeace works in a non-violent way by studying problems and suggesting viable solutions, by lobbying governments and businesses to change bad practices, such as drift-net fishing, and by making people aware of irresponsible activities, such as unsustainable levels of fishing and the dumping of toxic pollutants. Sometimes, Greenpeace intervenes directly. Pictured above, supporters protest about whaling activities in Icelandic waters. Contact a Greenpeace office in your nearest major city to find out how to offer your support.

listed in our Resources Directory (see p. 272). Work towards having effective marine park areas and no-take zones declared. Subscribe to natural history and diving magazines and add your vote to campaigns they orchestrate for the protection of the environment. Work with the public aquarium in your area to learn about local and global marine issues and ways to act. The Internet and the World

Wide Web are also great tools for learning and for sharing your observations and ideas for solving problems. If you dive regularly, record shark sightings to help to add to our knowledge about various species. Make notes while your memories are fresh and send them off with photos, if possible, to magazines, or groups such as the American Elasmobranch Society (see p. 275). Report any unusual objects or dramatic changes in numbers of marine creatures in areas you visit regularly. Such changes may indicate a problem that can be fixed by prompt local action.

Your every act affects the natural world in some way. Strive to know what these effects may be and work to make them helpful to land and sea. Live so that your effect on the world enhances its diversity and wonder.

When once [the ocean deep] has been seen, it will remain
forever the most vivid memory in life, solely because of its
cosmic chill and isolation, the eternal and absolute
darkness and the indescribable beauty of its inhabitants.

Half Mile Down,
CHARLES WILLIAM BEEBE (1877–1962), American scientist

CHAPTER THREE

IN *the* FIELD

PLANNING a FIELD TRIP VACATION

Careful planning is essential to ensure that your encounters with sharks and rays are safe, environmentally sound, exciting, and memorable—for all the right reasons.

Sharks and rays can be found in all the world's oceans, but because they occur in smaller numbers than other species of fish, they can sometimes be hard to locate. In some areas, access to sharks and rays may be fairly easily gained, and little planning is required. Caribbean reef sharks in the Bahamas or stingrays at Grand Cayman, for example, can be found there all year round, and day trips provided by local dive centers or dive resorts will virtually guarantee sightings. If you are fortunate enough to live near an ocean environment that sharks or rays inhabit, perhaps all you need do to see them is to don mask, fins, and snorkel, and wade in off the local beach.

Many species are not only unique to certain countries, but they may congregate in an area for only limited seasons. The whale sharks at Ningaloo Reef in Western Australia are an excellent example of this— they congregate there only during late March, April and May. To meet up with them may involve traveling long distances, and proper timing of your trip is critical.

Some sharks and rays are found in remote locations. For example, to see the silvertip sharks in Papua New Guinea or the sharks and rays in the Galapagos Islands, you may have to take a trip on a live-aboard dive boat for 7 to 10 days to reach the area.

When planning your trip, contact a dive-travel specialist experienced in dive-vacation packages. Some vacation

ERODED BY TIME *The Natural Arch near Darwin Island in the Galapagos. A great white shark (above) glides past*

I must go down to the

eas again, to the lonely

ea and the sky.

ea Fever,
OHN MASEFIELD
878–1976), British poet

ackages provide encounters
vith just one species, but
ecause some of the congre-
ations are seasonal, you may
e able to combine several in
he one trip. For example, if
ou were to take a trip to
ustralia during March or
April, it would be possible to
ee gray nurse sharks in New
outh Wales and great white
narks in South
ustralia when the
veather is favorable,
efore pursuing
ghtings of whale
narks at Ningaloo
eef from March
May.

IELD GUIDES
ND BOOKS
he best way to
nd out what
ptions are available
or shark and ray
ncounters is to
udy reference
ooks and a well-
espected field guide
edicated to this
ubject. The Field
uide section in
iis book (page 132)
rovides an intro-
uction to 68 species of shark
nd 20 species of ray. The
ppearance, behavior, and
abitat of each species is
iscussed. *Encounters with
harks and Rays* (page 226)
atures 21 sites worldwide
here you are likely to view
ecific sharks and rays.

BIODIVERSITY *Tropical coral reefs
(above) and temperate zone kelp
forests (left) are famously diverse
communities. In both, sharks and rays
are dominant predators.*

SURFING THE NET
Another good source of
information is the Internet.
Many operators, dive-travel
agencies, and divers with
experience of shark and ray
sightings communicate on the
Net. Be aware that some of
the information may not be

accurate, and further research
will be necessary to maximize
your chances of an encounter.
Animal behavior can vary,
weather can be unreliable and
even the best dive operator
can experience problems that
affect the normal operation
of the tour. Nevertheless, the
Internet is a good place to get
ideas, information and many
contacts that can be checked
out directly with the dive
operators on the Internet.

67

PREPARATION

*The best preparation for a field trip is to gather
as much background information as possible and
to be aware of the hazards such a trip may involve.*

Gathering information prior to going on a field trip is a time-consuming, but rewarding, task. Many avenues are open to the intending traveler.

DIVE MAGAZINES
The national dive magazines of various countries are an excellent source of information about special-interest marine animal encounters. These magazines place accuracy above all other concerns. They will be first with news of discoveries and carry updates on existing information. Many of the advertisers in these magazines are dive operators and dive travel agencies.

BROCHURES
Although travel brochures can provide good information about some of the facilities and features of a destination, they are never comprehensive and not always accurate. Such brochures might feature photographs of rarely seen shark or ray species. In other instances, the photograph may have been taken at a different location entirely. Always follow up on the information

EXOTIC LOCATIONS *Scuba diving at Ihuru, in the Maldives (above), and on the reef off Belize, in the Caribbean (left).*

offered in brochures and check details carefully with your dive-travel consultant.

PLAN AHEAD
Prepare yourself by studying up-to-date site maps of the area. These can be obtained from your dive-travel consultant. As your departure date nears, it is important to consult accurate short-term

and long-term weather reports for the area from recognized agencies.

DIVE-TRAVEL HAZARDS
With any foreign travel it's wise to check if a "travel advisory" has been issued by your government. For United States travelers, the US State Department operates a 24-hour hotline (see p. 272) that you can call for the latest word on political instability, epidemics, war, or terrorism. Another source is the World Wide Web at http://www.stolaf.edu/network/travel-advisories.html

Some of the most exciting destinations where sharks and rays can be found are in tropical areas where the dive traveler may be exposed to

THE BENDS *A diver receives oxygen treatment (right) for decompression sickness before being transferred to a recompression chamber.*

rtain health hazards. One of e most serious is malaria, a rus carried by the anopheles osquito and passed into the oodstream of the host when e mosquito feeds.

Travelers must be prepared r a number of minor ill- esses that can arise from a ange to their regular envir- nment. Ask your doctor to escribe a range of drugs to al with diarrhea, nausea, in and insomnia. Do not pect to find these drugs adily at your destination.

Always dive onservatively, do ot exceed the commended dive nes, and follow oper procedures. If ou don't, bubbles n form in the oodstream and you ay fall victim to ecompression ckness. This can ad to irreversible ain damage or ralysis if treatment a recompression amber is not gun quickly.

Many travelers nderestimate the ower of the tropical n, which burns iickly regardless of e time of day. If ou are severely irnt on the first day your vacation, it ay spoil the rest your trip. The opical Sun will rn you within 15 inutes. Cover up, ay in the shade, use enty of sunscreen, ep your dive-suit n in open boats, id wear a hat.

Never ignore oral cuts and scrapes,

which can become severely infected. Dive staff are experienced at treating these wounds, and you should seek their immediate help.

Learn to identify marine species that can cause harm and discomfort. These include fire corals, stinging hydroids,

sea jellies, coralliomorphs and venomous fish, snakes or shells. While these species do not attack people, ignorance can result in accidents.

TRAVEL INSURANCE
Once you book your trip, it is wise to take out travel insurance. This inexpensive option will provide you with compensation for the loss of your trip should you have an accident before or during travel, and offers other benefits, such as cover for medical expenses and lost baggage. Take out a policy recommended by your dive- travel consultant as it is more likely to be tailored to diving- related considerations.

DAN INSURANCE
Divers Alert Network is an American-based diving insurance and diving accident management service. DAN membership may be secured by paying an inexpensive annual membership fee (see Resources Directory pages 272–3). Members receive automatic emergency evacu- ation to the nearest suitable medical facility. This may include transfer to another country where a recompression chamber is available.

American residents also have access to other DAN insurance, including cover for travel, medical, disability and accidental death.

PREVENTING MALARIA

Prevention is better than cure, and it is important to defend yourself against this disease when you travel in regions where malaria may be present.

• Obtain preventative drugs prescribed by a doctor who has up-to-date knowledge of the latest malarial prevention for the areas you wish to visit.

• Check with the doctor that these drugs are compatible with diving.

• Make sure that you commence the prescription prior to entering the malarial area. Most important, continue to take the drugs for the required time after leaving the area as the virus can survive, dormant, in your bloodstream for up to four weeks.

• Avoid being bitten. The anopheles mosquito is most active at dusk and dawn, so cover up with light-colored clothing and use plenty of repellent. Stay out of the jungle and stay on the water as much as possible.

• If you have a choice, keep in mind that live-aboard boats will expose you to far fewer mosquitos and other bugs than shore-based accommodation.

• Learn to recognize the signs of malaria and report any symptoms immediately. People living in malarial areas are experienced at treating an outbreak.

• If symptoms appear after your trip, tell your doctor that you have been in a malarial area and insist on complete testing.

GETTING CLOSER

A good dive-travel agency will take the time to determine your expectations and level of experience before helping you plan a trip to your chosen destination.

Choose your dive-travel agency carefully. Try to ensure that the consultants are reputable and experienced, as well as environmentally responsible.

DIVE OPERATORS

Enthusiasts who want to encounter sharks and rays will find they need the services of a dive operator to organize air and scuba equipment, a dive boat, accommodation, and shark cages or other specialized equipment or support. These dive operators also know the best dive sites, the species and behavior of sharks and rays in their area, and other marine life of interest to the dive traveler.

Operators who are skilled in the field soon make a name for themselves that becomes respected worldwide.

DIVE-TRAVEL AGENTS

Dive operators are represented worldwide by specialist dive-travel agents. These consult directly with dive travelers wishing to plan a vacation or excursion that can include encounters with marine life. Dive-travel agents have first-hand experience of the area you wish to visit. They also have video promotional tapes, brochures and photographic material that provide information about the destination, the dive operator, and any special features of the area.

It is very important to make your expectations known to your consultant. A good dive-travel consultant will always try to ensure your expectations are met. If it is important to you, always ask about weather patterns and seasons. If you don't, your consultant may assume this is not an issue for you. Some shark and ray enthusiasts are unconcerned that it is cyclo season in a particular area if that is the best time for them to see sharks and rays.

Once you have agreed on the trip you want, the dive-travel agency will put together a package that will include flights; transfers; accommodation; and a diving package that includes boats, divemaster services, scuba cylinders and weights. If you do not have your own diving equipment check if it is cheaper to take hire package from your local dive center or to hire at your chosen location.

If your trip involves a live-aboard dive boat, meals will be included. This is rarely the case if you are staying at shore-based resort

DIVE CENTERS

Today's dive center provides a much wider range of service than just

SCUBA SCHOOL *Last-minute briefing (right) from the divemaster. A dive vessel at Roach Island, off the north-east coast of Australia.*

uba training and gear
les. The modern dive
nter offers specialized
aining; scuba
uipment sales, hire
d service; and
derwater photo-
aphic equipment and
otography training.
ost important, it offers
oup trips guided by
experienced tour
ader/divemaster.
any dive centers have
travel consultant on the staff
ho will understand your
eds and expectations. The
ve operators also have
ained and experienced staff
the dive destinations who
n provide information to
ients through their local
ve centers.

ROUP TRAVEL
here are many advantages to
rticipating in a group diving
cation. The solo dive
aveler cannot take advantage
the experience of a tour
ader who has local
owledge of the area, and
e ability to smooth out
ccasional difficulties during
e trip. Dive-tour leaders are
ten qualified divemasters or
structors who have an
timate knowledge of unique
arine life and shark or ray
havior. They are skilled in
elping group members

improve their diving skills
during the trip. Group trips
are also very social, and
new divers will soon feel
welcomed into the group.

LIVE-ABOARD VERSUS SHORE-BASED DIVING

At many locations that are
known as "hot spots" for
sharks and rays, there is a
choice of staying at a shore-
based resort or participating in
a 7 to 10 day trip on a live-
aboard dive boat.

The main advantage of
shore-based facilities is a
greater variety of other
interests that may suit non-
diving partners and children.
Also, there is usually the
option of a shorter stay and
fewer dives, which makes a
budget vacation possible.

Live-aboards, however,
provide the best value for
money. Your trip aboard will

UNLIMITED GEAR *is
available from dive
centers such as this (left).
Live-aboard dive boats,
like the Telita (below),
offer divers every comfort.*

include unlimited
diving, all meals
and refreshments, a
greater range of
dive sites, and
much more oppor-
tunity to meet
special creatures—such as
sharks and rays. Going diving
on a live-aboard trip is
much simpler and more
comfortable. The vessel is
often at the dive site for many
hours, so divers can choose
their own dive times.
Equipment is carried on
board, and showers and food
are readily available. Live-
aboard dive groups are smaller
and more intimate.

Keep in mind that the
quality and performance of
the various dive operators can
often differ greatly. Ask for
recommendations from your
dive center or dive-travel
agency, or from friends who
have already experienced
enjoyable trips. In the highly
competitive world of the
diving industry, if one deal is
cheaper than another, be
wary. There is always a very
good reason for it.

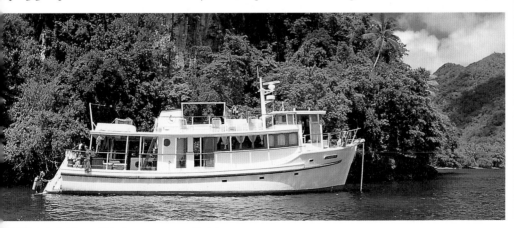

EXPANDING *the* KNOWLEDGE

Sharks and rays provide an opportunity for divers and snorkelers to enjoy an encounter with some of the world's most graceful and magnificent creatures.

A most important aspect of any shark or ray encounter is your behavior, so you must understand and "read" the behavior of the species of sharks or rays you are likely to meet.

APPROACHING SHARKS AND RAYS

If you wish to get close to a shark or ray, keep in mind some simple guidelines. Always dive in a small group. When you see a shark or ray, stay still, or move very slowly. The creature will be less intimidated and will probably approach you. Slow your breathing to minimize the noise of your exhaust bubbles. If you need to swim close, take an indirect path to the animal, swimming on a converging course.

Manta rays are exceptional among sharks and rays in that they sometimes seem to enjoy human contact. Some have been known to instigate contact and return to a dive group repeatedly. However, such encounters are rare, and divers should not encourage them. You should never initiate contact with any wild animal. To do so could adversely affect its health and behavior. Whale sharks are often greatly stressed by divers attempting to touch them.

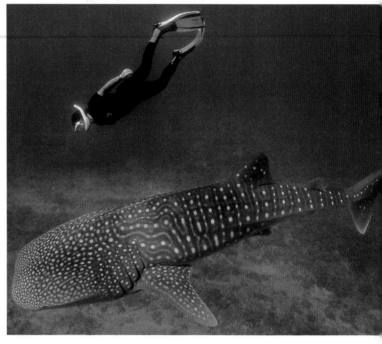

GIANTS OF THE DEEP *The whale shark (above) grows to at least 40 feet (12 m). A marbled ribbontail ray (below right) grows to more than 5 feet (1.5 m).*

PERSONAL DIVING EQUIPMENT

Dive travelers should ensure that their equipment is complete and in perfect order. Check your diving skills and proficiency, and all your gear, by having a practice dive before a trip. Should this not be possible before the trip, do it as a check-out dive with the divemaster as soon as you are at the location. The sea floor or the confines of a shark cage surrounded by sharks is a very unpleasant place to discover that your regulator or mask is. leaking, your air is low, your battery has gone flat in your dive computer, or your weight belt is slipping.

Pack your certification car and dive log with your equipment. All dive operato: require proof of certification and some will demand a record of dive experience before taking you on an advanced dive. This is a lega necessity in some countries.

KEEPING A RECORD OF OBSERVATIONS

Divers or snorkelers can contribute a great deal to marine science or conservation if they are willing to record their observations. Sharks and rays are hard to study in their own habitat, and too few scientists and

QUID SPACE *Diving from [fi]shing trawler (right) in the [Ma]ldives. As well as a dive [log]book (below right), keep [rec]ords of your observations.*

[M]arine biologists are [av]ailable to monitor [th]e behavior, health or [m]ovements of rays [an]d sharks adequately. [O]ften it is the casual [ob]server or the dive [op]erators and staff [w]ho are in the best [po]sition to observe [sp]ecial behavior, new [dis]coveries, or any [cr]itical changes.

Your observations are [va]luable only if you record [th]e data properly and take [gr]eat care to be accurate and [ob]jective. Do not jump to [an]y conclusions that might [m]as your ability to observe [ac]curately. Simply write [ex]actly what you witness, [an]d let the experts do the [in]terpreting. An important [po]int to remember is to carry [a] waterproof slate and pen, [an]d to record everything [im]mediately—it's surprising [w]hat you can forget during [th]e time span of a dive. [R]emember to note any [co]nspicuous markings or [sh]apes. These can help to

identify a species or even a known individual.

Try to record the date, time, depth, and water temperature. Include any details of tides, currents, weather, or moon phase. These can be important clues to mating or movement patterns. Also, take note of the surrounding habitat in which the behavior took place—for example, the ocean surface, mid-water, on a reef, among kelp, or on a shipwreck. It was observations such as these that established that sand tigers congregate to mate during a certain month every year on the wreck of

the US submarine *Tarpon*, in the Atlantic Ocean near North Carolina in the United States.

Avoid disturbing the animals' natural behavior by your presence on the scene. Try to stay still, breathe slowly, and don't get too close. Include observations of injury, improper or illegal fishing activities, or evidence of stress on the animals. Keep in mind that what you don't see can also be important. If the sharks are supposed to be there and they are missing, record it. Provide copies of your observations to the dive operator, shark and ray conservation groups, and marine science authorities.

Photographic flash units do not disturb marine life, so if you are a photographer, so much the better. Send photographs with your recordings to one of the natural history or recreational diving magazines. Other readers may have a similar story to tell.

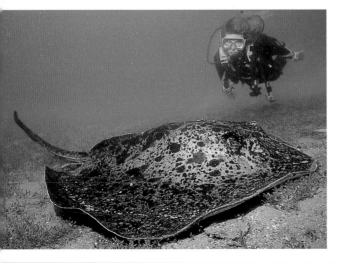

ENCOUNTERS
with SHARKS and RAYS

For the most part, sharks and rays do not pose a threat to

humans. They are not aggressive animals—they are

usually prepared to live and let live.

Having swum among sharks for generations, indigenous people of Polynesia and Melanesia are well aware of their behavior. Yet they do not live in fear of them, and shark attacks among these people are very rare. They have a spiritual relationship with these sea creatures and will not kill

them. In some cases, they believe that sharks are the reincarnated souls of their deceased family members.

Most other cultures do not share this attitude toward sharks and rays, being, at the very least, wary of these

creatures. Indeed, if you are snorkeling or diving in areas where you are likely to encounter sharks and rays, you should be especially careful. There are a number of precautions you should take, and guidelines to follow

KNOWING THE QUARRY *People of Papua New Guinea (right) are on good terms with sharks. The silvertip shark (below) is territorial and not to be trifled with. This giant black stingray (far right) was seen in Queensland, Australia, and the zebra shark (top right) in the Red Sea.*

GUIDELINES FOR SHARK AND RAY ENCOUNTERS

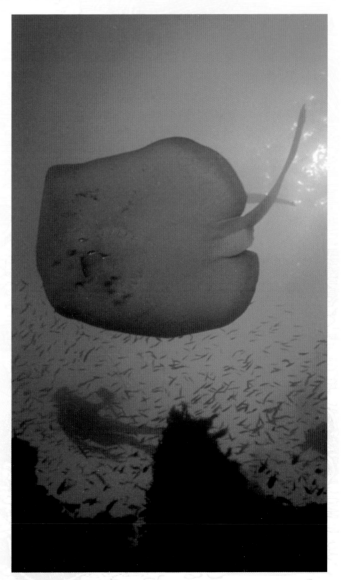

Never panic. Most approaches by sharks and rays are motivated by simple curiosity. Do not assume that you are in trouble.

Maintain eye contact. If you want to retreat, do it in a slow, controlled manner.

Don't be afraid to move toward these creatures. Move slowly so as not to intimidate them. They are wary of other large predators, and they will often swim away rapidly. The exception to this is a reef shark defending its territory. Do not approach any reef shark that is swimming with an exaggerated side-to-side motion with its back hunched, and its pectoral fins down. Instead, calmly and quickly leave the area.

Avoid periods of low light (dawn or dusk) and low visibility. At these times, a shark could mistake you for its natural prey.

On the surface, avoid excess splashing. To a shark, you will appear to be a disabled animal and you will attract the wrong kind of interest. Underwater, swim with slow, deliberate strokes so that you will appear to be another healthy predator, and sharks will be wary.

Avoid areas where people are spearfishing. A struggling fish transmits distress signals that sharks are able to pick up from miles away.

If baits are used to attract sharks into the area, pay careful attention to the ocean current and make certain you are always up-current of the bait. Any object in the odor corridor carried along by the current will attract sharks.

Make sure the dive boat is up-current and not far away.

Beware of any small, light-colored object that contrasts with your equipment, especially if it is hanging loosely. Sharks can mistake white fins, gloves, a white underwater slate, or torch for a piece of bait.

Diving in a group can be safer. When you are finished, leave the site as a group because sharks will become bolder as numbers reduce.

Never touch, surround or try to contain a shark or ray. They must always be allowed plenty of room to retreat, or they may panic and rush you in a frantic attempt to escape.

If a shark becomes overly curious and approaches too close for comfort, a hard punch on the nose will usually cause it to retreat rapidly. Some divers carry a shark billy (any short, blunt rod) for just this purpose.

Always remember, although they are not aggressive, there is no such thing as a harmless shark or ray. Each can and will defend itself if threatened, and this is the natural response.

PROTECTIVE EQUIPMENT

Over the years there have been many attempts to provide effective protection for those professionals who must work with sharks and rays.

During the past 60 years, many strategies designed to protect swimmers and divers from sharks have been developed and tested (see pp. 54–5). Until very recently, all have failed.

PROTECTING THE PROFESSIONAL

During the Second World War, the United States Navy put its faith in a chemical shark repellent. The sharks swam right through it. They also kept swimming through other repellents, such as air bubble curtains, sound wave barriers and dyes. Mesh netting has been installed at a number of beaches to create a safety barrier for bathers. But, unfortunately, these nets kill a great number of harmless sharks, rays, turtles, dolphins, and many other marine animals.

Divers developed a numb[er] of strange, and unsuccessful, devices. Dressing a diver as a black-and-white sea snake w[as] one unusual strategy put to the test—until it was realize[d] that some sharks eat sea snake[s]. Weapons with a detonating device were developed to shoot any aggressive shark. But, since most shark-attack victims never see the shark coming, these weapons were directed at sharks that were mostly harmless. A hypodermic gas device called a "shark dart" was als[o] developed. This killed the shark, after first inflating it and rendering it harmless. However, because the dart had to be fired into the shark[']s stomach, it was effective onl[y] on sharks swimming by rath[er] than ones that were attacking.

A very effective device— a stainless-steel suit of chain-mail—was finally developed by Australian underwater photographers and shark

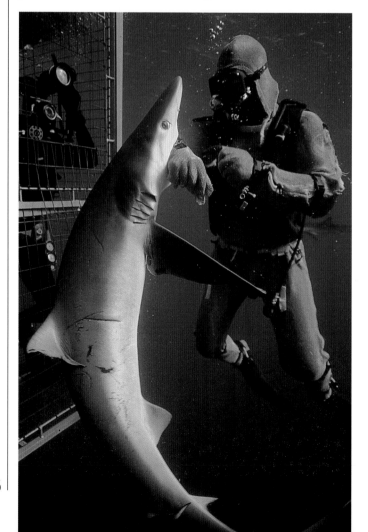

TESTING TIMES *Developing the protective stainless-steel chain-mail su[it] involved close contact (above) and tryi[ng] to get a shark to bite it (left).*

PROTECTIVE DEVICE *The POD (below) disrupts signals picked up by a shark's natural detectors, the ampullae of Lorenzini, situated along its face.*

xperts, Ron and Valerie Taylor. This suit has become andard equipment for film akers, dive guides, and cientists who work with arks. However, it does have ome disadvantages, and must e used only by experienced pecialists trained in its use. can restrict movement, and s weight prevents it from eing discarded easily in an mergency. It is also possible at a very large shark could rush or tear the garment.

A recent major reakthrough, how- ver, promises to rovide the ultimate rotection from ccidental shark tack for all divers, horkelers, and water port enthusiasts.

is a device called he shark POD (or rotective Oceanic evice). It has been gorously tested by the South frican Natal Sharks Board and y Ron and Valerie Taylor.

The shark POD is a ompact accessory that fits nto a diver's scuba cylinder. is connected to a wire that ins from the POD to a small ate attached to the diver's n. A switch is provided to nable the diver to turn it on efore entering the water, and warning light reveals that he unit is on and working. he unit can be switched off the water should the diver ant to get closer to sharks or

rays. A red light display indicates the remaining battery life, giving the diver time to surface and replenish both battery and air supply.

The POD repels sharks at close quarters by creating an electrical force field around the diver that totally disrupts the shark's ampullae of Lorenzini. These are the natural electrical detectors situated along a shark's face that it uses to detect minute electronic signals emitted by potential prey. This disruption cannot be tolerated by sharks.

Tests have shown that the shark POD is very effective, does not injure sharks or rays and has no effect on other marine life, as these creatures do not have ampullae of Lorenzini.

The Natal Sharks Board is currently developing a version that can provide a complete screen for a beach or bathing area. Once this has been perfected, the meshing of our beaches against sharks would become unnecessary. This would relieve the community of a major annual expense, and much innocent marine life would be spared.

SHARK PARTNERS

Both Australian-born, Ron (b. 1934) and Valerie (b. 1935) Taylor originally shared a common interest in spearfishing, at which they both excelled, and underwater photography. Working independently and together, they have notched up a list of extraordinary films and TV documentaries, including *Playing with Sharks, Shark Hunters, Blue Water, White Death,* and *Inner Space.* The Taylors' focus of interest has altered over the years to one of committed conservation of all marine creatures, no matter how fearsome. They now work tirelessly for better understanding of the denizens of the deep, especially the much-maligned and misunderstood shark. Valerie and her husband pioneered the use of a protective mesh diving suit made of stainless steel, which made possible photographic work among sharks without the photographer being confined to a shark cage. More recently, the Taylors have been helping to test the POD.

UNDERWATER PHOTOGRAPHY

Capturing encounters with sharks and rays on film can be a thrilling and satisfying exercise for many dive travelers.

Fortunately for both the amateur and professional photographer, great advances in technology mean that successful underwater photography is now possible.

CAMERA EQUIPMENT

The complete beginner might choose a disposable camera in a waterproof housing. This is an inexpensive system that calls for no technical knowledge of photography. Such cameras produce a good result, particularly in shallow, clear, sunlit, tropical waters.

More serious photographers prefer amphibious 35 mm cameras with interchangeable lenses, underwater strobe lighting, variable focus, and exposure control. Such features allow a much wider range of photographic composition and the means to deal with low light levels or limited visibility.

Advanced or professional photographers should consider combining a current model auto focus 35 mm SLR (single lens reflex) land camera with one of the many excellent waterproof camera housings that are now available. These systems provide a very wide choice of lens options that allow photography of small, medium, or very large

RECORDING THE COLORS *of sea stars and coral in Hawaii (above); and a special amphibious camera (above left).*

sharks and rays. Auto focus, auto exposure, and motor drive film transport features are invaluable for action shots of fast-moving subjects.

TYPE OF FILM

Sharks and rays are often encountered near the water surface where light levels are good, so

any slide or print film with a medium sensitivity rating of ISO 50 or 100 is suitable. In deeper water, below 30 feet (10 m), the photographer can use a strobe (flash unit) to provide extra light and restore natural colors. Films with sensitivity ratings of ISO 200 are often used for fast-action subjects photographed in available light situations. Choose a film that favors the blacks, whites, and subtle shades of color common among shark and ray species.

TECHNICAL CONSIDERATIONS

Photographing sharks and rays frequently involves the use of available natural light so it is very important to be aware of the position of the

FINGERTIP CONTROL *Strobe units and cameras are securely mounted on a bracket for maximum flexibility.*

PRACTICAL CONSIDERATIONS

A dive buddy willing to act as a rear guard can be very valuable—particularly when the photographer is pre-occupied with composing pictures of one shark while other sharks are about. Since chum is often used to attract sharks, and baits are provided to over-come their natural caution, the sharks will often become very excited and curious. It is not unusual for several sharks to approach at once. A second set of human eyes is useful at this point.

Photographers may sometimes find it necessary to extend their camera and upper body through the windows of shark cages to obtain a good angle. The shark you can see is not a problem, but another shark approaching from the side could be. Once again, a vigilant companion is vital.

…n. To ensure that details of …e shark or ray are revealed, …y to position yourself so that …e Sun is always coming at …a angle over your shoulders. …void photography around …idday when the Sun is …irectly above you.

When a strobe is used to …rovide light, the angle of the …un in relation to the subject … not so critical, but beware …f suspended matter in the …ater that may be emphasized …y the strobe light and spoil …e image. This effect is …rmed "backscatter" and it …n be avoided by using low …ower settings on the strobe …d longer strobe arms. Some …ommon sources of back-…atter in shark photography …e chum—a mixture of …roducts used to attract sharks; …articles of shark bait used for …eding sharks once they …rive; and plankton—a …atural food source of whale …arks and manta rays. Also a …roblem are the small bubbles …onstantly created by the …ovement of shark cages, the …ve boat, or the wake from …ther snorkelers' fins.

To ensure clear, sharp …ages underwater, avoid …ooting until you are less …an a few yards from the …bject. If the subject is a very …rge shark or ray, you will …ed a 15 mm or 20 mm

wide-angle lens to capture the whole creature. Lenses of the 60 mm, 35 mm or 28 mm variety are useful for portrait shots of the face, details of the body, or for complete images of smaller species.

Because many sharks and rays are dark in color, the camera's light meter may be less accurate than normal and may tend to give an over-exposed image. You can compensate for the dark color by overriding the camera's automatic exposure functions and setting them manually.

approaching from the side could be. Once again, a vigilant companion is vital.

The diver needs to exercise care whenever making a close approach to any large shark or ray, even if it is a harmless species. A whale shark, for example, can break bones or knock a diver unconscious with its tail. Be particularly careful always to leave space for a shark or ray to retreat and remember that they all have some method of defense, such as biting, ramming, or a powerful tail slap.

UNDERWATER FILMING

Words seem inadequate when you describe diving with sharks and rays to others, but underwater videos convey all the wonder and excitement.

The variety of compact video camcorders and well-designed watertight housings on the market today makes it possible for anyone to capture all the underwater action and drama of shark and ray encounters.

CAMERA EQUIPMENT

Video cameras, or camcorders, are the world's most user-friendly cameras. They are effective in low light, fully automatic, and simple to operate. Not only do they provide more than one hour of continuous recording time, but the results can be viewed almost at once. This means that any missing or poorly recorded images can sometimes be re-shot before you leave the site.

A compact model is the best choice of camcorder and the most popular format is Video 8 or High 8. The size of these compact camcorders makes them ideal for use in an underwater housing.

The best watertight housings are made of aluminum and feature magnetic switches, water alarm, interchangeable lens optics,

and many controls. Basic acrylic housings are also available and are sometimes cheaper. Although they have certain limitations, if you are on a restricted budget, it is still possible to get good underwater images with cameras in these housings.

TECHNICAL CONSIDERATIONS

To capture good images of sharks and rays you will need a housing with wide-angle lens optics to encompass large species, and a zoom control that enables you to use a telephoto option to capture small or shy species.

WATERTIGHT HOUSINGS *(above) a specially designed to make video equipment feel lighter under the water.*

Filters are also available to offset the excessive blue of tropical water or the predominant green cast of temperate water. They work well, but should not be used in shallow water less than 10 feet (3 m) deep, as the filter color will dominate and distort the natural color.

Because video camcorders respond even in very low light, underwater lighting wi not be necessary. There will be a lack of bright colors at greater depths, but few shark

CLOSE *It is possible to video the
most intimate life happenings of reef
creatures and the fascinating reef itself.*

...d rays are colorful. The
...ded feature of movement
...d action will compensate
...r any lack of color, but the
...thusiast keen on recording
...thful color could consider
...ding underwater lighting to
...oot more colorful species.
...lthough flash and strobe
...its do not disturb marine
...e, stronger lighting may.
...heck with local operators to
...e if any lighting restrictions
...ply in a particular area.

PRACTICAL
CONSIDERATIONS

...nce the camcorders are
...tomatic, most problems are
...used by the operator. To
...sure quality footage, the
...mera must be held steady to
...event wobble. Keep the
...tion in the center of the
...ewfinder so that the
...tomatic focus does not need
...o hunt for focus, and shoot in
...quences of wide shots,

medium shots and close-ups.

Beware of air bubbles on
the lens—these bubbles are
created by snorkelers' fins,
scuba exhaust, dive-boat
propellers, shark-cage
movement and breaking
waves. The bubbles cling to
the camcorder lens port and
become very pronounced
once the image is reviewed
on the television screen. Wipe
your hand regularly over the
port to remove them.

THE HUGE MANTA RAY *(below), with
long, gray remoras attached, presents an
exciting scene. A photographer's buddy
must keep a vigilant watch (right).*

EDITING

Do as the professionals do and
plan a "shot list" of everything you think you will need
to make an interesting and
cohesive short story. Shoot
everything on the shot list,
including any unexpected
encounters, before you return
home. Finally, edit the useful
shots into an action-packed
short story by dubbing across
from your camcorder to your
home video cassette recorder.

LEARNING *to* SCUBA DIVE

Scuba diving is a sport that must be taken seriously. Training with a qualified instructor is essential before you will be accredited as a diver.

Swimming with scuba is simple and relatively non-strenuous. Any healthy person aged more than 12 years can learn to scuba dive. It is essential, and, in fact, mandatory, to complete a training course before you attempt any scuba dive. Any lack of knowledge of such topics as pressure changes and decompression, and a lack of training in the correct assembly and use of the equipment can lead to serious injury and death.

DIVING TECHNIQUES *must be mastered in a pool (left) before those who qualify for certificates venture into the ocean. Below are two divers with a school of colorful milletseed butterflyfish.*

Dive centers offering scuba courses can be found in most cities and towns, or at most tropical resorts around the world. The Open Water Diving course is the one most likely to suit your needs.

It is essential to learn from a qualified instructor who is a current member of one of the instructor agencies with worldwide recognition and credibility. Participants who qualify at the end of the course receive a certification card that enables the holder to purchase or hire diving equipment, and participate in diving activities. Without this qualification, participants will now find it almost impossible to dive anywhere in the world.

GETTING STARTED

The best source of dive centers in your area is the telephone directory. Contact several centers and carefully compare the inclusions of their training programs. Most will offer a full-time or part-time training schedule. A full-time course should consist of at least four or five days' training. Part-time courses should provide a minimum of two complete weekends for the practical training, plus night lectures. Be wary of shorter courses, and check to see if all of the following are provided: diving equipment, air fills, textbook, logbook, dive tables, pool fees, boat diving, certification card, and any necessary accommodation.

Check the student-to-instructor ratio. Instructional agencies usually insist on a maximum of eight students for every one instructor. If the agency assigns assistant instructors or divemasters to a class, this does not necessarily mean they can increase student numbers.

The practical training component of your course must include five pool session and a minimum of four ocean dives, utilizing the best part of four cylinders of air.

Find out what you can about the dive center and its instructors. Keep in mind tha the instruction you get is onl as good as their experience, ethics and professionalism,

gardless of any affiliation
ey may have with any
rticular instructor agency.

COMMENCING YOUR
TRAINING

medical examination is
quired before the start of
ur course to determine that
u are fit to dive. A diving
edical form must be
mpleted, which identifies
y medical considerations
ique to diving, such as
hma, diabetes, heart
nditions, and sinus
d ear cavity
nditions.

You will be
ued a training text
th self-study
ides and quizzes,
hich should be
idied before the
mmencement of the
propriate lectures or
ving sessions.

Initially, you will be
troduced to all the skills and
ills of equipment assembly
d use in a swimming pool,
a very shallow dive site
at provides calm, sheltered
iter. Once you are
mpetent at these skills, you
ll progress to open-ocean
ving. Do not allow yourself
be rushed into the ocean if
u are not proficient with
ese skills. If you have
osen a good program, there
ll be time for the instructors
provide extra instruction.

ESORT COURSES

any dive resorts also have
structors on staff to provide
ining. This is a good option
you do not have time to
rn at a local dive center.
ie classroom, pool and
ining dives will, however,
t into the opportunity to
ly explore the area. If the
ort course is your preferred

BASIC TRAINING *consists of classroom lectures (right) and practical work in a pool or shallow water. A small group of divers (below) sets out on a great adventure.*

option, try
to schedule a longer stay so
that you can pursue good
diving opportunities in the
area after the completion of
your scuba course.

INTRODUCTORY DIVES

For the beginner who just
wants to dip a big toe in the
water, many resorts or dive
centers offer introductory
dives. These are a single-day
diving experience with a
minimum of training, which
allows potential enthusiasts to
give the sport a try.

Such introductory dives do
not count towards certification, but they can provide
special experiences, unique
encounters with marine life,
and kick-start you into the
fascinating world of divers.

ADVANCED SKILLS

Should you wish to continue
your diving training, there
are many programs with
advanced and specialty courses
available. Check with your
local dive center.

The Advanced Open
Water diver program will
introduce you to better
navigation and orientation
skills, deep diving and night
diving. This should be
completed as soon as possible
after your Open Water
Diving course.

Other courses to consider
are those in rescue diving,
deep diving, wreck diving,
underwater photography, and
even shark diving. All these
diving programs will improve
your knowledge and skills in
these specialized areas.

83

SCUBA—
WHAT YOU NEED *to* KNOW

Once you are feeling confident that scuba diving is the right sport for you, it is a good idea to start purchasing your own gear.

When diving, you will feel more comfortable if you wear good-quality diving equipment that has been selected just for you. Your instructors will provide valuable advice on equipment selection, and instruct you on the fine points of using, maintaining, and servicing your equipment. Keep in mind that the advice they give is more important than the price of the equipment. Your instructors will place your welfare and future enjoyment above anything else, so it is often a false economy to shop around elsewhere to try to find a cheaper deal.

REEF DIVING from a yacht (below) in Fijian waters. A diver in the South Pacific (bottom right) studies a gorgonian fan. The dive computer (above left) is an important piece of gear.

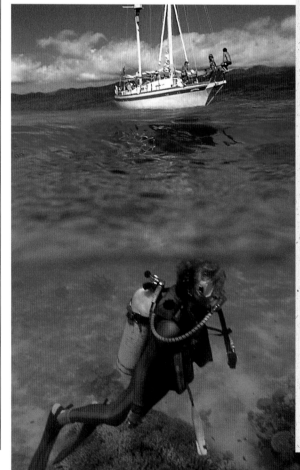

SCUBA DIVING

The basic rules of safe scuba diving can be summarized as follows:
• Never dive without obtaining adequate professional training.
• Always evaluate the conditions carefully before diving.
• In an emergency, do not panic.
• Never drink alcohol before diving.
• Never dive beyond your limits.
• Never hold your breath during an ascent. This can cause severe damage to your lungs.
• A good guide is never to surface faster than your smallest exhaust bubbles.
• Do not dive to the limits of your dive tables and do not dive deeper than the depths for which you have been trained.
• To reduce the risk of decompression sickness, always do the deepest dive of the day first, the deepest part of any dive first, and take a safety stop at 12–15 feet (4–5 m) for three minutes after each dive.
• Do not attempt specialized dives without specialized training. Examples of specialized dives are deep diving, cave diving, wreck diving, night diving, and penetration diving (the deep penetration of wrecks and caves).
• Never dive with equipment that is faulty, obsolete, or in need of service.
• Never succumb to peer pressure, or be afraid to call off a dive.
• Local knowledge is invaluable, so always seek it before diving in an area or dive site that is new to you.
• Avoid airplane travel for 24 hours after a dive

SCUBA EQUIPMENT

Currently, equipment that is considered mandatory for the modern diver includes:

➤ A face mask that is low-volume, and has a nose pocket (with the option of prescription lenses for divers requiring corrected vision; alternatively, contact lenses can be used inside the face mask).

➤ A snorkel that is contoured, and has an exhaust valve and a water deflector.

➤ Boots with zippers and reinforced soles.

➤ Fins with an open heel and adjustable quick-release straps.

➤ Gloves that are flexible and close fitting, with reinforced fingers and palms.

➤ A small, stainless-steel dive knife with a serrated edge and a quick-release sheath.

➤ An exposure suit with ankle-to-wrist coverage (anything less is not a dive suit). It should be of a thickness suited to deal with the local water temperatures.

➤ A comfortable weight belt.

➤ A regulator. This delivers air to the diver in two stages. It should have a balanced twin-stage function—a good-performance first stage and simple second stage. It should also feature effective exhaust deflectors.

➤ An "octopus" regulator. This is a back-up second stage, specially designed for the purpose of dive-buddy rescue.

➤ A pressure gauge that indicates the air remaining with color-coded low-air calibration.

➤ A depth gauge.

➤ A dive cylinder. This is optional for the traveling diver, who will probably use a dive cylinder supplied by the tour operator rather than taking this item.

➤ A Buoyancy Control Device (BCD), which consists of secure tank bands to hold the dive cylinder, and a secure adjustable harness. It should, if possible, be weight integrated, so that the diver has the option of wearing dive weights in the BCD instead of on a weight belt.

➤ A dive computer. This is a multi-level computer that indicates the dive time remaining, ascent rates, decompression information, and options for the amount of time you can spend on the bottom during your next dive. It also records information from up to 10 completed dives in its user-retrievable memory.

➤ A dive watch that is waterproof to about 650 feet (200 m).

➤ A compact dive light with a powerful beam for night diving, or a large dive light with a wide beam for cave and wreck diving.

➤ Accessories. These should include a whistle, a compass, an underwater slate and pencil, a safety buoy, a chemical light stick, a strobe light, and waterproof dive tables.

➤ A dive-gear bag. This should be large, water resistant, and have compartment pockets and strong nylon straps.

SNORKELING— WHAT YOU NEED *to* KNOW

Snorkeling is easy. Almost anyone of any age can participate,

and even beginners can enjoy the experience.

norkel divers should never feel compromised by any lack of scuba diving skills or equipment. The world's most beautiful coral reefs are accessible to the snorkeler and, indeed, snorkeling is considered the best way to encounter some species of sharks and rays (such as stingrays at Stingray City in the Caymans or reef sharks and stingrays at Lord Howe Island, off the east coast of Australia).

SELECTING SNORKELING EQUIPMENT

Your enjoyment of snorkeling can be heightened by making use of modern equipment and learning some snorkeling skills. Take the time to select a good-quality, low-volume face mask that will provide excellent vision, and allow the option of prescription lenses for optical correction if required. Select a high-quality snorkel with a water deflector

to prevent much water from entering, and a purge valve to expel the excess if it does.

Spend a little extra on high-performance fins. They are far more comfortable, and if you are following sharks or rays, you will need plenty of power. Consider a light-weight exposure suit that will cover you from wrist to ankle. Some excellent Lycra ones that are non-restrictive

A WORLD HERITAGE AREA *Lord Howe Island (above) lies off the east coast of Australia. Snorkeling amid schooling hussar (below).*

are available, and these will retain some body heat while also protecting you from coral, stingers, and sunburn.

Check with your local div center for snorkel classes. There are quite a few skills that instructors can show you

SEA STARS *at Manado, Indonesia (left). The coral reefs surrounding the many small islands there teem with life.*

person on the surface keeping a sharp watch.
• Tow a buoy with a dive flag in areas where other boats are likely to be.
• Take a course in CPR (cardiopulmonary resuscitation) and basic lifesaving skills.
• Always respect marine life and avoid touching and damaging reefs.

JACQUES-YVES COUSTEAU

The growing popularity of the sport of snorkeling has largely been made possible by innovation and improvement in the gear available. Until comparatively recently, exploration of ocean life was restricted to the surface close to land or to what could be seen from the confines of a diving suit. More than anyone else, French-born Jacques-Yves Cousteau (b. 1910) has liberated observers in this so-called "inner space". For many years, he pioneered dramatic improvements in diving techniques, and captained the research vessel, *Calypso*, which sails the oceans of the world collecting data. By co-inventing the aqualung, he released divers to move as freely in water as they did on land.

Cousteau has won great renown as a dedicated oceanographer, film-maker and writer. His books, translated into many languages, include *The Silent World* (1953), *The Living Sea* (1962), and *Cousteau's Amazon Journey* (1984). A widely screened TV series, *The Undersea World of Jacques Cousteau*, successfully raised awareness about the need for research into and conservation of ocean life. His films include an Oscar-winner, *The Golden Fish*, and *Cousteau: The First 75 Years*. His remarkable work has awakened a sense of wonderment in people all over the world to the compelling marvels of ocean life.

Don't be embarrassed to go to your local pool and practice until you feel confident about your skills and equipment.

Practice slow, but steady, controlled swimming with a minimum of splash and maximum thrust. Practice duck diving to the bottom and equalizing pressure on your eardrums by holding your nose and very gently forcing some air into your inner ears as you descend. You should not force yourself deeper if you feel any pain. This procedure equalizes pressure on the eardrums, and prevents pain and possible injury to the inner ear.

Learn to extend your time underwater by deep breathing before a dive to expel excess carbon dioxide. Never take any more than five or six deep breaths, or you may hyperventilate and lose consciousness while you are underwater.

SNORKEL DIVING

Before you go snorkeling, practice in a pool or confined water until you are confident

in and competent with your equipment.
• Before the excursion, obtain local knowledge from dive centers or dive operators.
• Evaluate currents, waves, visibility and ocean conditions prior to diving. Choose safe entry and exit points.
• Do not descend if you are suffering from nasal congestion or sinus problems.
• Never hyperventilate. Avoid deep, rapid breathing beyond 6 to 10 deep breaths.
• Avoid any excessive surface splashing.
• Always dive in pairs. Have one person down, and the other

BOATING *and* FISHING

Many sharks and rays are killed each year because of ignorance or lack of understanding on the part of boating and fishing enthusiasts.

Today, the waterways and oceans off our coasts are busy with a continual stream of traffic consisting of ships, power-craft, yachts, and jet-skis. These craft all take a toll on the many species of sharks and rays that spend much of their time on the surface—some of which may already be close to being classified as endangered species. It is not uncommon to see whale sharks, the largest and most gentle of all sharks, displaying the scars of encounters with watercraft. Some have had an entire fin torn off by a propeller blade.

Today's conservation-minded boaters and sailors should keep a careful watch for any creatures just beneath the surface so that the injuries to marine animals can be reduced. People on watch

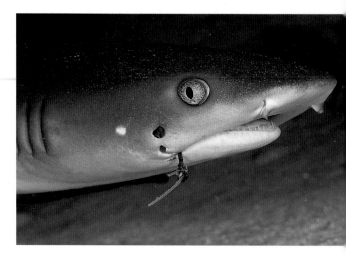

should wear polarized sunglasses that allow a much improved view through any glare on the water surface.

UNINTENDED CATCH

It is not unusual for fishing enthusiasts to find they have accidentally caught a shark or ray. The correct management of the problem can go a long

way toward preventing the death of an innocent creature

Take great care—it is very important to avoid injuring

ACCIDENTAL DAMAGE *The whitetip reef shark (above) may have escaped being caught, but a hook remains lodge in its jaw. The whale shark (below) has probably had its dorsal fin and tail tip amputated by a boat propeller.*

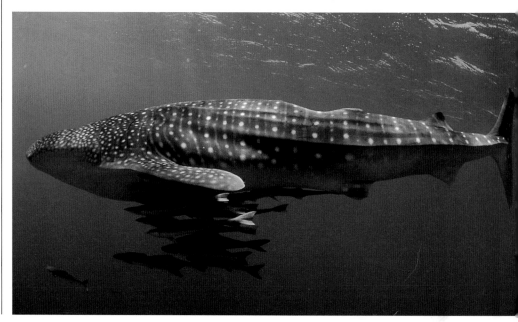

UNNATURAL HAZARDS

A discarded fishing net snares some angelsharks and Port Jackson sharks (left). This shark's mouth (below) was damaged by a hook and line.

ourself. Bring the creature as close as possible, but not so close that you are at risk from its teeth or barbs. Do not use a gaff or any instrument that will injure the animal. Cut the line as close to the hook as safety permits. Avoid the temptation to remove the hook. To do so is hazardous to you, and the creature will struggle so much that it will probably be injured, or die later from the stress.

Consider fishing with hooks made of regular, rather than stainless, steel. Such hooks will rust away reasonably quickly if they are left in the mouth of the fish. A shark or ray that is encumbered by a hook and attached wire leader could become tangled in the wire and either suffocate, or starve slowly to death.

PROTECTED SPECIES AND PROTECTED AREAS

Ignorance is no excuse. It is the responsibility of fishing enthusiasts to make themselves aware of which shark and ray species are protected, and of restrictions to fishing areas. They should also know about prohibited fishing practices.

Sharks, rays, and other forms of marine life are now under a great deal of pressure from overfishing, loss of habitat due to development, diminishing fish stocks, accidental by-catch, and pollution of all kinds, so our acts of conservation are vital.

APPROACHING SHARKS OR RAYS WITH BOATS

An informed skipper can contribute greatly toward a worthwhile shark or ray encounter that is safe for all involved. The boat operator should be aware of certain procedures.
• Never drive the vessel directly toward the creature.
• Steer a parallel course. Move approximately 100 yards (90 m) ahead, then turn across the animal's course and drop the divers in its probable path.
• If the passengers are non-divers, stop the vessel in the animal's path and turn off the motor.
• When divers or snorkelers are in the water, have a lookout on watch at all times and be ready for an urgent pick-up.

There is, one knows not what sweet mystery about this
sea, whose gently awful stirrings seem to speak of some
hidden soul beneath.

Moby Dick,
HERMAN MELVILLE (1819–91), American novelist

CHAPTER FOUR

SHARKS

IDENTIFYING *and* CLASSIFYING SHARKS

To recognize a shark, you need a good understanding of its external features, and sometimes a quick eye and a keen memory.

Classification and description of the 350 or so species of living sharks is based on the science of taxonomy, in which the morphological characteristics are used to group closely related species. Early modern taxonomists, such as Carolus Linnaeus (1707–78), did not fully understand evolutionary relationships among organisms and often used superficial features to form these groups.

ANATOMY OF A SHARK *The diagram below shows the key external characteristics of a typical shark. The pygmy or dwarf shark (above) reaches a maximum size of 10 inches (25 cm).*

Modern shark taxonomists use shared characteristics that have appeared in species throughout evolutionary history, such as the way the upper jaw is attached to the skull, how the skeletal structures are arranged, and the shape of the teeth. Since such features cannot be readily observed in living animals, the keys we have for the identification of most organisms are still based largely on external features that can be observed or measured with relative ease. These are not necessarily important evolutionary markers.

THROUGH THE AGES

The basic body plan of sharks has been conserved for hundreds of millions of years. The features of extinct fossil sharks, such as *Cladoselache*, are found today among living species, such as the whale shark, *Rhincodon typus*, which can be more than 43 feet (13 m) in length, and also th unrelated spined pygmy shark *Squaliolus laticaudus*, which reaches only about 10 inches (25 cm). The identification of different shark species usually involves information on relative sizes of the animals, placement and shape of fins, and detailed anatomical features, such as tooth shape.

Sharks can be separated into the higher taxonomic level of order by observation of basic anatomical features. For example, the angelsharks (Squatiniformes), sawsharks (Pristiophoriformes), and dogfish sharks (Squaliformes) can be identified by their lac of an anal fin. Once this featu is known, it is relatively easy to differentiate among the three orders by the shape of the body and head. Some other important identifying features at the order level are the number of gill slits, the presence or absence of dorsal fin spines, the position of the

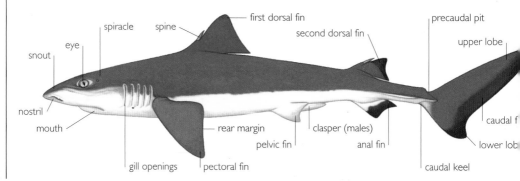

first dorsal fin — spine — second dorsal fin — precaudal pit — spiracle — upper lobe — eye — snout — nostril — mouth — gill openings — pectoral fin — rear margin — pelvic fin — clasper (males) — anal fin — caudal keel — caudal f — lower lob

Squatiniformes

Flat body, ray-like

No anal fin

Pristiophoriformes

Elongated snout

Body not ray-like

Squaliformes

Short snout

Hexanchiformes

1 dorsal fin,
6 or 7 gill slits

Carcharhiniformes

Nictitating eyelids

Mouth behind
front of eyes

Lamniformes

No nictitating
eyelids

Anal fin

No fin spines

LASSIFICATION

rtain external
tures that are
eful for grouping
arks (right)
olved in them
time passed.

Orectolobiformes

2 dorsal fins,
5 gill slits

Mouth in front of eyes

Heterodontiformes

Dorsal fin spines

outh, and the
esence or absence
a nictitating eyelid.

To identify species, shark
xonomists have developed
ist of external features and
ndard measurements.
hese include descriptive
atures such as the presence
absence of spiracles, dorsal
spines, an anal fin, a lower
be on the caudal fin, an
terdorsal ridge, caudal keels,
d nictitating membranes.
otal body length, interdorsal
stance, head length and
idth, fin length and height,
size and number of teeth,
ust also be measured or
unted. Collectively, these
atures usually provide the
vestigator with enough
formation to make a
ositive identification.

UNFAMILIAR SHARKS
To identify an unfamiliar
species of adult shark, first
examine the basic features,
body size, location of fins, and
shape of head. If, for example,
the shark is greater than about
16 feet (5 m) in total length,
the list of potential species
shrinks to only a handful that
includes the whale, basking,
great white, tiger, sleeper,
thresher, megamouth, and
great hammerhead sharks.
While a few species are very
small, less than 1 foot (30 cm),
most adult sharks range from
about 3–10 feet (1–3 m). In
these cases, shape of body,
color pattern, and fin placement may confirm the species.

While scientists using preserved specimens can spend
weeks making a tedious
examination of the external
features, internal anatomy,
and teeth, divers may
encounter a shark on a reef
for only a few seconds. When
trying to identify an unknown
species, a good knowledge of
distribution, habits, and
ecology may help to narrow
the field. For example, if a
6½ foot (2 m) requiem shark
was observed in the waters
off Hawaii, the choice can
be narrowed to about a dozen
possibilities. If it was observed
in blue oceanic water, the
candidates could be further
reduced by about half.

THE EVOLUTION *and* RADIATION *of* SHARKS

Sharks have dominated the oceans for more than 400 million years,

yet the sharks of today still look much like their ancestors.

The sharks, rays and chimaeras are all "cartilaginous fish," members of the taxonomic class Chondrichthyes. As the name implies, the skeletons have no true bone but are composed of cartilage, a soft, firm tissue with little, if any, calcification (similar to tissue supporting our nose and ears).

TWO MAJOR GROUPS

Living cartilaginous fishes fall into two groups. The Elasmo-branchii (sharks and rays) are characterized by five to seven external gill slits on each side of the head, placoid skin scales known as denticles, teeth that are replaced regularly, and an upper jaw that is not firmly attached to the skull as it is in mammals, birds, reptiles, and amphibians. The chimaeras, or ratfishes (Holocephalii), differ from sharks in that the gills are covered by a flap with only one opening. They also lack scales and have plate-like teeth for eating hard-shelled in-vertebrates. The upper jaw is firmly attached to the skull.

As a result of the lack of a hard skeleton, fossils of complete sharks (and ratfishes) are rare, and paleontologists must rely instead on finds of fossilized teeth, small dermal scales, and calcified vertebrae to piece together their evolutionary history.

Sharks appeared in the fossil record more than 400 million years ago in the Silurian and Devonian Periods. At this time, the early insects had appeared in primitive plant forests. Early amphibians had emerged from their aquatic habitat to invade terrestrial environments, but the dinosaurs would not arrive for nearly 200 million years.

Similarly, the oceans were teeming with small plankton life and the marine benthos was rich with widely varied forms of shelled invertebrate animals. This seemingly primitive era marked the beginning of the Age of Fishes, when many diverse groups of jawless and jawed fishes evolved to inhabit the wide marine oceans and fresh waters of the planet. Prominent among these were the ancestors of today's shark

EVOLVING FEATURES

The best known shark ancestors of the Devonian Period were members of the genus *Cladoselache*, which shared many of the features of modern sharks. These fish had five external gill slits, two well-developed dorsal fins with spines, pectoral and pelvic fins, and a powerful symmetrical tail. The upper

DENTAL RECORDS *A fossil tooth (a extinct* Carcharodon megalodon *sho a tooth of the great white shark. The hybodont (below),* Hybodus hauffianu

Cladoselache
about 40" (1 m)

*Long before the dinosaurs ruled
the world, sharks had already
evolved their basic powerful,
streamlined body shape, and
little modification has occurred
since the Devonian Period.*

Spined pygmy shark
about 10" (25 cm)

Whale shark
about 43' (13 m)

w was loosely attached to
e skull, and the lower jaw
as large, with many sharp
eth, each equipped with a
gle prominent central point
d smaller lateral cusps (*clado*
branched, *dont* = tooth).
nese features made *Clado-
ache* a swift predator, well
apted for feeding on fast-
imming fishes. This is
rified by impressions of
ge fish prey found in the
omachs of fossilized sharks.
ossils of later species show
at, over time, the teeth
derwent a wide range of
anges in size and number
cusps per tooth, which
obably reflected the
pansion of the shark's
eding habits in different
ological niches.

About 150 million years
er in the Triassic and
rassic Periods, when
nosaurs ruled the terrestrial
aches of the Earth, the
bodont sharks (*hybo* =
mp) were the dominant fish
edators in the oceans. Like
Cladoselache* ancestor,
ybodus* had two dorsal fins

that were preceded
by prominent spines
undoubtedly used for defense
against large predators. The
major changes in the body
were an elongated upper lobe
of the tail fin, the presence of
an anal fin, and small head
spines in males that may have
been used during courtship
and mating. Hybodont sharks
are also well known for the
presence of small, sharp teeth
in the front of the jaw, and
broader-based teeth at the
back, much as occurs in the
unrelated hornsharks (Heterodontiformes). The broad teeth
of some hybodont species
supported many small cusps
for grasping soft-bodied prey;
those of others were smooth
and flat and used for crushing
hard-shelled invertebrates.

DIVERSIFICATION

The expansion of the hybodont sharks was quickly
followed by the appearance of
most modern forms. The
sixgill and sevengill sharks
(cowsharks) were among the
earliest to appear in the fossil
record and are distinguished
by the presence of a single
dorsal fin rather than two.
With their upper jaw bearing
sharp, pointed teeth and those

in the lower jaw being broad
and saw-like, they can
efficiently remove pieces of
flesh from a large fish prey.
During this time, most of the
other modern shark families
also evolved, but the order in
which they appeared and the
evolutionary forces that drove
their rapid diversification
remain unclear.

Perhaps the most intriguing
fossil shark of all is *Carcharodon
megalodon*, the largest shark
ever to have lived and a close
relative of the living great
white shark, *Carcharodon
carcharias*. Fossil teeth of
C. megalodon are routinely
found from excavations dating
back 3 to 25 million years.
Reconstructions of the jaw
indicate that this shark
reached total lengths of at least
45 feet (15 m) and had a
mouth gape of about 6½ feet
(2 m). Using data on the
great white, we can assume
that a large megalodon
weighed more than 25 tons
(25,000 kg). This mammoth
carnivore probably fed on
large marine animals, such
as marine mammals, other
sharks, and dead whales, as
does its living relative.

THE BODY FORM
and FUNCTION *of* SHARKS

The shark's body is beautifully attuned to life in an unforgiving watery world. It provides the ultimate biological example of hydrodynamic efficiency and power.

Many features of the shark's body have evolved in response to the physical constraints of its dense aquatic environment. The internal skeleton of sharks and rays is composed of cartilage, an elastic tissue much higher in water content than bone. A skeleton of cartilage allows a high degree of body flexibility, provides protection and support for organs, and reduces total body mass. Skeletal parts that experience physical stress, such as vertebrae, jaws, and parts of the skull, are often stiffened by secondary calcification rather than by heavier bone. It is unlikely that large, modern sharks would be capable of such quick, agile movement had they evolved bony skeletons.

BIOLOGICAL TORPEDOES
A species that swims actively in the water column, such as the blue shark, usually has a fusiform (cigar-shaped) body.

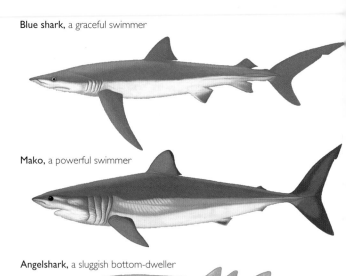

Blue shark, a graceful swimmer

Mako, a powerful swimmer

Angelshark, a sluggish bottom-dweller

The diameter of the body is greatest at about a third of the way back from the snout, and tapers off toward the tail. This shape lets water flow smoothly over the body as the shark swims and reduces turbulence along the skin.

Swimming power and stability are provided by the shark's well-developed fins. most sharks, the tail, or caud fin, creates forward thrust by wide side-to-side movement that produce an undulation the body. Special helically wound connective tissue fibe under the skin transfer much of the body's power directly to the tail. The unpaired dorsal and anal fins keep the body from rolling to either side during forward motion. The pectoral and pelvic fins, paired and displaced off the body midline, are used for li and control of movements.

The fastest sharks, such as the mako, are perhaps the

CONVEYOR BELT *The teeth of the swellshark (left) are arranged in rows and are constantly replaced by new ones produced at the back. The body shapes of sharks (above) have become adapted to their differing lifestyles.*

BODY SHAPE *The bottom-dwelling angelshark (left) disappears on the ocean floor.*

...imate biological example of ...drodynamic efficiency and ...wer. The snout and head ...e fused into a missile-like ...se cone, and the stream-...ed body is stout, and ...assive. Thrust is derived ...nost exclusively from quick ...eral motions of the ...mmetrical tail with only ...inimal flexing of the body. ...he pectoral fins are short ...th a small surface area to ...duce drag. Their stiffness ...lps the fish to maneuver at ...gh speed. The claspers of ...ales are retracted into special ...ooves behind the pelvic fins. ...ell-developed lateral keels ...the caudal peduncle act as ...rizontal stabilizers. These ...ift, biological torpedoes are ...pable of bursts of speed of ...miles per hour (36 km/h).

...OTTOM-DWELLERS
...contrast to species that are ...nstantly on the move, some ...e adapted for a life near the ...bottom. One extreme ...ample is the angelshark, ...hich has a flattened, ray-like ...dy and spends much of the ...y buried in the sandy bottom ...iting to ambush passing fish

prey. Sawsharks have a broad, flat-tened surface under the head that helps to detect and capture benthic inverte-brates. They retain the powerful tail for long-distance move-ment across their marine habitat.

The outer skin is composed of many tiny placoid scales, known as denticles, which are usually about ⅓₂ inch (less than 1 mm) wide. These are formed in the dermal layer of the skin. The surface of the denticles consists of hard enamel that covers a dentine layer and pulp cavity. The enamel crowns have multiple sharp ridges that reduce drag during swimming as well as protect-ing the animal from injury.

The jaw is beneath the skull so the opening of the mouth is usually behind the snout on the underside of the head. In large, predatory sharks, the jaw is highly adapted for grasping or cutting prey. The upper jaw (palatoquadrate cartilage) is loosely suspended under the skull by ligaments and connective tissue. The lower jaw (Meckel's cartilage) is connected to the upper jaw at the corners of the mouth and is covered by massive muscles used for biting. This entire mechanism is suspended from the skull by the hyoid cartilage.

The attachment of rela-tively small muscles between the jaw, skull, and adjacent cartilages results in a powerful, highly protrusible mechanism that can be decoupled from

the skull and thrown forward from the head during a bite. This enables predators, such as great whites and reef sharks, to bite off parts of prey that are too large to swallow whole.

THE TEETH

The teeth, formed from skin tissue, are arranged in ordered rows on both jaws. An enamel crown forms the primary cutting edge of the tooth, which in many species has additional lateral cusps or serrations. New rows of teeth form along the rear margins of the jaws, migrating forward as they become enlarged. This constant supply of sharp teeth emerges from the gums to replace those that are dulled or lost during use.

JAW ATTACHMENT

Like ancestral form, the jaw is normally positioned below the skull.

Like ancestral form, upper jaw remains close to skull as mouth opens.

Modern shark's upper jaw can detach from skull.

THE INTERNAL
ENVIRONMENT *of* SHARKS

Beneath the denticled skin of the shark lies a well-organized and coordinated biological factory that is designed for maximum efficiency.

RESPIRATION *The gill slits of a whale shark (above). The illustration (below) shows the heart, gill arches and direction of water flow. Water enters the mouth (and spiracles), passes over the gills and out the gill slits. Diagram (right) shows detail of water flowing counter to blood.*

A s well as being a superb hydrodynamic vehicle, a shark's body also controls many biological processes. Its internal organs share many features that are common in other fishes, but also show a number of special-izations unique to vertebrates.

RESPIRATION
Sharks and rays extract oxygen from the water to metabolize their food. The gills are found on five to seven vertical arches that form the walls of the external gill slits. In a separate chamber beneath the gills, the heart pumps oxygen-depleted blood to capillary beds in the arches. Water is pumped into the mouth and out across the gills counter to the direction of blood flow. This exchange system greatly enhances the rate and efficiency of oxygen diffusion into the blood. In fast-swimming species, water flows into the open mouth as the animal swims. In bottom-dwelling species, such as sawsharks and spiny dogfish, there are well-developed spiracles that serve as auxiliary water inlets when the animal is resting or using the mouth to feed.

DIGESTION
When prey is captured in the mouth, it is usually swallowed whole or cut into large pieces

oxygen-depleted water

gill filaments

gill arch

gill septum

afferent branchial artery

efferent branchial artery

capillari

seco
lame

oxygen-rich water

gill arches

ventral aorta

heart

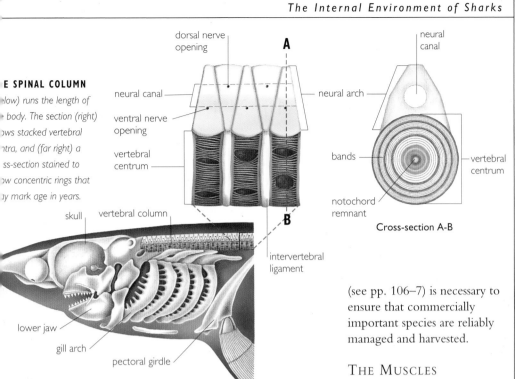

dorsal nerve opening

neural canal

ventral nerve opening

vertebral centrum

A

B

neural arch

neural canal

bands

notochord remnant

vertebral centrum

Cross-section A-B

E SPINAL COLUMN

low) runs the length of body. The section (right) ows stacked vertebral ntra, and (far right) a ss-section stained to ow concentric rings that y mark age in years.

skull

vertebral column

lower jaw

gill arch

pectoral girdle

intervertebral ligament

(see pp. 106–7) is necessary to ensure that commercially important species are reliably managed and harvested.

he stomach produces strong id and digestive enzyme cretions that, eventually, nulsify the food to a thin, up-like consistency. Large ones and other indigestible aterial in the stomach are ocked from entering the testine by a very small yloric opening and regurgi- ted later. The absorptive rface area of the intestine is eatly increased by internal oils that are wound like a iral staircase (spiral valve testine) or, in some species, e a long, rolled up sheet of per (scroll valve intestine).

ATER BALANCE

he concentration of minerals the body tissues of sharks is aintained by remarkable hysiological processes. In arine fishes, the concentra- on of salt is about three nes greater in the water an in the body, so there is a nstant tendency for dehyd- tion by loss of water across e gills. Sharks greatly reduce is loss by retaining urea, rived from the digestion of otein. They also produce an ganic compound, TMAO

(trimethylamine oxide), which helps to maintain osmotic balance. When excess sodium chloride enters the body after the animal swallows sea water or ingests prey, it is removed by secretions from a specialized organ called the rectal gland.

GROWTH

Lack of bony body parts in sharks and rays makes it hard to estimate age and growth rate of individual species. The vertebrae, which are partly calcified, can be stained to reveal concentric rings much like those seen in tree trunks, but we do not know if each ring represents a single year's growth. Additional research is necessary to confirm the meaning of each ring.

Tagging and recapture methods are another means of determining growth rates. Some species, such as the sandbar and dusky sharks, grow very slowly and may not reach sexual maturity for 15 years or more. Other smaller species, such as the sharpnose shark, reach maturity in three to four years. Information on growth rates and reproduction

THE MUSCLES

Most body muscle consists of white muscle fibers with relatively poor vascularization. These are an excellent source of power for brief bursts of speed. Normal swimming activity is produced by con- tractions of relatively small bands of highly vascularized red muscle along the sides of the body. Red muscle can be used almost indefinitely for sustained swimming.

The fast-swimming lamnid sharks (great white, mako, and porbeagle) have developed a counter-current vascular system ("rete mirable") in the red body muscle and viscera. Heat that would be lost in blood leaving the muscle is retained locally by warming the cooler, oxygen-rich blood as it enters. In this way, the muscle maintains a tem- perature 9 to 15 degrees Fahrenheit (5–8° C) above that of the surrounding water and produces more power when burning oxygen. This provides faster cruising and bursts of speed useful for following large prey, such as tuna and mackerel, and also when diving to deep, cold waters in search of prey.

VISION, SMELL, TASTE, *and* TOUCH

Sharks have at least eight well-developed sensory systems and a large brain, which makes it rather illogical to think of them as primitive.

Even today, sharks are often presented as sluggish, instinctive, and uncalculating predators that possess poorly developed sensory systems and rudimentary brains. This view stems from their long fossil history, and the assumption that they are less advanced than the more recently evolved vertebrates. Nothing could be further from the truth.

VISION

The location of the shark's eyes on the sides of the head provides it with an excellent field of vision, in almost all directions. The eyeball is elliptical with a clear central cornea, and the globe wall is made of a white fibrous sclera. The amount of light entering the eye is regulated by a well-developed iris, which contracts and expands to change the size of the opening, called the pupil.

A clear, nearly spherical lens behind the pupil can be moved to focus images on the retina which lines the inner surface at the back of the eye. Within the retina a photoreceptors, called cones These provide color vision and good detail in daylight.

Images seen during twilig and at night are mediated primarily by rod photoreceptors. Compared to cones, the rods provide relatively poor detail, but th

THE SENSES OF THE SHARK *The diagrams (below) show the componer of the various sensory systems and th location on the body. For an explanat of how they function, see the text on this and the following three pages.*

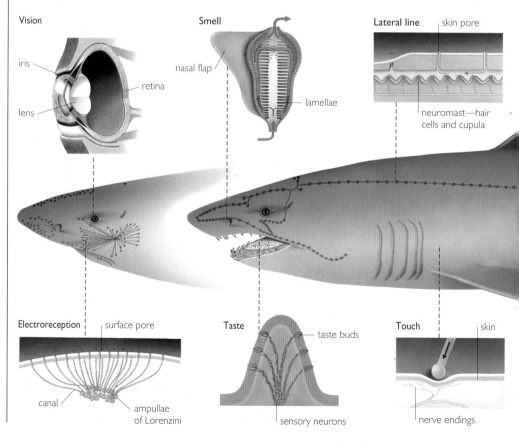

Vision
- iris
- retina
- lens

Smell
- nasal flap
- lamellae

Lateral line — skin pore
- neuromast—hair cells and cupula

Electroreception — surface pore
- canal
- ampullae of Lorenzini

Taste
- taste buds
- sensory neurons

Touch — skin
- nerve endings

e highly sensitive in
w-light conditions and
xcellent discriminators
tween light and
ark objects.

Another such
aptation to low-
ght conditions is the
petum lucidum, which
located behind the
tina. This structure is a
yer of minute mirror-
ke crystal plates that
nctions as a biological
hotomultiplier, reflect-
g any light that passes
rough the retina back
ain onto the photo-
ceptors. Sharks and
ys feed during the
riods of dusk, night,
d dawn, so this is an
pecially useful
aptation for them.

MELL

he sense organs for
nell are found within the
vo olfactory sacs under the
out. Each sac is covered by
flap of skin that channels
ater into the chamber
d across the sensory
mellae. Water, along with
ay dissolved molecules or
spended particles, flows
rough the series of small
lleys between the lamellae,
hich are lined with olfactory
ceptor cells.

Molecules such as
nino acids, the building
ocks of proteins, bind
the surface of the
ceptor cells and evoke
ural discharges that are
rried to the brain for
ocessing. Researchers
ve reported a neural
sponse to solutions
glycine, and also
havioral responses to
h extracts at concentrations
about 1 part per 10 billion
rts of water.

THE SHARK BRAIN

Contrary to popular belief, the relative size of the brain in sharks and rays rivals that of some birds and mammals. Like the brains of all vertebrate animals, the shark brain consists of hundreds of thousands of specialized cells known as neurons. Neurons receive electrical impulses from the various sensory systems of the body, process information in different regions of the brain, and send control commands to the muscles of the body.

The hindbrain processes information from many sensory systems, controls movements of the head and jaw, and is also a relay station between the higher brain centers and the spinal cord. The cerebellum coordinates body movements and may even be capable of motor learning. The tectum receives and integrates visual, electrosensory, lateral line, and other sensory information (see main text and pp. 102–3).

Below the midbrain is the diencephalon, which regulates the production of hormones, controls behaviors and activity patterns, and acts as a relay station for information passing to the forebrain. Finally, the forebrain, which is especially well developed in stingrays and mantas, receives information from the olfactory, electro-sensory, and lateral line systems (see also pp. 102–3). Much work remains to be done to determine how the forebrain controls the behavior of sharks and rays.

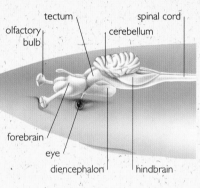

tectum
spinal cord
olfactory bulb
cerebellum
forebrain
eye
diencephalon
hindbrain

TASTE

Like the olfactory system, the sense of taste is specialized to detect biological compounds. There are taste receptor cells on small taste buds that cover small bumps inside the mouth. They are best stimulated by direct contact with items such as food. The shark normally uses this sense to decide whether the food item it has captured is palatable.

SUPERSENSITIVE *With its elaborate nostrils, the hornshark (above) is able to detect microscopic amounts of chemicals.*

TOUCH

Tactile sense in elasmobranchs is mediated by a network of nerve endings beneath the surface of the skin. Free nerve endings are simple, unspecialized touch receptors near the skin surface. They discharge impulses briefly when the overlying skin is depressed by as little as 0.0008 inch (20 μm). In Wunderer corpuscles, a more defined organization is seen, with the nerve endings tightly coiled into small capsules lying deeper in the skin layer. These structures respond both to direct touch and to the fin or body bending.

Finally, the Polou-mordwinoff endings are thought to be stretch receptors for muscle fibers of the fins of rays, providing information on muscle length and contraction rate.

BALANCE, HEARING, LATERAL LINE, *and the* ELECTROSENSE

Signals relayed through a system of amazingly sophisticated sensory organs keep the shark fully informed about what is going on within and around it.

Sharks and rays have exquisite sensory organs for balance (vestibular system), hearing (auditory system), and detecting prey (lateral line and electrosensory systems). In all these sensory systems are hair cells—small receptors that excite sensory neurons when a physical force is applied to them. The hair cell is ubiquitous among vertebrates, including the organs of balance and hearing within our own ears.

INNER EAR *The inner ear of a shark serves balance and hearing functions.*

endolymphatic pore
endolymphatic du
anterior semicircula canal
macula neglecta
posterior semicircula canal
horizontal semicircular canal
sacculus
lagena

THE VESTIBULAR SYSTEM

The vestibular system is a complex of fine membranous organs designed to maintain the shark's orientation, balance, and control of body movements. Inside each ear are three fluid-filled semi-circular canals, at right angles to each other and firmly embedded in the otic capsules of the skull. As the shark turns its body, or moves its head from side to side during swimming, the fluid in the canals that are within the plane of

rotation presses against a vane of hair cells, and stimulates nerve impulses to the brain.

Attached directly below the semicircular canals are the three otolith organs. The hair cells of each of these organs are arranged in a carpet-like layer known as the maculae, suspended vertically (the sacculus and lagena) or horizontally (the utricle) within the inner ear.

A conglomeration of hard calcium granules, known as

otoconia, rests on each macu and, depending on the orientation of the body, will produce a shearing tug on th hair cells due to the force of gravity. Signals from these organs let the brain know about the position of the boc relative to gravity and also te it in which direction the body is moving.

HEARING

Although sharks and rays lac any external evidence of wel developed ears, the hearing is very acute. In field studies, many shark are regularly attracted to sounds like those made by struggling fish played through underwater speakers. Recent work suggests that the macula neglect

SENSORS *Along the lateral line, which runs down the shark's head and sides, are special hair-cell receptors that provide the animal with an amazing fund of information. Ampullae of Lorenzini are visible on the nurse shark (right).*

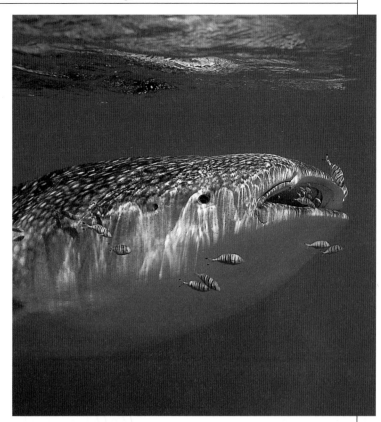

HYPERSENSITIVE *The whale shark (right) uses its extraordinary electrosense to locate the fish on which it preys.*

...probably the organ of hearing. These tiny, paired hair-cell organs, located near the top of the skull above the semicircular canals, lack otoconia. It is currently proposed that sound-pressure waves traveling through the water, such as those produced by the movements of fishes or unusual acoustic disturbances on a reef, are channeled down tiny cartilaginous tubes in the top of the skull where they enter the inner ear to stimulate the macula neglecta.

LATERAL LINE

The lateral line of sharks and rays is an important means for detecting water movements made by prey and potential predators. Sensory hair cells are arranged in tiny clusters less than 1/50 inch (0.5 mm) long, known as neuromasts (see p. 100). On the surface of the skin there are superficial neuromasts, often referred to as pit organs, that detect water movements (velocity) relative to the surface of the body. These organs are distributed across the shark's body, and are especially well positioned along the tail of the stingray for detecting an approach from the rear by a foraging hammerhead or bull shark.

The lateral line canal neuromasts are also found within an extensive network of small, water-filled canals immediately below the surface of the skin on the head and sides of the body. Neuromasts among the skin pores are stimulated by water movements within the canal that result from differences in pressures at the pores. This makes them sensitive to water acceleration. Much of the canal system on the head lacks surface pores altogether, which means that these neuromasts are relatively insensitive to water disturbances on the skin. Laboratory research indicates that, when stimulated, the unpored lateral line system in the stingray probably functions as a specialized touch receptor for use when handling prey.

ELECTROSENSORY SYSTEM

The electrosense is perhaps the most intriguing and mysterious sensory system of the elasmobranch fishes. This sense is used to detect and locate prey, and in stingrays also to locate mates during the reproductive season.

Each of the electrosensory organs, known as ampullae of Lorenzini (see p. 100), consists of a small chamber (the ampulla) lined with hair cells, and attached to an insulated tube filled with a conductive jelly. Many ampullae are grouped, like small grapes, in three to five clusters on each side of the head and lower jaw. From these, the tubes radiate to pores at separate locations on the skin, so that these small "biological cables" can sample voltage potentials at different locations.

The weak bioelectric stimuli produced by prey originate primarily from their biological membranes, and appear to the shark or ray as a weak electrical aura around them, even when the prey is buried in the sand. Sharks and rays use the electrosensory system to detect voltage gradients as low as 5 nano-volts/cm, or 5 billionths of a volt measured across a distance of only about 1/2 inch (1 cm). The strength of the bioelectric fields produced by small organisms falls off rapidly with distance from the source, so the effective range of the electrosense is usually less than 1 foot (20–30 cm).

THE SHARK'S LAIR

*Each species of shark is exquisitely adapted for life in
one of the many vast realms of the world's oceans.*

Sharks inhabit almost every marine ecosystem on Earth. Nearly all coastal regions of the world have large populations of small, bottom-dwelling sharks that are almost always an important component of the local marine ecosystem. Temperate latitudes are usually dominated by small requiem sharks, hornsharks, catsharks, houndsharks, spiny dogfish sharks, and sometimes angelsharks. These species frequent rocky algae-laden reefs, muddy bottoms of bays, and open sandy habitats. Their major food source is a rich abundance of small fishes, and a selection of bottom-dwelling invertebrates, such as crabs, shrimp, and mollusks.

The most common sharks associated with the bottom on tropical reefs include the collared carpetsharks catsharks, nurse sharks, zebra sharks, and wobbegongs, although not all may be present on any single reef. Like their counterparts in temperate zones, most small tropical reef sharks feed heavily on bottom-dwelling invertebrates and small fishes.

LARGE SHARKS

The larger sharks are also commonly found near coastal areas, but differ from most smaller sharks by swimming constantly over large ranges. In temperate latitudes, these include the large sevengill sharks, which are common visitors to shallow waters along the shoreline and the deeper continental shelves.

Great white sharks are seasonal visitors to many temperate coastal waters near rookeries and haul-out sites for seals and sea lions. Other large species, such as sand tigers and many requiem sharks, frequent coastal areas adjacent to their normal distribution ranges above the continental shelves.

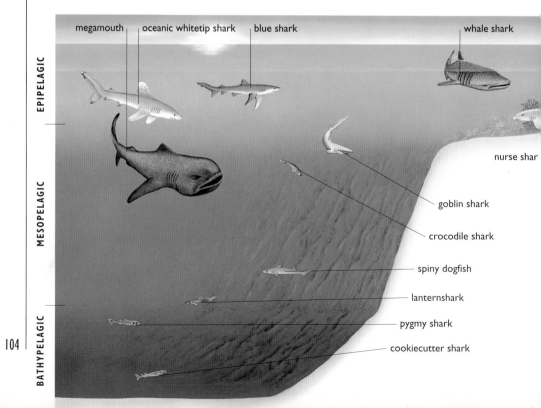

EPIPELAGIC

MESOPELAGIC

BATHYPELAGIC

megamouth | oceanic whitetip shark | blue shark | whale shark

nurse shar

goblin shark

crocodile shark

spiny dogfish

lanternshark

pygmy shark

cookiecutter shark

TO EACH HIS OWN *The bull shark (left) scours sandy bottoms, while the whitetip reef shark (far left) feeds at night and rests during the day in quiet places such as mangrove bays (below) and reef caves.*

In tropical reef habitats we find relatively large, mobile species of requiem sharks, including many well-known species, such as the gray reef, Queensland, whitetip reef and silvertip sharks of the Indo-Pacific, the Caribbean reef shark, and lemon sharks. The largest members of circum-global tropical reef sharks include the tiger shark, great hammerhead, and bull shark.

FINDING FOOD

Many species live in the open ocean. Blue sharks are quite common in temperate pelagic waters both near and far from land. Other oceanic visitors to coastal areas are the mako, salmon, and porbeagle sharks, which often follow coastal migrations of their fish prey. In tropical oceans, blue sharks avoid the warm surface temperatures and swim at greater depths where the water is cooler. Mako sharks are commonly found among tuna schools in tropical seas. The most common open-ocean requiem shark is the oceanic whitetip, which feeds on fishes and cephalopods.

There are three families of very large sharks that are known to filter feed on small oceanic plankton. The most commonly encountered planktivore in temperate waters is the basking shark, which has extremely long gill slits and reaches a length of about 30 feet (10 m). These sharks feed on tiny zooplankton in coastal areas with a rich upwelling of nutrients.

Another planktivore found in tropical and subtropical coastal seas is the whale shark, which reaches a length of 39 feet (12 m). The diet of the recently discovered megamouth shark (see p. 154) probably includes plankton, small crustaceans, copepods, and jellyfish.

THE WONDERS OF THE DEEP

The least-known realms of the shark are the deep mesopelagic waters of the open ocean, the slopes of continental shelves, and the abyss of deep oceans. The large and sluggish bramble sharks range from shallow shelf waters to the upper continental slopes. Velvet dogfish and gulper sharks are regularly collected at bottom depths of 2 miles (3,500 m).

The world's smallest sharks, including pygmy sharks and lanternsharks, inhabit the mesopelagic and bathypelagic regions. They show special adaptations to their gloomy environment, such as well-developed luminescent photophores that are probably used for visual communication in these dark depths.

Many of the most unusual species, such as goblin sharks and roughsharks, are found on continental shelves and on their upper slopes.

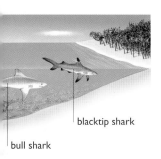

blacktip shark

bull shark

TERRITORIAL WATERS *Different ocean realms (left) are favored by various species of shark for a variety of reasons, including availability of food. As well as the preferred locality, coastal, reef, or open ocean, three depth levels are differentiated. Sharks are not illustrated to size.)*

SHARK REPRODUCTION

The reproductive strategies of sharks, which in many ways are more like those of birds and mammals than other fishes, serve to enhance the survival of their relatively few precious offspring.

Females of most fishes eject thousands (or millions) of small eggs to be fertilized outside the body by males. Female sharks, on the other hand, produce a relatively few large eggs that are fertilized inside the body by males. The gestation period, inside the female, may be as long as almost two years. So in many ways, a shark's reproductive system is more like that of mammals (including our own) and birds than that of other fishes.

THE JOURNEY BEGINS
Before or during the mating season, sperm is produced by male sharks within their testes,

paired organs found in the body cavity just below the backbone. Mature sperm are transported down a series of small ducts and, in some species, assembled into packets known as spermatophores. Sperm is then stored in the collecting ducts or specialized sperm sacs near the cloaca.

Mating in sharks is facilitated by the clasper organs of males, which develop from medial folds of the pelvic fins. During courtship a single clasper is flared, rotated, and inserted into the female's cloaca. In many

species it is anchored by spines or hooks. Sperm is then forced through the folds of the clasper into the female.

On the female side, small germ cells within the ovaries grow and develop into large, yolked eggs up to 1½ inches (4 cm) in diameter. After ovulation, the eggs pass through the ostium and enter the reproductive tract. They are usually fertilized one by one in the shell gland, and are encased in either a horny protective shell in egg-laying species (such as swellsharks and hornsharks), or a thin membranous covering in livebearers (such as requiem and hammerhead sharks). The fertilized egg

THE NEXT GENERATION *The diagram (left) shows the male and female reproductive organs of a typical shark. In the two egg case (right) the almost fully developed embryos of the lesser spotted dogfish are clearly visible.*

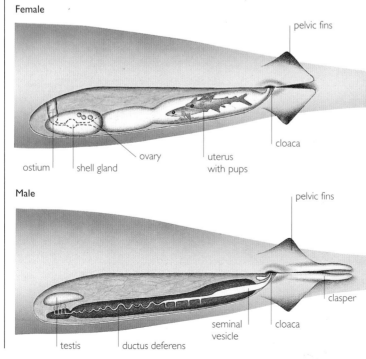

Female

pelvic fins

cloaca

ovary

uterus with pups

ostium shell gland

Male

pelvic fins

clasper

seminal vesicle

cloaca

testis ductus deferens

...en descends the oviduct and ...sses to the uterus, where the ...mbryo develops. Nutrients ...ss from the egg yolk by ...eans of the yolk stalk.

...OTHER CARE

...gg-laying, or oviparous, ...ecies deposit their eggs on ...e bottom substrate where ...e embryos develop, receiv- ...g nourishment entirely from ...e egg yolk. The egg case of ...ornsharks is soft when first ...d, and a female often picks ... up in her mouth and ...posits it in a crevice so that ...hen it hardens, it becomes ...edged. Catsharks have ...rse-like egg cases with long ...ndrils that twist around ...jects on the bottom. In ...bra, bamboo, and epaulette ...arks, there are sticky fila- ...ents instead of tendrils.

The majority of sharks are ...viparous, livebearers, and ...e embryo develops entirely ...ithin the uterus. Most ...ecies show aplacental vivi- ...rity in which the embryo is nourished entirely by the yolk but is not released by the mother until fully developed. In others, the embryo remains in the mother's uterus even after the yolk sac has been fully absorbed. In the tiger shark, the uterus provides additional nutrient-rich secretions that are thought to be absorbed directly by the embryo. Embryonic sand tiger sharks receive supplemental nutrition through sibling cannibalism. The first-born consumes its siblings, then continues to feed upon hundreds of unfertilized eggs produced by the mother.

In species with placental viviparity, the spent yolk sac forms a connec- tion with the uterine wall and absorbs nutrients from the mother. These are passed to the embryo via the yolk stalk umbilicus. In other species, the yolk stalk shows leaf-like elabora- tions that absorb nutrients directly from the sur- rounding rich uterine fluid.

Sharks and rays do not guard eggs or newborn young. The young are small versions of their parents, active swimmers, and begin to feed almost immediately.

THE MATING GAME

Most oviparous sharks mate for a brief period each year and lay eggs that hatch 3 to 15 months later. The repro- ductive cycle for viviparous sharks is often limited by the gestation period. Small species may mate annually and give birth to live young from a few months to about a year later.

For example, sharpnose sharks, which reach a maximum size of about 40 inches (1 m), carry 1 to 7 young for 10 to 12 months. At the other extreme is the spiny dogfish shark, which takes nearly 2 years for up to 20 young to develop to a viable size.

Larger sharks, such as the blue shark, may have litters of more than 100 pups after a gestation period of 9 to 12 months. In the other large requiem sharks, such as the blacktip, the gestation period is 10 to 12 months, and they are thought to give birth only in alternate years, but this is by no means certain.

SHARK BEHAVIOR

Most sharks have a diversity of often complex behaviors related to feeding,
mating, and social interactions that we still don't fully understand.

Although inhospitable to humans, the ocean realm has very few boundaries that can contain the movements of sharks. Scientist divers are able to spend only a few hours at a time in the water, and are limited in their movements to relatively short distances and shallow depths. In contrast, the streamlined bodies of large sharks are designed to carry them over great distances each day, and they are also capable of rapid, deep dives. As a result of the shark's wide-ranging journeys in the ocean, information on their behavior is usually limited to brief snapshots of their daily lives.

Activity patterns are often closely tied in with a shark's daily feeding. The blue shark, whitetip reef shark, catsharks

SIGN LANGUAGE *The agonistic display (above) of the gray reef shark. Hammerheads (below) schooling with Pacific creole fishes, Galapagos Islands.*

Side

Front

Top

Aggressive behavior   Non-aggressive behavior

and many other species feed primarily at night, but only a few species are known to feed mainly during daylight hours. These include the bonnethead shark, which takes crabs, shrimp, and small fishes in bays and along sandy beaches. Lemon sharks are especially

active around dusk and daw but these are only the times major activity. Like most predators, sharks feed whenever there is an opportunity.

SAFETY IN NUMBERS
Sharks are known to occur both as solitary individuals a

various groupings. For example, tropical reef species, such as blacktip reef, gray reef and lemon sharks, are often observed by divers as solitary individuals in search of food. At other times, these same species are seen swimming together in small groups, apparently engaged in hunting or social activities.

Research in the Sea of Cortez has identified a large population of scalloped hammerhead sharks that forms schools on seamounts during the day, then moves off at night to feed on fishes and squid. Some species, such as the pelagic blue shark and bottom-dwelling bonnethead sharks, often form large, single-sex schools or schools of similar-sized individuals. There may be biological reasons for these aggregations, including the avoidance of larger predators, habitats that have preferred food items, optional birthing grounds for females, to name only a few.

PECKING ORDER

Many social interactions are observed within schools or groups of sharks. While feeding on whale carcasses, large white sharks will often aggressively chase away or even severely bite smaller individuals of the same species, and will ultimately do most of the feeding. Dominance hierarchies between species over food are also common, such as the interaction between reef whitetip sharks (low dominance), gray reef (middle dominance), and silvertip (high dominance). Similar hierarchies also clearly exist for many species in non-feeding situations. For example, male bonnethead

sharks will display a threat posture known as a "hunch" toward others in the group, and physically bump and bite females or smaller males.

Perhaps the most spectacular and well-documented of the shark's social behavior is the agonistic (ready for combat) display demonstrated by the gray reef shark of tropical Pacific reefs. When approached by a diver at rapid speed or cornered against the reef, the shark will exhibit a threat display in which it arches its back, depresses the pectoral fins, and moves in an exaggerated swimming motion. This is a graded behavioral display in which the intensity of the display increases with the level of the shark's agitation.

If a shark in an intense display is further pressed, it will probably attack the source of the threat. Because the agonistic display of the gray reef shark occurs in non-feeding contexts, it may be a form of territorial defense, but it seems to be unrelated to defense of any specific site, so it may represent some defense of personal space or be anti-predator behavior.

COURTSHIP

All species of shark yet studied engage in some form of complex social reproductive behavior because the male must copulate to fertilize the female's eggs. In many species, a male closely follows a female during the mating season with its nose near the female's vent, which is probably a way of obtaining chemical information about her reproductive condition. During courtship, a male may aggressively bite the back,

COURTSHIP AND MATING *A diver observes a group of Port Jackson sharks mating (below). It is hard to gather data for species living in some remote habitats.*

flanks, and fins of the female, inflicting severe wounds, but this seems to stimulate her willingness to copulate.

Near the end of courtship, the male usually grasps the female's pectoral fin in his mouth, flexes a single clasper and rolls on his side to insert the clasper into the female's cloaca. In most large reef species, the pair will rest together for a few minutes on the bottom during sperm transfer, but some large species continue to swim while they copulate.

In smaller species, such as catsharks, which are more flexible, a male will often coil its body around the female during copulation without biting her fins. While nearly all of our information on shark mating comes from reef-dwelling species, almost nothing is known about the sex lives of the large pelagics because of their inaccessible environment and wide range.

FOOD *and* FEEDING

Each species of shark occupies a specific feeding niche within its habitat, and provides an important link in the flow of energy through the Earth's oceans.

Contrary to popular myths, sharks are not scavengers of the deep, feeding indiscriminately on garbage or anything that crosses their path. They are carnivores occupying nearly all feeding levels of all marine food webs. Most small sharks associated with reef systems or bays are major predators of large invertebrates, such as crabs, shrimp, worms, squid, and small bony fishes. Snails and sea urchins, which are primary grazers on fields of benthic algae, are also important prey for hornsharks and some other small species.

The diet of the wide-ranging requiem sharks of reef habitats includes larger bony fishes, squid, cuttlefish, and octopus. Large tiger sharks, usually found in the deeper regions of tropical reef systems, consume a wide variety of vertebrates,

MODIFICATIONS *The teeth of sharks (above) show adaptations to cope with their various diets. Stages in the biting action of the great white shark (below): the mouth begins to open; the snout lifts as the upper jaw protrudes; the lower jaw slips forward; and closes again on the prey.*

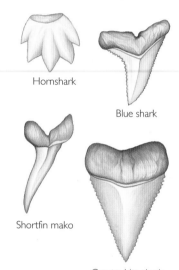

Hornshark

Blue shark

Shortfin mako

Great white shark

including large fishes, turtles and sea birds. Even large marine mammals, such as seals, sea lions, and dolphins, are preyed on by adult great whites and other large sharks.

HUNTING STRATEGIES

Each species of shark usually hunts in a certain way. Many small reef sharks, such as hornsharks and smooth-hounds, are benthic foragers that move over wide areas of the reef or open sand bottom

in search of invertebrates. Other benthic species, such the wobbegongs and angel-sharks, are ambush predators. Their bodies are camouflage by cryptic colors and pattern that match their background. They lie concealed on the bottom until an unsuspecting small fish or crustacean come close enough for a strike.

Many ambush predators also use trickery. For exampl the wobbegong mimics benthic algae, and the nurse shark rolls its pectoral fins under the body to mimic a small reef crevice. Both of these strategies are designed lure unsuspecting small reef fishes into what looks like a safe shelter. Other sharks are pursuit predators that activel chase down their fleeing pre Blacktip reef sharks move in groups over coral reef flats during the day in search of surgeonfishes and mullet. Gray reef sharks cruise the edges of coral reefs at dawn and dusk, pursuing prey fishe

Hammerhead sharks commonly roam the sandy

Stage 1

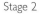

Stage 2

ef flats in search
stingrays, which
ey pin to the
ottom with their
ead and devour.
ne of the most
usual predatory
haviors is that
reef interior
nters, such as reef
hitetip, nurse, and
aulette sharks.
he bodies of these
ecies are so
tenuated and
exible that they
n swim into small
oles in search of
dden crustaceans
d fish prey, only
emerge from
nother hole on
e other side of
e reef.

ETHAL
/EAPONS

arks show many
atomical and behavioral
laptations for feeding, with
e dentition of the jaw being
rticularly efficient. Species,
ch as the hornsharks and
onnethead sharks, that con-
me armored invertebrates,
ve small, sharp teeth at the
ont of the jaw for grasping
eir prey, and flat, molariform
eth at the back to crush the
rd shell before swallowing.
arger requiem sharks have
at, triangular teeth with

"BITE AND SPIT" THEORY

Adult great white sharks are the major predator of elephant seals and sea lions, such as the group at right. These animals bask at the surface in many temperate coastal waters of the world. Surfers and skin divers are also sometimes attacked at the surface by great whites in these areas.

One similarity between encounters with both humans and marine pinnipeds is that the initial attack frequently involves a single, massive bite that inflicts a major, often fatal injury. Usually no flesh is removed until the subsequent bites.

This predatory behavior, unique to the great white shark, has led researchers to propose the "Bite and Spit" hypothesis. The prey is released after the first quick and powerful killing bite, aimed to incapacitate the victim. This behavior is thought to reduce the chance of injury to the shark during, for example, prolonged contact with a large, struggling elephant seal. Such a formidable opponent usually has dangerous teeth and nails and could weigh more than 1,000 pounds (500 kg).

serrated edges to cut large fish and cephalopods into pieces before swallowing.

This tooth design reaches its climax with the large, triangular and serrated teeth of the lamnid great white shark, which can easily cut a 22 pound (10 kg) chunk of blubber from a whale body in a single bite.

Other species, such as the mako and sand tiger sharks, have long, thin, needle-like

teeth that have become adapted for grasping large fish. The jaw and associated muscles form a highly efficient mechanism for the rapid capture, processing, and manipulation of many types of prey.

In the great white shark, the feeding action begins when the head and snout are lifted, and the lower jaw is simultaneously depressed. Once the jaw is fully open, muscle contractions force the forward rotation of the upper jaw, which detaches from the skull and comes completely out of the mouth. This action creates this predator's powerful and awesome bite.

Stage 3

Stage 4

DAILY MOVEMENTS *and* MIGRATIONS

As advanced technologies tap into the ocean's secrets, we are gradually

building up a picture of the way sharks use their environment.

Migration from tagging
stations off US coast

Migration from other
tagging stations

EPIC JOURNEYS *The map (left*
shows the migratory patterns of
the blue shark around the Atlan
Ocean, as revealed by an
extensive tagging program.
Individual animals may travel
incredible distances each year.

Cooperative Shark
Tagging Program, is
sponsored by the Unitec
States National Marine
Fisheries Service and ha
been in operation since
1962. To date, more
than 87,000 sharks of
46 species have been tagged
by scientists and fishers off
the eastern seaboard of Nortl
America. Of these, there hav
been nearly 4,000 returns
covering 30 species.

Sharks are classified in
three categories based on the
migratory patterns. Local
sharks are non-migratory
species, such as the bull shark
nurse shark, and bonnethead
shark. These sharks are
found near the shore or abov
reefs, and seem to range
within an area of only a few
hundred miles.

Coastal pelagic sharks
occur in deep waters above
continental shelves. These
include large species, such
as the dusky, sandbar, tiger,
and blacktip sharks, that are
capable of migration distance
in excess of 1,000 miles
(1,600 km). The sandbar
shark, for example, is known

Spanning vast distances
between continents, the
world's oceans provide
highways for the global migrations of many pelagic sharks.
Other species never venture
far from major landmasses,
but travel long distances
parallel to the shoreline or
adjacent continental shelf.

Many such migrations are
to follow movements of their
prey while others are related
to mating activities or
pupping of the young. Much
of our current understanding
about shark movements
comes as a result of
tremendous human effort,
and with the advent of new
technologies, knowledge
continues to expand.

MAJOR MIGRATIONS

Because of seasonal changes
in many local shark numbers,
fishers and researchers realized

long ago that sharks make
large-scale migrations.
Much of the relevant data
about these movements
comes from long-term tagging
programs supported primarily
by government agencies,
researchers, and sport and
commercial fishers.

The main tool is the dart
tag—a numbered, labeled
plastic streamer attached to
a nylon or stainless-steel barb.
Sharks are captured by hook
and line, identified to species,
sexed and, if possible,
measured. The dart, attached
to an applicator pole, is
inserted under the skin
usually near the first dorsal
fin. The shark is then released
unharmed to continue with its
normal movements. If it is
later recaptured, data on size,
date of capture, and location
are sent to the tagging agency.

The largest of these, the

migrate from the north-
astern seaboard of North
America to southern Mexico.
Highly pelagic sharks, such
as the mako and blue shark,
make long, often trans-
oceanic migrations across the
deep basins of the Atlantic.

The longest linear move-
ment by an individual was
recorded for a blue shark
tagged off the coast of the
northeast United States and
recaptured 300 miles (500 km)
south of the Equator, a travel
distance of 3,740 miles
6,000 km). Multiple recap-
tures of tagged blue sharks
indicate regular transatlantic
migrations over distances
greater than 10,000 miles
6,000 km). Although shark
tag and recapture data are
relatively scarce in the Pacific,
it is probable that blue sharks
make similar long migrations
between the coast of North
America and Asia. While dart
tagging is still valuable, it
will be new technologies,
such as satellite telemetry,
that will eventually unravel
the mystery of the global
movements of sharks.

DAILY MOVEMENTS

New technology has
emerged that is
helping to record shark
movements in their
everyday environment,
too. In recent years,
many scientists have
used ultrasonic tele-
metry transmitters, which are
attached to the shark and
tracked with a hydrophone
from a boat or by a diver.
These devices can be fitted
with sensors to monitor
depth, swimming speed,
body or water temperature,
or even stomach pH.
Telemetry studies of the
blue sharks off Santa Catalina
Island, California, show that
at certain times of year,
individuals spend daylight
hours not far offshore. After
dark, they move in closer,
presumably to feed.

Other studies show that
tiger sharks associated with
Pacific reefs move over
a home range as large as
14 square miles (40 sq km)
each day and make frequent
vertical dives along the reef
slopes at night, probably to
feed. Other
tropical reef
species, such as
the gray reef shark, may cover
areas of about 11 square miles
(30 sq km) each day. Within
a given species, smaller sharks
generally have smaller home
ranges than do larger adults.
For example, juvenile lemon
sharks, which live in shallow
reef flats near mangrove
habitats, have a home range
of less than ½ square mile
(1 sq km), while adults use
20 square miles (50 sq km)
or more.

Sharks also seem to pay
visits to particular areas at
regular times. For example,
hornsharks found on
temperate rocky reefs were
observed to forage in the same
area of the reef each day, rest
in the same area of the rocky
reef in the afternoon, and
return to shelter in a single
cave each night. Similarly,
telemetered large gray reef
sharks visit specific regions
of the reef each day.

BUILDING THE PICTURE

A lemon shark swims past
a monitor (top) that picks
up a signal from an ultrasonic transmitter implanted
in its body. A numbered
tag from the University of
Miami (above) carries
instructions and a return
address. A tiger shark
(right) being tagged.

CHAPTER FIVE

RAYS

The secret pit of the ocean holds a universe of
tangled infinities.

JOSEPH MACINNIS (b.1937), Canadian ocean explorer

IDENTIFYING and CLASSIFYING RAYS

Rays are among the most distinctive of the cartilaginous fishes but their classification is difficult and the subject of spirited ongoing scientific debate.

There are almost 600 living species of rays from some 18 families. Their body shapes have become highly modified and specialized. They are flattened in various ways and the pectoral fins and part of the body are joined to form a distinctive structure known as the "disc." This is typically wider than deep and may be wedge-shaped, oval, circular, or triangular. Members of major families are easy to recognize, but species can be confusingly similar in form.

DISTINCTIVE FEATURES

Some shark groups, such as angelsharks and sawsharks, also have enlarged pectoral fins that resemble a small disc, but their gills are on the sides of the head. Rays, on the other hand, have five (or six) pairs of gill slits on the under-surface. In many ray groups, the head forms part of the disc and when the head is separate, the pectoral fins join the head in front of the gill slits. In bottom-dwellers, the eyes and spiracles are usually on top of the head. In a few blind electric rays, the eyes are covered with skin and difficult to see.

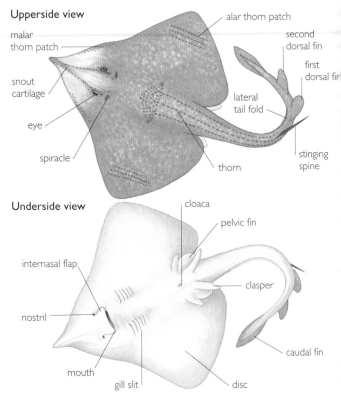

Upperside view

malar thorn patch
snout cartilage
eye
spiracle
alar thorn patch
second dorsal fin
first dorsal fin
lateral tail fold
thorn
stinging spine

Underside view

internasal flap
nostril
mouth
gill slit
cloaca
pelvic fin
clasper
caudal fin
disc

Some ray charactersistics are very useful for identification, for example, snouts that resemble saws, electric organs enlarged pelvic fins that are joined to form discs, and lobe or horn-like projections on the snouts. The sexes can be distinguished at an early age. Male claspers are important in distinguishing species, because their shape and structure varies not only among families but also within them. They have been used extensively to

BODY LANGUAGE *Identifying the parts of ray (above). A bluespotted ribbontail ray (left) in Mabul, Malaysia*

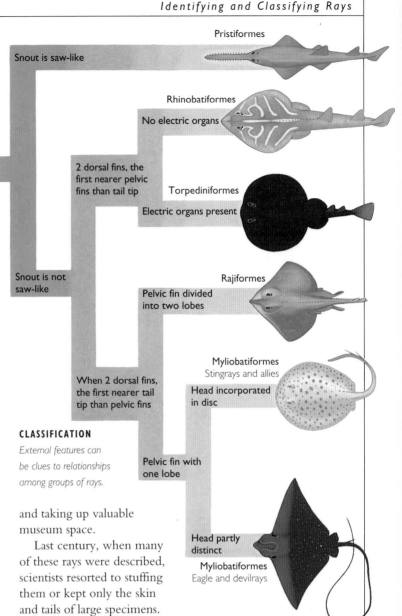

Pristiformes

Snout is saw-like

Rhinobatiformes

No electric organs

2 dorsal fins, the first nearer pelvic fins than tail tip

Torpediniformes

Electric organs present

Snout is not saw-like

Rajiformes

Pelvic fin divided into two lobes

Myliobatiformes
Stingrays and allies

Head incorporated in disc

When 2 dorsal fins, the first nearer tail tip than pelvic fins

CLASSIFICATION

External features can be clues to relationships among groups of rays.

Pelvic fin with one lobe

Head partly distinct

Myliobatiformes
Eagle and devilrays

tinguish close relatives d also to assess evolutionary ationships between genera d species. The skin, thick many rays, is either ooth with a coating slimy mucus or may ve a protective armor strong bony tubercles thorns. Size, shape, and cation of these special types denticle varies from species species, which is important identification.

WHAT SIZE TELLS US ith more than half of the ecies exceeding 20 inches) cm) in length, rays are hong the largest fishes. The l, which is often damaged, ries greatly in length from e specimen to another, so entists prefer to express size width. The gigantic manta y may exceed 22 feet (6.7 m) width and weigh several ns. The smallest, the short- se electric ray, is less than inches (10 cm) wide and eighs less than 1 pound)0 g). The average adult te varies greatly from family family. While all numb- hes are smaller than 3 feet) cm), the range for sawfish ecies is from 5–25 feet .4–7.6 m), and the highly verse skates, with more than)0 species, vary from 8 inches 8 feet (20 cm to 2.5 m). Our knowledge of ray xonomy is increasing only wly. Unknown species rk in the ocean depths, rticularly in the Indo- cific where more than) new species have been scovered in the past decade. shore species are often istakenly identified and ed further study. Large ults can be bulky and avy, making them difficult collect, transport, and store,

and taking up valuable museum space.

Last century, when many of these rays were described, scientists resorted to stuffing them or kept only the skin and tails of large specimens. Many such specimens are now lost or in poor condition.

GATHERING CLUES
Male and female rays can differ in shape and color, as can the young. To identify features that distinguish one species from another, taxono- mists need to examine several specimens, including juveniles and mature males and females. For many species, this simply has not been possible.

When trying to identify a ray, it is important to note its external features. Is the disc large or small compared to the tail? Is the head separate from the disc? Is the tail broad and muscular, long and whip-like,

or short and narrow? Does the tail have dorsal and caudal fins and where are they? All these important initial observations are needed to identify the ray's family group.

Beyond this point, the identification becomes more difficult and a knowledge of the species occurring within the area is usually needed. Each region has a unique ray fauna, with the species often having narrow distributional ranges. If you know where the ray was caught, the number of options can be reduced. Details of color, denticles, and placement of thorns are also vital clues.

THE EVOLUTION *and* RADIATION *of* RAYS

Given the difficulties in studying these interesting animals, it may be some time yet before the ray's evolutionary history is fully unraveled.

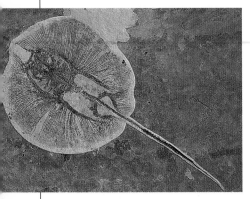

Rays evolved from sharks but there has been much debate about which groups are the oldest, and the sequence of their evolution. They belong to a major group of cartilaginous fishes called Squalea, which includes dogfishes, sixgill and sevengill sharks, angelsharks, and sawsharks. Ancestral rays may have resembled sawfishes and probably evolved during the age of the dinosaurs.

Guitarfishes and their relatives are thought to be among the oldest ray groups, and eagle rays, devilrays, and stingrays are the most recently evolved. Skates may be the immediate recent ancestors of either shovelnose rays or electric rays. Some ichthyologists believe that electric rays

evolved before sawfishes. Yet another theory says that electric ray groups may have evolved from an ancestral guitarfish. The picture is unclear, so several classes of batoids have been proposed.

THE FOSSIL RECORD

The earliest known fossil rays date back to the Jurassic Period, more than 150 million years ago (mya). Most species are known from only a few teeth, denticles, and spines, but well-preserved whole bodies of ancient guitarfishes have been found. The appearance of these rays has changed little with time.

Sadly, the fossil record of many groups is incomplete. We know from examining the distributions of living rays and from Earth's geological history that several groups

roamed those ancient seas for even longer than the fossil evidence suggests. While ray fossils of the Cretaceous (65–145 mya) are comparatively rare, they are common throughout Tertiary sedimen (25–60 mya). Many such fossils are represented only by teeth, but whole fossil animals, including the stingra *Heliobatis*, trapped in coastal lakes when sea levels fell and the oceans receded, have bee found in shales from the Gree River, Wyoming, USA.

The oldest known fossil skates were found in sedimen of a prehistoric sea dated to the late Cretaceous, some 70 mya. It has been suggeste that these rays colonized the Pacific and Atlantic via an ancient marine pathway, the Tethyan Sea. But it is also probable that an old group o skates had an ancestor in the

ANCIENT AND MODERN *The white-spotted guitarfish (right) shares many characteristics with its fossilized ancestor* Heliobatis *(above) taken from Eocene deposits more than 35 million years old.*

s around Gondwana-
d, the ancient south-
n supercontinent. This
oup, which includes
rough skate, *Raja
suta*, has species still
ing in the coastal seas
South America, New
aland, and southern
stralia. These three
gions were connected
Antarctica in the Cre-
eous Period, but later
fted apart. Since skates
not migrate across
en oceans, they must have
ed there before the break-
of Gondwanaland (about
mya). The oldest Antarctic
sils date from 50 mya.

IDE DISTRIBUTION
ving rays, very successful
hes, are found in all oceans
d seas on Earth. They are
luable in determining the
olutionary structure of the
rld's fish faunas because
ne of the groups contain
cies that are closely related
t which have very restricted
tributions. The eggs of
ny bony pelagic fishes drift
the open sea and are often
nsported to areas far from
ere they were laid. Young
s, on the other hand,
born alive or hatch
m eggs laid on the
ttom. Dispersal
yond their existing
ge depends almost
tirely on the move-
nts of the mother.
Unlike bony fishes,
ich produce eggs
mbering millions in
ne species, rays have
ry few young at the
d of quite a long gestation
riod. This limits how
idly their populations can
rease, so they rely instead
the survival of the few
ung they produce. If their

numbers are affected by
external influences, such as
overfishing or loss of habitat,
the survival of the species
could be threatened.

Ray distributions also vary
greatly from group to group.
Sharkfin guitarfishes, devilrays, and sawfishes occur
throughout the tropics but
seldom visit cooler temperate
waters. The ubiquitous skates
live around the shelves and
slopes of oceanic islands and
all continents but have never
been found near the coral
islands of the Pacific. These
are the dominant rays in cool
waters but they are mostly
confined to deeper waters
in the tropics. Few of the

families have restricted distributions, although the shorttailed
electric rays (Hypnidae) are
confined to Australian seas, and
the river rays (Potamotrygon-
idae) are native to the South
American rivers and lakes that
drain into the Atlantic Ocean.

RICH DIVERSITY
The shortnose electric rays
(Narkidae) have an unusual
distribution that includes the
Indo-West Pacific (from
Indonesia to Japan) and New
Zealand, but not Australia.
Within some families, genera
may be quite restricted. Stingarees (Urolophidae) and whiprays (*Himantura*) have groups
of species that occur in the
Indo-West Pacific and
off Central America but
are quite distantly
related to each other.
Other groups have
diversified greatly in
some regions but less
in others. Stingrays are
much more diverse in
the Indian Ocean than
in the Atlantic.

The richest ray
faunas are in the Indo-
Pacific, from South Africa to
Japan and Australia. About a
third of all species occur
off Australia and Indonesia.
Atlantic faunas are smaller but
still contain endemic species.

DISTANTLY RELATED GROUPS
*The thornback skate (top), and the
widely distributed sparsely spotted
stingaree (above), probably have
similar body forms because of the
similarity of their lifestyles.*

THE ANATOMY *and* BIOLOGY *of* RAYS

The secret lives of rays can be glimpsed by studying their anatomy and, in many cases, this is the best evidence we have.

We know details of the biology and ecology of only a small number of ray species. For example, while we are aware that most species live and feed on or near the bottom, we generally have a poor understanding of the more intimate aspects of their lives. Fortunately, a basic profile of a ray's life can be gleaned by examining its body features, such as shape, color, size, mouth structure, fin details, and internal anatomy. This field of study, known as ecomorphology, is becoming increasingly useful in predicting the lifestyles of many species of fish, including rays.

BODY SHAPE

Ray families vary greatly in shape, which makes them ideal subjects for ecomorphological studies. Their discs are well adapted for either a bottom-dwelling life or for swimming almost continuously above the bottom. The extent of flattening of the disc, its musculature, and its overall shape reflect the animal's preferred lifestyle. The tail, which is separate from the disc, is variably developed. The shorttailed electric rays (Hypnidae) have probably the shortest tails of all fishes. In contrast, the long, skinny whip-like tails of some stingrays, often several yards long, are among the longest found in fishes. In guitarfishes, the tail is comparatively broad, muscly, and powerful.

The dorsal and caudal fins vary greatly in shape, size and position among species. In some sawfishes and guitarfishes they are tall and shark-like, but in most other rays they are small. In the stingrays and eagle rays they are absent or rudimentary. One or more venomous stinging spines on the tail of many stingrays and stingarees are used to repel attacks by predatory sharks. Some eagle rays and butterfly rays also have stinging spines.

INTERNAL FEATURES

Ray skeletons, made almost entirely of cartilage, are highly modified, with the strong skull very flattened and a chain of small vertebrae that extends to the tip of the tail. The snout of guitarfishes and many skates is kept rigid by cartilage that extends from the front of the skull. This cartilage is absent in some species, such as the stingarees and stingrays, which need

ADAPTATIONS *The narrow, flattened stingaree cranium (top left) allows its flexible snout to grub for food. Cownose rays have flattened upper tooth plates (above) for crushing crabs and mollusks. The stingaree's nostrils and mouth (left) house a well-developed sensory system for locating prey. A bat ray (right) consuming squid eggs.*

TAIL STORIES
The stingray's whip-like tail (top) carries a venomous spine; the shovelnose ray's (above) is for swimming power.

ighly flexible snouts to grub
r food. An animal's skeleton
ops the body from flopping
d provides attachment
oints for its muscles. The
y's disc is supported by
umerous thin, pectoral-fin
rtilages. These cartilages are
attened, densely packed and
tend over most of the disc.

The brain of a ray is small
d simple compared to that
f a dolphin or a seal, but in
tio to body weight it is
rprisingly large. In fact, this
tio is similar to that found in
arsupials and birds. Of the
rtilaginous fishes, rays are
nong the best endowed
ainwise, with the manta ray
aving the largest brain of all.

All rays are carnivorous but
ost occupy a level below
at of sharks in the food chain
erarchy. Where sharks are
portant predators on reefs
d in open water, rays play a
ore significant role as
edators on soft substrates.
rge rays, including several
rpedo rays, stingrays, and
ates, are known to feed on
hes. However, small mobile
vertebrates, such as sand
orms, crustaceans, and
ollusks, are more important
etary items. Algae and
dentary invertebrates, such
sea tulips, anemones, corals,
d sponges, are rarely eaten.

FEEDING STRATEGIES

As the majority of rays are
bottom dwellers, the mouth is
located on the undersurface.
Most rays feed by trapping
prey against the substrate with
their disc. Food is directed to
the mouth by maneuvering
the disc over the prey, or by
manipulating the victim by
means of the flexible disc
flaps. Rays can be quite
selective feeders and the
various shapes of their mouth
and teeth are an indication of
their food preferences.

The bowmouth guitarfish,
for example, has a contoured
mouth with small, tightly
packed, flattened teeth for
crushing hard-shelled invertebrates. Eagle and cownose
rays have a series of flattened
tooth plates, rather like beaks,
to crush crabs and mollusks.
Torpedo rays have a very
arched lower jaw studded

with small spiny teeth. This
can be thrust forward to suck
up small fishes from the substrate. The cavernous mouth
of the plankton-feeding manta
ray is at the front of the snout.
The teeth, which are not
important in feeding, are
minute and covered in skin
in the lower jaw and totally
absent in the upper jaw.
Skates and most stingrays have
compact rows of strong,
pointed teeth in both jaws for
simultaneously holding and
crushing struggling prey.

The part of the sensory
system used to find and gather
food is well developed in rays.
Sawfishes and most guitarfish
have long, slit-like nostrils just
forward of the mouth. The
nostrils of other rays are partly
covered with a broad, fleshy
lobe, known as the internasal
flap. This is covered in
sensory pores and usually
reaches the mouth.
The pores form part
of the ampullae of
Lorenzini—an
electroreceptor
system for detecting
electric fields
produced by the
nerves and muscles
of other animals.
Rays use them to
detect predators,
prey, and other
members of the
same species.

THE HABITAT *of the* RAY

*These highly successful animals have adapted to all kinds of
habitat and have found niches in oceans and seas all around the globe.*

The majority of rays live exclusively in the sea, but some spend part of their lives in estuaries. A few have even invaded fresh water, living in rivers thousands of miles from the coast. Rays are important in marine communities, playing an integral part in the day-to-day life of the sea. Each has a discrete role—the common perception of a particular ray being just another ray is quite wrong.

For example, the lives of rays found in estuaries differ markedly from those living on outer continental shelves. Similarly, species living together in one area are biologically distinct from each other in some way. They may eat the same food, but they will have different seasonal distributions, reproductive methods, or prefer to live on different types of bottom. Most rays are highly efficient, and in some regions appear to have ousted bottom-dwelling bony fishes such as soles and flounders.

BALANCING SALINITY

Rays living in estuaries must be able to overcome potentially severe ionic stresses from fluctuating salinity. In high-salinity environments, such as the sea, water diffuses out through permeable membranes of living cells in a process known as osmosis, and salts are gained. In fresh water, the reverse occurs, water diffuses into the animal, and salts are lost. Animals living in either environment need to balance their salt and water concentrations to survive. In brackish estuaries, this is made more difficult because the salinity of the water is changing continuously as river water mixes with the sea.

To achieve a balance, the ray adjusts its internal osmotic pressure to minimize the transfer of water through its membranes. In the sea, rays supplement chloride levels in the blood and tissue with nitrogen compounds, such as urea. Apart from some water taken up through the membranes of the gills and mouth, their bodies are almost impermeable, so rays can live in estuaries for short periods without the osmotic stresses experienced by bony fishes. Rays that live full-time in fresh water, such as the ocellate river ray below, have more difficulty. These rays need to reduce their osmotic concentration. To compensate, they have very well-developed kidneys and endlessly excrete large quantities of weak urine to remove excess water and minimize ionic losses.

DIFFERING LIFESTYLES

Rays occupy a variety of habitats in the sea. They are found inshore in very shallow water but extend offshore down into the abyss to depths exceeding 10,000 feet (3,000 m). Some rays are predominately pelagic, swimming tirelessly in midwater and rarely resting on the bottom. Others lie on or bury themselves in the substrate, only swimming off the bottom to browse for food, reproduce, or escape from predators. However, unlike some bottom-dwelling bony fishes, none of the rays live in burrows.

The habitat needs of rays are evident from their body

GLASS WALLS *This ray likes to rest on the smooth wall of its aquarium tank at Underwater World in Perth, Australia.*

apes and may be quite
ecific. A rounded, flattened
ody is ideally adapted to
urying itself in the substrate.
he disc is amazingly flexible
ear its margin, which is
nportant for swimming,
urying, and feeding. The
ectoral fins of pelagic ray
roups, such as eagle rays and
antas, are pointed and have
rong lateral muscles for
rolonged swimming. Most
ecies prefer sandy and
uddy bottoms, but a few
ve mainly on rocky reefs,
a grasses and coral. The
angrove whipray, *Himantura*
anulata, wraps its disc around
e tops of small coral heads
ombies) with its tail hanging
ut sideways. Adults, which
ay be more than 5 feet
.5 m) wide and 10 feet
 m) long, make an impres-
ve sight in this pose.

In aquariums, skates often
efer to rest on the smooth,
ertical glass walls, rather than
n coarse rubble or rocky
ottoms. Other rays living on

reefs seek refuge
on sandy patches
among corals or
under ledges.

SEASONAL CHANGES

Some habitats are
used seasonally or
for only part of the
day. Estuaries, tidal
flats, and mangrove
swamps are very
important feeding
areas for many
tropical rays but
few live there
permanently.
Instead, they move
into these areas on
the incoming tide
and retreat as it
recedes. Others
move into some
particular habitat for part of
the year, perhaps to breed,
and such seasonal migrations
can be highly consistent from
year to year.

Beyond the continental
shelf break, demarcated by the
655 foot (200 m) isobath, lies
the open ocean. Much of the
deep-sea floor is muddy ooze.
Some deep-water skates use
their long, firm snouts,
covered in sensory pores,

to grub around in the soft
upper layers. The equally
long, but softer and more
flexible snout of the sixgill
stingrays (Hexatrygonidae)
appears to be used like a
finger to probe more deeply
into the sediments for food.

OCEANIC MYSTERIES

Devilrays live throughout
tropical seas and migrate
across the open oceans in
water many miles deep. Their
activities when far from shore
are not well understood, but
we believe they remain quite
close to the surface.

One species of stingray is
primarily oceanic and may
venture into deep water.
Unlike coastal rays, which
typically have pale bellies, the
pelagic stingray (*Pteryoplaty-*
trygon violacea) is black all
over. Our knowledge of its
distribution in the open seas
is based on specimens hooked
accidentally by longline
fishermen catching tuna.

HABITAT PREFERENCES *A blue-*
spotted ribbontail ray (top left) shelters
under a ledge near Bunaken Island,
Indonesia, while the stingray (below) is
more at home swimming near the sandy
sea floor surrounding the Bahamas.

LIFE CYCLE *and* REPRODUCTION

Nature has equipped these creatures with marvelous ways to handle the hazards that arise during the dangerous time of conception and birth.

Rays use two types of reproductive strategy, egg laying (oviparity) or a form of livebearing (ovoviviparity) in which there is no placental attachment of the embryo to the mother. In all species, male rays, like sharks, fertilize females internally using their claspers, the modified inner edges of the pelvic fin. Claspers are present as a pair of minute lobes near the cloaca in young males at birth. They expand greatly in late adolescence and become firm with the development of internal cartilage when the male reaches sexual maturity. They are made up of many small cartilages, but their anatomy varies greatly among the ray families and even within certain genera.

The end of the clasper, known as the glans, carries many tiny structures, which may include hooks, spines, discs, plates, spongy tissue, and grooves. When the glans opens during copulation, these structures are responsible for maintaining contact within the female, as well as holding and transferring the semen. Lubricating fluid is produced in secretory glands at the base of each clasper. In some rays, this fluid may also block the female's oviduct, to prevent her from being fertilized again by another male.

COURTSHIP AND DEVELOPMENT

Copulation can appear violent and takes place in a variety of positions, either belly to belly, or back to belly with the

PROPAGATION *A giant black stingray with its pup (top). Detail of a pair of male claspers (above) belonging to the eastern shovelnose stingaree. The ends are modified to hold the male in position while the sperm is delivered.*

claspers greatly twisted. The male often initially follows the female with his acutely sensitive snout close to her cloaca in search of chemical "green lights." Courtship usually includes some degree of nibbling or biting of the disc. The teeth of mature male skates are more slender and pointed than those of females, and probably help them to grasp the female during copulation.

Eagle rays use their flattened tooth plates to gouge the female's fins during courtship. Copulation can last just a few minutes or go on for hours, depending on the species. The act may take place on the bottom or in midwater. In each case, the teeth and body spines are important in helping the male maintain his position. In some skates, the male moves beneath the female and holds himself in place by the retractable alar thorns on top of the pectoral fins. Females may mate with several males in succession.

Skates are the only rays that do not give birth to live young. They lay leathery egg cases that are anchored or attached to the bottom. These are rectangular with long tendrils at each corner. Part of the egg case is usually sticky and shell bits and sand become attached,

eighting the egg case to the
ottom. Embryos may take
ore than six months to
evelop so the cases have to
e tough enough to avoid
eing eaten by predatory
vertebrates and fishes. Some
arine snails use their horny,
sping tongue to bore holes
the case and siphon out
e contents.

In the ovoviviparous rays,
e developing embryos either
vallow nutrients secreted
om the mother's uterus (as
torpedo rays), or absorb
utrients via string-like
tensions of the uterus that
ach the gut through the
iracles (typical of stingrays,
gle rays and butterfly rays).
newborn pup is sometimes
ore than 50 times heavier
an the unfertilized egg.

ROTECTIVE MEASURES
harp parts of young rays are
kely to damage the mother
birth and in the uterus.
oung sawfishes have a snout
ke the adult's, so the entire
w and its teeth are soft,
exible and covered with a
embranous sheath at birth.
he snout straightens and the
eth harden soon after.
imilarly, the stinging spines
venomous rays are soft at

THE MATING GAME

The breeding strategies of rays, which vary considerably among groups, are known for only a few of the more common species, such as the mating fiddler rays below. Round stingrays are segregated by sex outside the breeding season, with females occupying deeper parts of the continental shelf. Both sexes reunite inshore in late winter and spring to breed. In the morning, patrolling males locate

receptive females, who make themselves obvious by resting on the substrate in harems, their bodies often in stacks. Groups of sexually inactive females, those we think may have already mated or are not reproductively active, remain buried in the shallows. During the afternoon, these females emerge to feed among sea grasses and the males become inactive. This daily cycle continues over a fortnight or so.

birth. Some skates and stingrays that are very thorny as adults are born almost devoid of denticles. On the other hand, some mothers, for example, female electric rays, must avoid stunning and possibly killing their young. It has been found that torpedoes stop producing shocks in the presence of their pups and can be safely handled by humans. After the young are born, the rays

revert to their usual habit of delivering shocks.

Rays have long gestation periods and produce relatively small litters, which makes them highly vulnerable to population collapses from over-fishing and habitat degradation. Many species also have a restricted range of distribution.

These two factors make the group more fragile than most other marine animals, including bony fishes. Despite their obvious vulnerability, we have been slow to recognize their plight and their numbers continue to decline. Rays play an important role in the sea and the implications of their loss on the ecosystem are unknown.

BIRTH PANGS *A sparsley spotted stingaree (left) in the process of giving birth, and a newborn stingaree pup (above) with umbilical cord still attached.*

SURVIVAL *and* DEFENSE

All animals face risks and rays have developed a powerful and
surprising armory to defend themselves in the battle to survive.

The ray's ability to avoid and ward off predators is vital to its survival. Although they are relatively large fishes, they still have enemies and are a major food item for some species of shark. The ray's defensive armory includes electric organs, venomous spines, and hard bony thorns, also known as scutes. They can also make themselves difficult to detect by lying concealed in the silty or sandy substrate.

ON THE DEFENSIVE

The stinging spines (or stings) of rays, which are modified dorsal-fin spines, lie on top of the tail. The nearer the sting is to the tip, the more useful it becomes as a defensive weapon. It is a hard, flattened structure that tapers to a sharp point. The edges are serrated so that once driven into a victim, the sting either remains or tears the adjacent tissue when withdrawn.

Venom is produced and delivered in two narrow grooves running lengthways along the undersurface of the sting. The whole structure is covered by a thin skin which, when ruptured, releases its venom into the victim. Humans are frequent victims of ray stings but injuries are usually less severe than in shark attacks.

Longtailed rays, such as whiprays (*Himantura*), can use the tail to lash out when startled. The tail's effectiveness as a whip is lessened by the resistance of water, but this is partly compensated for by a covering of short sharp thorns that can severely lacerate unprotected skin. Despite this capability, these rays seem to use their tails on humans only in defense.

Sawfishes have been observed using the top of the snout as a bat to knock fishes away and laterally as a saw to lacerate. Large sawfishes can stun or kill fish as big as a grouper.

The shock-generating organs of the electric rays are

among the most powerful found in fishes. Large torped rays can produce shocks of more than 200 volts. This is sufficient to knock humans off their feet or to stun an unsuspecting diver. Apart from defense against sharks, these organs are probably used to communicate, and to locate and stun prey. A kidney-shaped electric organ

NON-SLIP GRIPPERS *The small teeth (above) of a shovelnose ray hold its prey firmly while it is crushed before swallowing.*

FENSIVE ARMORY *A porcupine ray ht) has a very rough upper surface sisting of plate-like denticles and rp thorns (also present on the outer ;). The green sawfish (below) uses saw both to cut and as a bat.*

located lengthways near the iddle of each side of the sc. Shocks can be delivered will but quickly weaken in tensity. Some electric rays e known to rush at intruders deliver a shock, but prey d predators alike are usually ocked accidentally when ey wander over a concealed y or strike it on the back.

JRVIVAL TACTICS

ays rarely use their teeth to aliate. Eagle rays can bite if stressed, but are not likely do so to deter predators, hough surf fishers have had gers crushed when removing ooks from a ray's mouth. umans have also been bitten the fingers when feeding ngrays. Recently, an ocean- um attendant who was earing only scuba gear and imsuit when hand-feeding a oup of large whiprays, was verely lacerated by an over- uberant ray.

The sensory capabilities of ys, such as sight, smell, bration, touch, and electrical and magnetic impulses, are very well developed. The animal uses them in combination to survive. Signals to the brain supply the ray with a full picture of its surroundings. Rays are known to detect and use magnetic fields to locate prey, and they are also thought to use this sense to move along compass headings and detect ocean currents. Large rays migrating across open ocean, where senses such as sight and smell are of little use, probably use these capabilities to navigate.

Rays have their share of parasites. Particular species of rays become infected with adult tapeworms when they eat a smaller fish with a dormant cyst of the worm in its flesh. Digestive juices in the ray's stomach enable the cyst to hatch and the tapeworm grows to adulthood in the alimentary canal of its host. These worms, which may eventually grow to several yards in length, lay eggs that are passed into the sea with the ray's feces. These, in turn, may infect the ray's prey, thus continuing the life cycle.

Sometimes, small flattened crustaceans (copepods) and worms (monogeneans) are seen crawling on the skin within the ray's mucus, particularly on the head, near the cloaca, and on the tail. Unless present in large numbers, these parasites are rarely injurious to the ray.

MOVEMENT
and PROPULSION

The acrobatic gliding and rolling maneuvers of manta rays are well known

to divers, but all rays ripple and glide with seemingly effortless grace.

Because they move in ways that vary greatly from group to group, the body shape and fins of rays are highly adapted to a pelagic existence or, more typically, to a life on the bottom.

POWER AND GRACE
To understand the role of fins in movement, let us compare a ray with a glider. The pectoral and pelvic fins of the ray are equivalent to the wings, elevators, and ailerons of the glider, controlling horizontal stability and up-and-down movements. The tail fin and rudders (dorsal and caudal fins of the ray) are often more responsible for

EFFORTLESS MOTION *Startled by something on the floor of the Coral Sea, a mangrove stingray (top) stirs up a great flurry of sand. A smoothtail mobula leaps out of the water (below).*

vertical stability, sideways movements, and steering.

Propulsion is mainly achieved either from the tail, by horizontal or lateral movement, or the pectoral fins, by vertical movement. Strongly built guitarfishes and sawfishes have powerful tails and relatively small pectoral fins compared with other rays. The tail muscles are arranged more as in sharks, and they move by laterally undulating the entire back half of the body. The pectoral fins are rather stiff and, rather than

being flapped, are used provide vertical control and stability. These rays also have well-develope dorsal and caudal fins, a do sharks, which enhan the swimming efficiency of the tail. The long lower lobe of the sharkf guitarfishes provides lift

Most rays have a wel developed disc, formed most from the pectoral fins. The tails vary from very short to several times longer than the discs. Except in some electri rays, the musculature is weak and plays a lesser role in propulsion. Skates and stingrays move by vertical undulation of the disc, either by flapping or sending ripple-like waves along the flexible disc edge. These ripples flow either from front to back to move the ra forward, or in reverse.

If only one side of the dis is moved independently, the

...ING PROGRESS *Ripple-like
...ves along the edge of the disc
...ble the stingray (top) to move.
...at ray (right) changes direction
...moving only one side of its disc.*

...ect is like using oars
...one side of a boat: the
...rotates. Movements
...parts of the disc also enable
...ray to dive, climb, turn,
...nk, or stop. Low-speed,
...ely controlled movements,
...t achievable by other
...ttom fishes, make rays
...credibly maneuverable. This
...es them a great advantage
...seeking prey, enabling
...em to move around in the
...ud while still partly buried.
...Some electric rays, such as
...mbfishes, use both disc and
...l to move. On the bottom,
...licate movements of the
...ge of its round disc allow
...e animal to forage around
...wly. Above the bottom,
...uses its well-developed tail
...d vertical fins to swim.

...ISTANCE SWIMMING
...antas, cownose rays, and
...gle rays are well adapted to
...ife that involves extended
...riods of swimming in open
...ater. Most have long whip-
...e tails that serve no purpose
...propulsion. Their powerful
...ctoral-fin muscles enable
...e stiff outer disc to flap like
...e wings of a bird. The

center of the head and body
are raised slightly on the
downstroke and lowered on
the upstroke. Unlike birds,
they can flap one wing at a
time to turn rapidly or beat
a swift retreat by zigzagging
away at great speed. This
ability is used to foil predatory
charges by sharks.

Unlike some bony fishes
that drift passively in water
currents or attach themselves
to larger fish, rays are active
continuously in open water.
Some whiprays may seem
passive at times when they
ride on the backs of larger
individuals, but apart from
brief periods when copulating,
they do not stay attached, as
do lampreys and remoras.

Many rays are covered
with a thick, slimy mucous
coating to reduce drag. The
mucus smooths out irregular-
ities on the body surface and
reduces surface tension. Apart
from some stingrays and
skates, rays seldom have large
denticles and many are
entirely smooth. The skin

denticles make the body
stiffer, so electric rays and
stingarees with smooth skins
generally have highly flexible
discs capable of extremely
delicate movements.

Rays lack the swim bladder
of bony fishes and large oily
liver that most sharks have to
maintain neutral buoyancy, so
unless they swim, they
sink to the bottom.
However, their enlarged
pectoral fins give them
one advantage over
sharks. The flattened
disc enables a ray to
glide for long distances
between active move-
ments, which provides
obvious benefits in
conserving energy and
may be useful in surpris-
ing prey. With their huge,
lightweight discs, butterfly
rays glide silently over the
bottom searching for food and
looking like stealth bombers.

BEATING A RETREAT
Rays are surprisingly good
at retreating quickly from
their resting position in the
substrate if disturbed by a
predator. They can turn
quickly and accelerate rapidly
at right angles to their original
position. Others, including
eagle rays and guitarfishes,
prop on the tips of their
pectoral fins in a racing start.

These animals differ in the
way they retreat—eagle rays
bear off by flapping one
pectoral fin before acceler-
ating, while guitarfishes twist
the body and accelerate by
using the tail. The powerful
pectoral discs of eagle and
manta rays enable them to
move at great speed. Some
species have been observed
skipping along the surface,
often leaping several yards
clear of the water.

BEHAVIOR *and* CONSERVATION

With new technologies, studies of less accessible marine creatures,

such as rays, are now possible, and we are slowly gaining an

understanding of their place in the ecosystems of the sea.

The ecological role and behavioral complexity of rays have never been fully appreciated by humans. Because of their more fearsome reputation, sharks have generally stolen the limelight. Rays were once thought of as simple animals with uncomplex behaviors, but we now know them to be complicated animals with rather large brains and very well-developed sensory systems.

Knowledge of their behavior is still based largely on observations made by underwater divers and photographers, and studies of captive rays in oceanariums. Unfortunately, few of the species have been studied—they are generally less visible than terrestrial predators of a

similar size and, among our marine fauna, they are considered less glamorous than seals and dolphins.

SOCIABILITY

Rays are basically sociable animals, often occurring in large groups of hundreds or even thousands of individuals. By sheer weight of numbers, schooling eagle rays may pose a nuisance to shellfish farms and they can decimate oyster beds. Farm managers place protective net fences around sites to keep them away, or sometimes try to entangle them in mesh nets. Rays resting in confined spaces, such as sand patches

among reefs, will often rest top of each other. Their ski is sensitive to touch and it h been observed that they see to go into a trance if stroke

Solitary rays are commor seen among bony fishes at cleaning stations on coral reefs. They swim slowly above the bottom with gills and jaws open so that small wrasses can access the mout cavities and spiracles to remove waste tissue and mucus. Parasites are also removed from the body.

They also share symbioti relationships with other bon fishes, such as trevally, pilot fish, cobia, and remoras, which either swim together with the ray or attach themselves to its skin. These fish feed on food rejected by

SYMBIOSIS *Cleaner fish at work inside a manta ray's open mouth (top), and southern stingrays (right) hitching a ride by swimming on top of each other.*

CONSTANT COMPANY
The Pacific manta ray is usually accompanied by cleaner fish, in this case orange clarion angelfish, and often has remoras attached to its body.

Experiments on rays have shown that their strong instincts are supplemented by a reasonable learning capacity. Round stingrays (*Urobatis halleri*) have been conditioned to move to specific sites within a circular tank to obtain food. Correct strikes were rewarded with a herring meal, incorrect movements were given a solid prod. Using a reward system, bat rays have been taught to fetch little floats on their snouts.

VARIETY OF USES

Humans have used rays for many purposes through the ages. Japanese Samurai warriors used rough stingray skin covered in large denticles on the handles of their swords to provide grip. The tails have been used to make clubs and necklaces, the stings for spear tips, the skin for leather, and the flesh for food.

Large tonnages of rays are still being caught around the globe with little regard to their long-term sustainability as a resource. Catches are being monitored in only a few regions, so ray survival is becoming quite a serious conservation issue.

ray or disturbed from the ⸱tom by the beating of the 's wings. Some rays live ⸱ne, presumably only ⸱ializing to mate. Like ⸱rks, they sometimes occur ⸱single-sex groups outside ⸱ breeding season.

⸱JRIOSITY

⸱ys also differ greatly in ⸱ir response to humans in ⸱ir natural environment. ⸱ge stingrays are often ⸱uisitive and will approach a ⸱er cautiously. Sometimes ⸱y will threaten divers by ⸱ckly raising the tail over ⸱ back in a scorpion-like ⸱nner. The raising of the tail ⸱a fixed upright pose by ⸱all stingarees is thought to ⸱a territorial response. ⸱Some whiprays swim in ⸱cles in front of an intruder ⸱h their long tails raised and ⸱ling in an ominous display ⸱defiance. Eagle rays and ⸱aller stingrays tend to be ⸱ and will depart rapidly if ⸱roached. Giant mantas are ⸱atle and seem to be unafraid ⸱humans in the sea.

RAYS IN MYTH AND MEDICINE

The venomous barbs of rays, such as that of the southern stingray at right, earned notoriety long ago. Aristotle described rays as dangerous, and the Greeks noted that rays retained their venomous properties well after death. These powers were considered so great that plants and trees were expected to wither and die if a sting was scraped along their bark. It was believed that the flesh was also poisonous—native tribes in parts of the Indo-Pacific placed a taboo on eating it. Even today, artisanal fishermen of the region are reluctant to eat rays, and cut off the tails to avoid being stung. In Malaysian folklore, there are tales of a leviathan ray that lived beneath a gigantic sea mushroom.

The ray's sting is also thought to have magical properties. Malaysian witch doctors produced a magical potion, consisting of burnt and powdered spines mixed with fruit and needle-shaped crystals (calcium oxalate) derived from plants. Powdered and blended with the Christmas rose (hellebore), ray stings were used as an anesthetic in dentistry by the ancient Greeks. (Interestingly, alkaloids removed from hellebore are used today in the treatment of heart disease.) The Greeks also used the sting as a charm—when removed from a live ray and attached immediately to a pregnant woman's navel, it was thought to promote an easy labor.

In a world older and more complete than ours they move more finished and complete, gifted with extensions of senses we have lost or never attained, living by voices we shall never hear.

The Outermost House,
HENRY BESTON (1888–1968), American writer

CHAPTER SIX

SHARKS FIELD GUIDE

USING *the* SHARKS GUIDE

Knowing as much as possible about sharks and their appearance can only enhance your explorations of the watery world below the surface.

The accounts and illustrations in this field guide will help you to appreciate a wide range of sharks. Some are familiar sights over reefs and sand flats around the world. Others are much more infrequently seen. Using the guide, you may be able to confirm the rarity or perhaps novelty of a shark you see, photograph, or find as part of a catch. You might even discover a little-known shark, and your observations could help to advance scientific knowledge of these extraordinary creatures. To this end, some rarely seen species have been included in the guide in the hope of enlisting your assistance in the search for new information, to help unlock the secrets of the sea.

*The **main photograph** shows as much of the species as possible, given the constraints of photographing such wild creatures in circumstances and conditions that can be difficult.*

*The **common** and **scientific names** of each species. The species are grouped according to taxonomy.*

*The **text** provides information on the appearance of the shark, its common names, habitat, and where and what to look for when you want to find it. It also gives clues on how to differentiate between similar species, and supplies information, where known, about the shark's migratory habits and methods of reproduction.*

Triakidae: Houndsharks

Soupfin Shark
Galeorhinus galeus

FIELD NOTES

■ Widespread: west coast of North America, east coast of South America, northeast Atlantic, South Africa, southern Australia, New Zealand
■ Varies throughout the world, but up to 6½' (2 m)
■ Not encountered by divers
■ Abundant

The soupfin shark is also known as the school shark or tope. It is a moderately slender shark, bronzy gray on the upper side and pale underneath. It has an unusually large subterminal lobe on the caudal fin. The small second dorsal fin is about the same size as the anal fin.

The soupfin shark is usually found on continental shelves and continental slopes in temperate waters. It feeds mainly on fish, squid, and octopus near the seabed or in the water column. Often preferring to congregate in schools, it lives to be more than 50 years old.

Although considered harmless, it is a very shy creature and encounters are unlikely. It will flee long before a diver arrives in its vicinity. Large numbers of new-born pups are sometimes caught inshore by anglers.

This species migrate distances so pregnant f can give birth in coole Sharks tagged in Eng. Ireland have traveled (1,530 miles [2,460 Canary Islands (1,5 [2,525 km]). Shark Californian region recaptured off Brit (1,000 miles [1,6

The soupfin shark is ovovivip sizes vary—a litter of 52 pups is known. After a gestation of 12 pups are born, 12–14" (30–35 Discrete, inshore nursery areas in Australia, Argentina, and Female sharks rea 8 to 10 year every se This rate sc n t r

Close-up of the eye of the
166 *soupfin shark, showing the free*

Secondary photographs show details of particular features or amplify some aspect of the shark's habitat or behavior.

This *illustrated banding* at the top of the page is a visual pointer to indicate that the page is about a shark species.

This **panel** refers to the family of sharks that the species belongs to.

Triakidae: Houndsharks

Carcharhinidae: Requiem Sharks

Triakidae: Houndsharks

Gummy Shark

Mustelus antarcticus

FIELD NOTES
- Southern Australia
- Females to 5½' (1.77 m); males to 4½' (1.45 m)
- Harmless
- During the day, year-round
- Abundant

he gummy shark takes its name from its teeth. They are flat, and arranged in a ent-like pattern, ideal for ng rather than cutting its This includes a wide variety topus, squid, crustaceans, and ound on the sandy and rocky oms where it dwells.

The gummy is a slender, bronzy gray shark h numerous white spots and sometimes black ots on its back and sides. A thin ridge runs ong its back.

The dusky smoothhound (*Mustelus canis*) of ne western Atlantic is another of the 20 or so species of the genus *Mustelus*. It is a slender shark, uniformly gray in color, and similar in biology and diet to the gummy shark.

Both species occur mainly in temperate waters on the continental shelf from the shore down. Some also dwell on the continental slope: the gummy shark to depths of 1,150' (350 m), the dusky smoothhound to 1,900' (580 m). They are abundant, and divers will often see them lying on the seabed in shallow coastal waters. Since they are harmless, they can be approached quite safely.

Tagging has shown that a small number of female gummy sharks make long migrations

across the ocean off southern Australia—the longest known journey is about 1,140 miles (1,840 km). Most travel only relatively short distances.

The gummy shark is ovoviviparous. After a gestation of about 12 months, pups 12–14½" (30–36 cm) long are born in coastal areas. There are between 1 and 38 pups in a litter, with 15 being the average. They live for about 16 years. In the past there was concern about declining stocks, but these days they are fished sustainably—for their meat, which is popularly known as "flake."

teeth of the lower jaw

167

Silvertip Shark

Carcharhinus albimarginatus

FIELD NOTES
- Widespread in tropics from East Africa to Panama; not in the Atlantic
- 10' (3 m)
- Aggressive, but not a significant risk
- During the day, year-round
- Common

y large and rk gray in non name ective all their arrow orsal ert like m sharks that are he reef edge in lar to those of nus

e ideal ey feed water, ral er sive

dorsal fin

Silvertip sharks are viviparous; females usually have 5 or 6 pups to a litter, but there can be as many as 11. The young hatch after 12 months.

Experiments conducted using underwater sound have shown that silvertips are attracted to low-frequency sounds, probably because these frequencies mimic the sound made by an injured fish, potentially an easy meal.

169

Quick-reference Field Notes panel
- *Distribution range of the shark*
- *Size*
- *Possible risks when encountering the shark*
- *Best time of day or year to observe the species*
- *Information on population numbers*

Color illustrations supplement the text by showing some basic features of the shark.

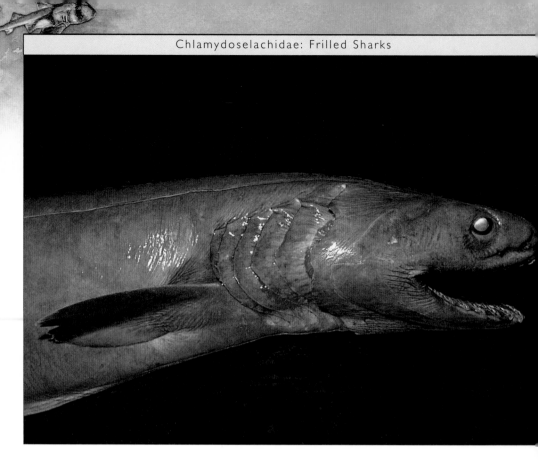

Frilled Shark

Chlamydoselachus anguineus

The frilled shark, or eel shark, has a long, slender body with an elongate tail fin, which gives it an almost eel-like appearance and one of its common names. A single small dorsal fin is located well back on its dark chocolate brown body, directly above the large anal fin. The pectoral fins are short and rounded. This shark has six pairs of large gill slits—most sharks have five—the first pair of which joins under the throat. The gills are surrounded by frilly margins of skin—hence the common name of frilled shark. Its snout is short, while the lower jaw is long, with the mouth almost at the tip of the snout rather than under the head.

The frilled shark's teeth have broad bases with three sharp cusps separated by two small intermediate cusps. Little is known about its diet, but with such teeth, it probably feeds on small deep-water fishes and squid.

Very little is known about the biology and ecology of this shark, the only living member of the frilled shark family. It is found on the bottom shelves and upper slopes around continents and large islands. Occasionally, it is seen near

FIELD NOTES

■ Eastern Atlantic, western Indian Ocean, western and eastern Pacific

■ Up to 6½' (2 m)

■ Harmless

■ Occasionally seen at the surface

■ Not uncommon

the surface in open waters, but it usually lives at a depth of 330–4,260' (100–1,300 m), so the only chance of observing it is from a deep-water submersible. It is sometimes collected a bycatch during bottom trawling

Female frilled sharks bear 8 t 12 live young, about 16" (40 cm long. Gestation is probably one to two years.

Thoughts on this shark's evolution are contentious. Some think it is a direct descendar of the primitive cladoselache sharks (see p. 94), but others say it is closer to modern forms.

snout with distinctive teeth and frilled gill margins

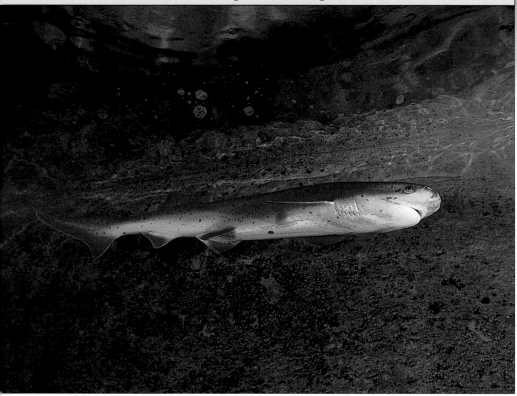

Broadnose Sevengill Shark

Notorynchus cepedianus

The broadnose sevengill shark is immediately recognizable because of its seven pairs of gill slits—most shark species only have five pairs. Its other unusual feature is a single, small dorsal fin. It has a wide head with a short, blunt snout and small eyes. It is a large and powerful shark. Its silvery gray to brownish back and sides are speckled with numerous small dark and white spots, while the underside is pale. Juveniles have white margins on their rear fins.

The seven gills and distinctive spots of a broadnose sevengill shark.

(135 m). Although the species is widespread, it is not particularly abundant. It will often come close inshore in shallow bays and inlets, but does not rest on the seabed. This might explain why it is not commonly seen by divers. There are no records of it attacking people (except for divers in aquariums), but it will scavenge on human corpses. It is potentially dangerous. In captivity, it is aggressive when attacked, and it struggles vigorously to escape when captured.

Males mature at about 5' (1.5 m), and females at about 7' (2.2 m). They bear live young in shallow bays. Litter sizes vary, and can be as large as 82 pups. The pups are about 16–18" (40–45 cm) when born.

The teeth of the broadnose sevengill shark are very effective for cutting. The teeth of the upper jaw are jagged with cusps, except for a single middle tooth; the teeth of the bottom jaw are comb-shaped. The shark's diet includes other sharks, rays, bony fishes, seals, and carrion. It bites pieces of flesh from other sharks caught by gill nets and hooks.

The shark lives in temperate waters on continental shelves, at depths down to 450'

137

Bluntnose Sixgill Shark

Hexanchus griseus

The bluntnose sixgill shark has a massive body, with a long and powerful tail, which it uses to swim in a strong, constant motion. A single dorsal fin is located to the rear of the body, slightly in front of the anal fin below. The eyes are small, and set on the side of the wide, short-snouted head.

The shark has six pairs of gill slits. Only two other shark species have six: the frilled shark (see p. 136) and the bigeyed sixgill shark (*Hexanchus vitulus*). The latter belongs to the same family as the bluntnose sixgill shark, and can be distinguished from it by its more slender body and large eyes. It has five rows of saw-like teeth on each side of its lower jaw, whereas the bluntnose sixgill shark has six rows of similar teeth. Its upper jaw has smaller recurved teeth with a single cusp.

This large shark is a voracious predator of other large fishes, such as

FIELD NOTES

- Worldwide in northern and cold temperate to tropical seas
- 5–16½' (1.5–5 m)
- Not dangerous unless provoked
- Most likely seen at night, year-round
- Common

sharks, billfishes, dolphin, cod, and flounder, which it can quickly cut into bite-sized chunks with its teeth. It also takes smaller prey, such as herring, squid, crab, and shrimp

The bluntnose sixgill shark is found both near the bottom and in the water column above continental and island shelves, at depths of 650–5,400' (200–1,800 m). It prefers dimly lit or dark waters, and is seen at night near the surface of the open ocean. Small sixgills move close inshore and forage near the bottom, but in coastal waters adults usually stay below 330' (100 m).

Females reach sexual maturity at about 14' (4.5 m). They produce up to 100 live young, about 28" (70 cm) long. Little is known about this shark's biology other than data from commercial fisheries— it is fished in many parts of the world for both its meat and its oil.

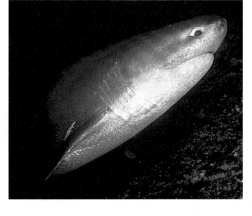

The broad, rounded snout of the bluntnose sixgill shark.

138

Prickly Shark

Echinorhinus cookei

The prickly shark is a spiny-skinned dogfish, one of two species of the bramble [sh]ark family. The bodies of both [sp]ecies are short and stout, the [he]ads slightly flattened. There is a [sm]all spiracle behind each eye and [in] front of the first of five pairs of [gil]l slits. Two spineless dorsal fins [are] located well back on the body [ab]ove the pelvic fins. Anal fins are absent.

The prickly shark is grayish brown with [wh]ite around the mouth and underneath the [sn]out, and black along its relatively large fin [ma]rgins. Its denticles, usually about ⅕" (5 mm) [wi]de at the base, are all over its body.

Little is known about the ecology [an]d habits of this shark. It is primarily [a d]eep-water species, dwelling in cold [te]mperate to tropical seas on conti-[ne]ntal and island shelves and upper [slo]pes at depths of from 36–1,390' [(1]1–424 m). Individuals are seen [oc]casionally in shallow waters. This [slo]w-moving species is probably a [su]ction-feeder of crabs and cephalopods [ne]ar the bottom. It also takes fishes such as [ju]venile sixgill sharks, flatfishes, and herring. [Fe]males reach maturity at about 8–10' (2.5–3 m)

FIELD NOTES

- Pacific, from the Americas to Hawaii, New Zealand, and Asia
- 13' (4 m)
- Harmless
- Rarely seen, except when taken by commercial fisheries
- Fairly common

long. They bear up to 24 live young, 16–18" (40–45 cm) long.

The related bramble shark (*Echinorhinus brucus*) gets its name from its much larger and very prominent spine-like denticles, about ⅗" (15 mm) in diameter at their base. They are scattered over the shark's body as well as on the underside of the snout in adults, and are sometimes fused into plates. The bramble shark is brown to dark gray above, with a lighter belly. It is most commonly encountered in the Mediterranean Sea and along the west coast of Europe and Africa.

skin and denticles of the bramble shark

Common Sawshark

Pristiophorus cirratus

The common sawshark is also known as the longnose sawshark. Like all the sawshark family, it is immediately recognizable from its saw-like snout with a pair of barbels. Because of this snout, it can sometimes be confused with sawfishes (see p. 204). However, the sawshark's five pairs of gills are on the side of its head, while the sawfish's gills are underneath. Also, the sawfish does not have a pair of barbels.

The common sawshark is a slender shark with a slightly depressed and flattened body. It has an attractive patterning of darker bands and brownish spots and blotches on a pale yellowish brown background. This shark is found only in

FIELD NOTES

■ Southern Australia, from southern New South Wales to mid-Western Australia

■ Females to 5' (1.5 m); males to 4⅓' (1.3 m)

■ Harmless unless provoked

■ Year-round

■ Common

temperate waters in southern Australia. The southern, or shortnose, sawshark (*Pristiophor nudipinnis*), also endemic to Australia, is found in a similar area. This brownish gray shark prefers to dwell on the inner continental shelf to depths of 230' (90 m); the common sawshark seems to prefer deepe water, on continental shelves and slopes to depths of about 1,015' (310 m).

Divers may find sawsharks lying on the sand bottoms. They are timid and harmless, but will strike with their snout if handled. They feed by trailing their barbels along the bottom to locate the small bony fish that they eat. The teeth on the snout are probably then used for stirring up sediment to rouse the prey and strike it.

The common sawshark lives for more than 15 years. Like all sawsharks, it is ovoviviparous. Mature females appear to breed every 1 to 2 years, carrying from 3 to 22 young, with about 10 being the average. After about 12 months' gestation, the pups are born in shallow coastal areas. They are about 11–14½" (27–37 cm) long at birth.

snout of the southern sawshark

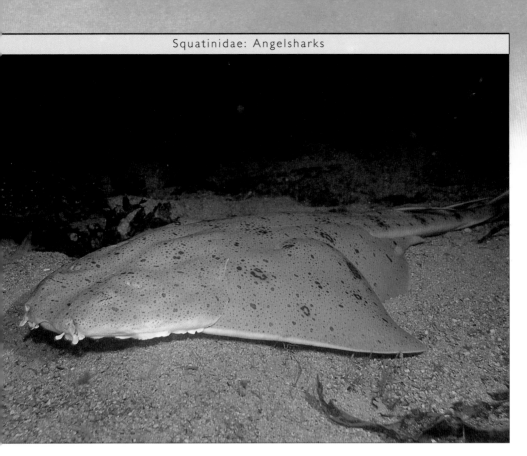

Pacific Angelshark

Squatina californica

A ngelsharks are unusual,
flattened sharks that are
often mistaken for rays.
ey used to be called monkfish
ause the strange shape of their
ads resembles the hood on a
nk's cloak. The dozen species
ge along temperate coasts from
llow waters to more than
65' (1,320 m) deep. They are
ique in having a blunt nose; the
ding edge of their pectoral fins
ree from the body; and the
ver caudal fin lobe is longer
n the upper.

The Pacific angelshark is easily identified by
large eyes, a conspicuous spiracle, and a
nerally brown-gray coloration. During the
y, it remains buried in sand on the bottom
th only its eyes and head exposed,
dy to burst upward out of the
d and ambush a fish or squid
th its protruding, trap-like
vs and numerous spiky
th. Occasionally, divers
y encounter a Pacific
gelshark swimming over
dy bottoms near kelp beds
depths of about 10' (3 m) and

FIELD NOTES

■ *Eastern Pacific, from southeast
Alaska, USA, to Baja California,
Mexico, and from Ecuador to
southern Chile*

■ *To about 5' (1.5 m)*

■ *Can bite if surprised
or harassed*

■ *Best seen at night*

■ *Once common, now reduced
due to heavy fishing pressure*

more. It can become aggressive
if harassed—a diver or angler
who foolishly grabs the tail of an
angelshark soon discovers how
quickly the shark can bite and
how painful the bite can be.

Males and females are mature
at about 3' (90 cm), and the
female is ovoviviparous, producing eggs that are retained within
her body. There are about 8 to
13 pups in each litter.

skin patterning

California Hornshark

Heterodontus francisci

Named for the spine in front of each dorsal fin, the California hornshark is one of nine living species of the family known as bullhead, horn, or Port Jackson sharks. The sharks of this family are unmistakable, with their blunt foreheads, pig-like snouts, and broad eye ridges. Their taxonomic name (from Greek for "mixed-tooth") refers to the small, pointed teeth at the front of the jaw and the blunt teeth at the rear. With these, they can grab soft-bodied fish and crustaceans, and crush sea urchins and the shellfish that they prefer.

California hornsharks have small dark spots on their bodies and fins. They live in cool, shallow waters, and lay curious, fist-sized, screw-shaped egg cases (always with a right-hand thread). The egg case is wedged into a rock crevice, and hatches after 6 to 10 months, depending on water

FIELD NOTES

■ Central California, USA, to the Gulf of California

■ To 4' (1.2 m), but most adults less than 3' (90 cm)

■ Generally sedentary; not dangerous

■ Day and night, year-round

■ Not uncommon; neither direct nor indirect sport or commercial fishing of species

The egg case of a California hornshark.

dorsal fin with horn spine

temperature. During the day, dive find the sharks, as well as their egg cases, resting among large rocks in shallow-wat kelp beds and at the base of boulders. At night, the sharks patrol for food out in the open.

California hornsharks a very popular in public aquariums. There, whi sitting placidly on th bottom, they def the commonly he belief that all shark must swim in order to be able to breathe.

Port Jackson Shark

Heterodontus portusjacksoni

The Port Jackson shark, also called the oyster crusher or tabbigaw, is very similar the related California hornshark e opposite). It is brownish gray, th conspicuous, dark, narrow pes in a harness–type pattern oss the shoulders. Two other stralian bullheads, the crested rnshark (*Heterodontus galeatus*) l the zebra hornshark (*Heterotus zebra*), have large crests ove the eyes and a dark striped ery respectively. Port Jackson sharks are ndant and survive well in aquariums. Although individuals may range over siderable distances, they favor certain reefs caves, and usually return to this ored spot to rest during the day. vers frequently encounter them hallow water, in caves, and r rocks and at the base of weeds. Groups of adults move nd out of shallow water ording to water temperature breeding conditions.

FIELD NOTES

■ Southern Australia, from Queensland to mid-Western Australia, including Tasmania; rare in New Zealand

■ To 5½' (1.7 m), but rarely larger than 4½' (1.4 m)

■ Generally sedentary; harmless unless handled

■ Mostly sighted at night, all year

■ Not uncommon

This species segregates by sex and maturity. In Australia, females and some males in the Sydney area move into shallow water in summer to mate. In August and September, females lay two eggs every 8 to 17 days among rocks in 16–100' (5–30 m) of water, often in a communal nursery. The female will wedge the pointed edge and flanges of the screw-shaped egg case into a rocky crevice using her mouth. The young hatch 9 to 12 months later and move into bays and estuaries. After a decade, they will have grown to 20–30" (50–75 cm) and have reached adolescence.

distinctive pig-like snout and pointy t teeth of the Port Jackson shark.

Necklace Carpetshark

Parascyllium variolatum

With its long, slender, and slightly flattened body, and its long but almost indistinct tail, the necklace carpetshark has a quite eel-like appearance. It is easily identifiable by its dark gray-brown body scattered with numerous white spots and the large black blotches on the edges of the fins. Most striking is the dark band, or collar, studded with small bright white spots that encircles the head like a necklace, hence its common name. It is also known as the varied carpetshark. Its spiracles are small, and its nostrils bear short barbels (probably for chemo-sensory purposes) and grooves that connect to the mouth.

Collared carpetsharks are closely related to nurse sharks and wobbegongs but are often mistaken for catsharks, which they resemble only superficially. Collared carpetsharks are distinguished by their mouth being located well in front of the eyes. The family has two genera: the *Cirrhoscyllium*, which have barbels on the throat, and the *Parascyllium*, which do not.

FIELD NOTES

- Southern Australia
- Less than 3⅓' (1 m)
- Harmless
- At night, year-round
- Common

The necklace carpetshark is common on shallow rocky ree[f] along the southern temperate coast of Australia. It feeds and active at night, and is often encountered by divers after dark. During the day it is difficult to spot because it rests either in caves or on the bottom, where it is perfectly camouflaged among the algae.

Little is known about this carpetshark's diet but it probably feeds on invertebrates and smal[l] fishes. It is oviparous, laying egg cases with curled tendrils that anchor the cases to the substrate.

This necklace carpetshark, one of seven collared carpetsharks, is being attacked by a voracious 11-armed sea star.

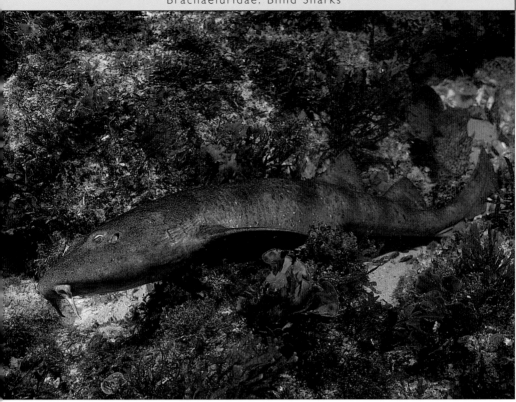

Blind Shark

Brachaelurus waddi

Blind sharks get their name from their habit of closing their eyes when caught by fishers. The blind shark, along with the blue-gray carpetshark (*Brachaelurus colcloughi*), make up the blind shark family. They are closely related to bambsharks, nurse sharks, and collared carpetsharks. Although often referred to as catsharks, they are related only distantly to them.

The blind shark has a stout, cylindrical, brown body, usually dotted with pale spots. Its two spineless dorsal fins are close together, with the first originating above the pelvic fins. It has very large spiracles positioned behind and to the side of the eyes. Its nostrils are well developed, with a pair of long, smooth nasal barbels, which are connected to the mouth by a groove that permits water that has passed over the olfactory organs to flow into the mouth. The blind shark

can be distinguished from the blue-gray carpetshark by the presence of a small (symphyseal) groove in the middle of the chin, which the blue-gray carpetshark lacks.

This shark inhabits shallow, warm temperate and tropical waters—it can occur in water just deep enough to cover it. It is also found on the continental shelf to about 490' (150 m). During the day, it shelters under ledges and in caves, and it is commonly observed by divers under ledges but is rarely seen out in the open. It emerges after dark to forage on the reef and the adjacent sandy areas for anemones, cuttlefish, and crustaceans.

Females reach sexual maturity when about 26" (65 cm) long, and give birth during summer to as many as eight young.

Snout and barbels from below (top) and from the side (above).

145

Tasselled Wobbegong

Eucrossorhinus dasypogon

Wobbegongs share many of the basic features of nurse sharks, blind sharks, bamboosharks, and collared carpetsharks. They have elongated bodies that are flattened, especially in the head region, and the two dorsal fins of similar size are set far back on the body. The broad, short pectoral fins are well adapted for a life on the reef bottom.

Tasselled wobbegongs are patterned with small, reticulated markings on a drab gray or brown back-ground; the underside is white. These unusual sharks are distinguished by a very broad, flat head. The upper jaw is sur-rounded by many finely branched dermal lobes

A tasselled wobbegong's jaw, with branched, fleshy tassels.

FIELD NOTES

- Western Pacific
- 10–13' (3–4 m)
- Dangerous when provoked, captured, or disturbed
- Year-round in many areas
- Common

is studded with sharp, narrow teeth, perfect for capturing the fish on which this shark preys.

Living in warm temperate to tropical seas, the tasselled wobbegong is a common member tropical reefs of New Guinea, the north Australian coast, and Indonesia. During the day, it is commonly found in caves on the reef, where it feeds on sheltering fish. At night, it emerges to feed on small fishes an invertebrates. Females are believed to bear live young, about 8½' (22 cm) long.

Divers are most likely to encounter smaller individuals, about 3⅓' (1 m) long.

that appear as fleshy flaps hanging down over the mouth. The chin and sides of the lower jaw are also decorated with small, reticulated fleshy tassels. Within this mass of tassels are branched nasal barbels and grooves that channel the water leaving the nostrils to the mouth. The mouth

Because of their markings, tasselled wobbegong are difficult to see against the sea floor. There have been many reports of attacks on divers. Most are provoked by divers pulling the shark' tail or accidentally stepping on it. But in some cases, the attacks were apparently unprovoked.

Ornate Wobbegong

Orectolobus ornatus

The ornate, or banded, wobbegong has large, black-bordered, saddle-shaped markings on the back. The body is flattened and wide from the head to the back of the trunk, where it quickly tapers to the tail. On each side of the head there are five or six dermal lobes. Each nostril bears a single barbel and there is a groove from the back of each nostril to the mouth. The teeth are long and slender, well adapted for grasping small fish prey.

This is one of four wobbegong species in the genus Orectolobus. While the relative position of these wobbegongs' fins is similar to that of the tasselled wobbegong (opposite), the fin lobes in Orectolobus are smaller in comparison to the body. Orectolobus also differs in having no dermal lobes or tassels on the chin or lower jaw. The back is smooth, which distinguishes sharks of this genus from the heavily tubercled cobbler wobbegong (Sutorectus tentaculatus), common on the southwest coast of Australia.

The ornate wobbegong is a large, common inshore inhabitant of temperate rocky and tropical reefs. During the day it rests in the open on rocky bottoms or table coral, or it sometimes hides under reef ledges. It becomes active at night, searching the reef for invertebrates and fishes to eat. Divers should be cautious because this species can easily camouflage itself against the sea floor, and it is considered dangerous—numerous provoked and unprovoked attacks have been documented. Females produce litters of up to 12 pups, each about 8" (20 cm) long.

FIELD NOTES
- Western Pacific
- 10' (3 m)
- Dangerous, particularly when provoked, captured, or stepped on
- Almost year-round
- Common

Close-up of an ornate wobbegong's coloring. 147

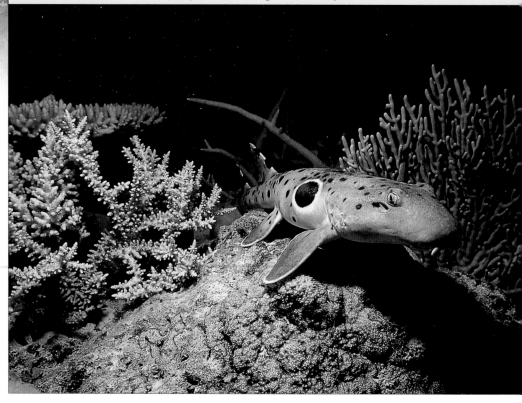

Epaulette Shark

Hemiscyllium ocellatum

The 13 species of longtailed carpetsharks are subdivided into the epaulette sharks (*Hemiscyllium*) and bamboosharks (*Chiloscyllium*). These usually small fish have thin, slightly flattened, elongated bodies. The two relatively large, spineless dorsal fins are about the same size. The anal fin, far back on the underside, is in front of the caudal fin, and separated from it by a notch. These short, stubby, paired fins are used by many species for "walking" across the bottom. Most juvenile longtailed carpetsharks have

FIELD NOTES

- Indo-West Pacific
- 3⅓' (1 m)
- Harmless
- Day or night, year-round
- Common

broad contrasting bands of colo on the body. In adult epaulette sharks these bands become spotted, and a prominent black spot develops above the pector fins. The yellowish or brownish body of *Hemiscyllium ocellatum* i covered with dark brown spots and the characteristic large black spot has a whit ring around it. Its nostrils and mouth are almost at the tip of the snout, which is short and rounded like all the epaulette sharks.

The solid bands of color of the juvenile carpetsharks fade or disappear altogether in adul bamboosharks such as the brownbanded bambooshark (*Chiloscyllium punctatum*). It is a uniform brown as an adult. However, the adult slender bambooshark (*Chiloscyllium indicum*) is covered with small dark spots and bars, and has small side ridges. It has rounded dorsal fins and the pointed snout typical of the bamboosharks.

Longtailed carpetsharks are common inshore on coral and rocky reefs and in tide pools. Dive often encounter adults, but juveniles are rarely seen because they hide within the reef. These nocturnally active sharks feed on small benthic invertebrates and fishes. Many species lay eggs.

Adult brownbanded bamboosharks congregating on the bottom

Nurse Shark

Ginglymostoma cirratum

No one is sure how the nurse shark got its name, perhaps from the sucking noise made by a feeding nurse shark, which sounds like a nursing baby. This fairly large bottom-dweller is uniformly brown to gray-brown and has large, rounded fins. Noticeable barbels protrude from the nasal openings in front of the corners of its small mouth. A small spiracle behind and below each eye allows it to take in water over the gills when breathing.

Common over inshore coral reefs in tropical waters, this is probably the shark that snorkelers and divers in the Caribbean see most often. Although sluggish during the day, it is active at night, when it feeds on bottom-dwelling invertebrates, such as lobsters and other crustaceans, as well as snails, clams, octopus, squid, and any fish slow enough to be caught by its great gulping

FIELD NOTES

- Eastern Pacific, from Mexico to Peru; western Atlantic, from Rhode Island, USA, to southern Brazil; tropical West Africa
- To 14' (4.25 m); rarely longer than 10' (3 m)
- Harmless unless provoked
- During the day, year-round
- Common, particularly in the Caribbean

and inhaling style of feeding.

Because they are abundant and easy to capture, handle, and transport, nurse sharks are common residents of public aquariums. Behaviorists have used them to study learning in sharks, and have demonstrated that nurse sharks can be taught to react to novel situations.

These ovoviviparous sharks conduct an interesting court-ship. Male and female swim in close synchrony, the male alongside or slightly behind and below the female. (Sometimes, a second male accompanies them to prevent the female from retreating.) When the male grabs the female's pectoral fin in his mouth, she rolls onto her back. He swims above her and inserts a clasper into her vent to deliver sperm.

A nurse shark resting on a reef in the Bahamas.

149

Zebra Shark

Stegostoma fasciatum

The zebra shark is a lovely creature, found over tropical coral reefs. Its very long, broad tail and its coloring make it quite distinctive. The juvenile shark has zebra-like stripes (yellow on black), which give the shark its common name. It takes on a yellowish brown color with dark brown spotting as it reaches adulthood. Because of this adult coloration, it is also known as the leopard shark. (It cannot be confused with the other shark known as a leopard shark, a very different, cold-water species of the eastern Pacific, from the houndshark family (see p. 168).)

FIELD NOTES

■ Widespread in the tropical western Pacific and Indian Ocean

■ To 11½' (3.5 m)

■ Harmless

■ More active at night, seen year-round

■ Common

The zebra shark has small barbels on its snout, a small mouth, and small eyes. Its teeth are pointed, with each tooth having two smaller, lateral, flanking points. Prominent ridges run along its flanks.

This is a sluggish species. Divers occasionally find one resting on the bottom during the day, propped up on its pectoral fins with its open mouth facing into the current in order to obtain oxygen more easily from the water. It poses no danger to humans. Its slender, flexible body allows it to wriggle into narrow crevices in the reef, searching for the shellfish, crustaceans, and small fishes upon which it prefers to feed.

The zebra shark is oviparous. It lays large, brown or purplish black egg cases, from 5–7" (13–18 cm) in length, that have fibers for attaching to the seabed.

Bunches of hair-like fibers secure the egg case of the zebra shark to the ocean floor.

Whale Shark

Rhincodon typus

The sole living member of its family, the whale shark is the world's largest living fish. Its massive, fusiform body reaches lengths in excess of 46' (14 m). It has alternating thin white vertical bars and columns of spots on a dark background, with ng ridges along the upper side of the body and a prominent lateral keel. The narrow mouth extends across the full width of its flattened head. The eyes are small and far forward on the head. Each nostril has a small barbel and the gill slits are long and extend above the pectoral fins. Above the relatively small pelvic fins are the first of two dorsal fins. The powerful caudal fin is semicircular.

This shark swims slowly near the surface, consuming small crustacean plankton, small fishes, such as sardines and anchovies, and even larger fishes such as mackerel. It has well-developed internal spongy filters at the gill arches, which help to retain small prey within its huge mouth. This

FIELD NOTES

- Western Atlantic, eastern Atlantic, Indo-West, central, and eastern Pacific
- Up to 46' (14 m)
- Harmless
- Seasonally, day and night
- Common in some regions

mechanism may impede the flow of water through the mouth during swimming, which limits the amount of plankton the shark can strain. So, as well as filter feeding, it can also pump water into its mouth to feed on concentrated patches of plankton.

The whale shark is found in all tropical and subtropical oceans, along coastal regions, and enters lagoons on tropical islands. It is mostly seen on the surface, where divers and snorkelers can swim with this gentle, curious creature (see pp. 262–3).

The whale shark is a livebearer. Pregnant females were recently found to contain hundreds of young, up to about 2' (60 cm) long.

revally disappears into the gaping mouth he filter-feeding whale shark.

Sand Tiger Shark

Eugomphodus taurus

FIELD NOTES

■ Western Atlantic, eastern Atlantic, western Indian Ocean, western Pacific

■ 10½' (3.2 m)

■ Dangerous only when provoked

■ Day and night; year-round in some regions, regional in others

■ Common

Depending on where you are in the world, the sand tiger shark may be known as the spotted raggedtooth or gray nurse shark. It is one of four species belonging to the sand tiger family, a group of large, fearsome-looking sharks that swim slowly with their mouths open, exposing long, narrow, needle-like teeth. Their bodies are stout, with two large dorsal fins. The elongated tails have a long upper lobe; there is a precaudal pit but no caudal keels.

The sand tiger shark has a short, flattened snout. Its dorsal fins are about equal in size, with the first located closer to the pelvic fins than to the pectoral fins. It is bronzy above, gradually becoming paler below. Juveniles have reddish or brownish spots scattered on the tail and rear of the body, which tend to fade with age. There are three rows of large teeth on each side of the midline of the upper jaw.

This shark is found in shallow bays, sandy coastal waters, and rocky or tropical reefs from shallow waters down to about 655' (200 m). Divers often find large numbers in aggregations around rocky outcroppings in offshore waters.

Essentially gentle sharks, they usually become aggressive only if provoked. Their diet consists of many species of large and small bony fishes, small sharks, rays, crustaceans, and squid.

The sand tiger shark is able to hover motionless in the water by swallowing surface air and holding it in its stomach, thus achieving near-neutral buoyancy. It is also known to make long coastal migrations for reproductive purposes. Reproduction is oviphagous. In each of the two uterine chambers, the first embryo to hatch, at about 6½" (17 cm) kills and devours the other developing siblings. The two embryos continue to feed on the other eggs inside the separate uterine chambers. After a gestation period of eight to nine months, the two live young are born, about 3⅓' (1 m) long.

A male sand tiger shark swimming, mouth characteristically open.

Goblin Shark

Mitsukurina owstoni

Perhaps the most mysterious, and bizarre, of all sharks, the goblin shark is the only species of its family. Its light pink body is tall but thin. The flesh has a soft, watery texture, which probably helps it to maintain neutral buoyancy, important in what is thought to be a slow-swimming species. The two dorsal fins are similar in size, while the anal fin is well developed. The tail consists almost entirely of a single long upper lobe.

This shark has an elongated snout flattened in the shape of a paddle. The nostrils are located immediately in front of the mouth. The teeth at the front of its narrow, pointed jaw are long and needle-like, ideal for grasping small fish. The teeth at the back of the mouth are small and form a crushing or grinding plate for processing captured prey. The goblin shark probably feeds mostly on small fishes, crustaceans, and squid, and its paddle-like snout is thought to feed the electrosensory system in detecting and capturing a potential meal.

In addition, its jaw is highly specialized to project rapidly from the head. This makes the goblin shark a very efficient predator, capable of quickly grasping or sucking prey into its mouth in a single bite.

Very little is known about the biology and ecology of this shark. It occurs near the bottom on continental and island shelves and slopes, at depths of about 3,940' (1,200 m). Living in such deep waters, it is rarely seen or collected. However, it is occasionally found in shallow water near shore.

Until recently, no one had seen a living goblin shark. Early specimens had been preserved with the jaw in the extended position, which gave the shark a very weird appearance. However, we now know that when its jaws are closed, the very protrusible upper jaw fits tightly against the bottom of the skull.

upper and lower teeth

153

Megamouth Shark

Megachasma pelagios

The accidental capture of a large, black, blubbery shark off Hawaii in 1976 was the shark discovery of the century. The creature had become entangled in a deep-water net line. It had a large head, a huge distending mouth about 3⅓' (1 m) wide, and numerous small teeth. But other characteristics indicated a relationship with the ecologically disparate white sharks and makos. A new genus, species, and family of vertebrates was created, known as the megamouth shark. Its scientific name comes from the Greek to mean "giant yawner of the open sea."

Only nine more megamouth sharks have been found. The first six were all large males; more recently, a 12' (3.6 m) female, a 16½' (5 m) female, and a small, 6' (1.8 m) male have been observed.

Not surprisingly, we know very little about the megamouth. It lives in the open ocean, often at great depths, which may explain the rarity of encounters. It appears

FIELD NOTES

■ Throughout the world's oceans

■ To 17' (5.2 m)

■ Harmless

■ Not likely to be seen by divers

■ Known from 10 specimens

to be a plankton feeder, like the whale shark (see p.151) and the basking shark (see p. 157). It swims slowly through the open ocean, filtering small shrimps and other prey from the water it goes. It spends the day feeding in deep water and comes up to shallower water at night. The silvery lining of mouth cavity is probably reflective, so that when shrimps and other luminous crustacean enter the open, cavernous mouth, they may encourage others to enter

upper and lower teeth

The great mouth filters huge amounts of water for tiny organisms

Pelagic Thresher

Alopias pelagicus

The pelagic thresher has a dark, countershaded body grading from gray above white on the underbelly. shares many of the features mmon to all the threshers (see 156), but the first dorsal fin of e pelagic thresher is closer to the ctoral fins. It has at least 30 rows small teeth in each jaw; all the th bear a distinct cusplet in the tooth notch.
Widespread in tropical and subtropical Indo-cific seas, the pelagic thresher is commonly served far from land, swimming at the surface. also frequents the seaward edges of coral reefs d submarine seamounts. However, it is shy, d difficult for divers to approach. Occasion-y, it makes excursions to depths as great as 0' (150 m). It feeds either near the surface or deep waters on small fishes and squid, which grasps and cuts with its small, sharp teeth.
The bigeye thresher (*Alopias superciliosus*), the gest of the thresher sharks, is known to reach ' (4.6 m) in length. It is easily distinguished m the others by the deep grooves above its ry large eyes, which are located almost on top the head. Its pectoral fins are long, curved on e trailing margins and rounded at the tips. is species occurs in nearly all tropical and

FIELD NOTES

■ Indo-Pacific

■ Up to 11' (3.3 m); tail comprises half the total length

■ Harmless and shy of divers

■ Spring and summer

■ Becoming less common in some areas because of heavy fishing

subtropical open oceans and coastal areas, from the surface to depths of about 1,640' (500 m). It is known to feed in the water column on pelagic mackerel, tuna, herring, and billfishes, as well as on bony fishes and squid near the bottom.
Female pelagic threshers reach reproductive maturity when about 8½' (2.6 m) in length. Embryos are cannibalistic in the uterus and only two live pups are born. These are almost 3⅓' (1 m) long. Bigeye threshers also bear cannibalistic pups, but litter sizes range from two to four, suggesting that some embryos coexist through gestation.

snout of the bigeye thresher

155

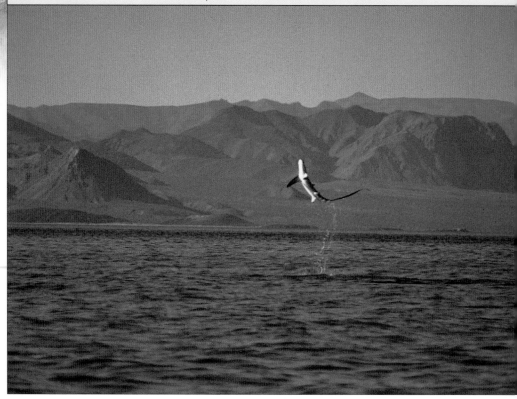

Common Thresher Shark

Alopias vulpinus

The common thresher is one of three thresher sharks. These large, pelagic sharks are immediately recognizable by their long tails. They have a short, conical snout, large eyes placed well forward on the head, and a husky, spindle-shaped body. The first dorsal fin is much larger than the second. The broad pectoral fins provide lift when swimming—these strong, active sharks have enough power to leap out of the water.

The jaws are relatively small, with remarkably efficient small, sharp teeth for capturing cephalopods and schooling fishes. They use the long tail to slap the water surface, frightening prey into tight groups to make capture easier.

Common threshers can be distinguished from their relatives by the position of the first dorsal fin, with its leading edge above the trailing edge

> **FIELD NOTES**
> ■ Western and eastern Atlantic, Indo-West Pacific, central Pacific
> ■ 16½–20' (5–6 m)
> ■ Not aggressive, but should be treated with caution
> ■ During the day, almost year-round
> ■ Becoming uncommon in many areas due to fishing pressure

of the pectoral fins. The pectoral fins are curved, with pointed tips. The body is dark blue-gray above, with a sharp, ragged break marking the edge of the white underside. There are prominent labial furrows at the sides of the jaws.

The common thresher shark is widespread in tropical and temperate waters. It is commonly seen swimming at the surface in coastal waters, but also occurs at depths of 1,15 (350 m) and more. It is best viewed from boat or by snorkelers in open water. While not aggressive toward humans, this is a large shark. Respect its power, and keep clear of its tail.

Females reach maturity at about 10' (3 m) long and produce four to six live young, about 5' (1.5 m) long. The thresher is targeted by fisheries for its fins and meat, and populations are diminishing in many coastal areas.

common thresher shark

Basking Shark

Cetorhinus maximus

FIELD NOTES

- Western and eastern Atlantic, western Indian Ocean, western and eastern Pacific
- 33' (10 m)
- Possibly dangerous when attacked
- Seasonal, according to region; during the day
- Common in some regions, but depleted in others

The basking shark is the second largest fish in the world, after the other plankton filter feeder, the whale shark (see p. 151). Its huge size makes it easy to identify, as do its very broad gill slits that extend around the top and bottom of the head. The grayish brown body is streamlined and stout, with a strong crescent-shaped tail fin and lateral keels. The short snout is narrow and conical, with huge jaws that expand laterally when the shark feeds.

Basking sharks are frequent visitors to cold and warm temperate waters, where they take advantage of plankton blooms in coastal regions. They often enter large bays to feed. You will see them close to shore, swimming slowly near the surface with mouth wide open to form a very wide "net" for capturing the plankton. Water passes into the mouth and across the specialized gill rakers, which strain out the plankton before the water

emerges through the gill slits. This feeding posture is in distinct contrast to the long but narrow mouth opening of a feeding whale shark.

Basking sharks are highly migratory, appearing seasonally in specific locations and supporting regional commercial fisheries—they are taken for their flesh and large liver.

Populations of basking sharks are often segregated by sex and size. Very little is known about their reproduction, but females reach maturity at about 13–16½' (4–5 m) long, and are thought to bear live young.

A feeding basking shark reveals its gill arches, which strain plankton from the water passing over them.

Great White Shark

Carcharodon carcharias

Also called the white shark, the white pointer, white death, and more, this is the largest flesh-eating shark. Star of film and literature, it strikes terror in many people, but little is known of its biology and behavior.

The great white shark is a robust, torpedo-shaped, conical-snouted species with a normal assortment of dorsal, anal, and paired fins. Unlike most sharks, but like other mackerel sharks, the upper and lower lobes of its tail are almost equal in size. This indicates that it swims constantly (because it must swim to breathe) and sometimes rapidly.

The great white differs from its relatives in having nearly symmetrical triangular teeth with serrated edges. It is also huge. It prefers shallow, cool, coastal oceanic waters, but is occasionally seen as close to the equator as Hawaii, USA. During the day, adults search for the seals and sea lions that are an important part of their diet.

Great white sharks are responsible for the majority of unprovoked attacks on people in cool waters and they can kill humans. However, the number of attacks is usually fewer than 10 a year. By diving inside a steel cage, it is possible

FIELD NOTES

■ Worldwide, along continental margins of all temperate seas and entering tropics

■ Largest said to be 21¼' (6.6 m) and 7,300 lb (3,285 kg)

■ Dangerous

■ Africa: Dec–Feb; Australia: Jan–May; Mexico: Aug–Sept

■ Nowhere abundant; protected in South Africa, Australia, Maldives, and California, USA

upper tooth

lower tooth

to see them in relative safety. Such dives are organized off Baja California, Mexico, in southern Australia (see pp. 264–5), and South Africa.

Females give birth to seven to nine live pup per litter, and are thought to produce only fou to six litters in a lifetime. The young do not mature until about 10 to 12 years old, so the species is extremely vulnerable to overfishing.

158

Shortfin Mako Shark

Isurus oxyrinchus

The shortfin mako shark is also called the bonito or mako shark. It is the most spindle-shaped shark of the mackerel family, with a long, conical snout, short pectoral fins, and a crescent-shaped caudal fin. Its back is indigo blue, and the belly white. Its teeth are visible even when its mouth is closed—long, slender, smooth-edged daggers. The less common longfin mako (*Isurus paucus*) has longer pectoral fins and a blunter snout.

The shortfin mako, the shark featured in Ernest Hemingway's novel *The Old Man and the Sea*, is well known as a sport fish, capable of spectacular leaps 20' (6 m) in the air when hooked and of achieving bursts of speed of more than 22 mph (35 km/h). It uses its speed to capture oceanic fish and squid. Large makos also catch billfish and cetaceans. One is known to have traveled 1,322 miles (2,128 km) in 37 days, an average of 36 miles (58 km) a day.

Shortfin makos live offshore in tropical and temperate waters, from the surface down to 490' (150 m). They are rarely encountered, but may be seen by open-water divers. They are dangerous and have attacked humans. However, attacks on fishing boats, when an angry mako leaps into a boat after being caught on the end of a fishing line, are more likely to occur.

Shortfin makos are viviparous, but lack a placental connection. Litters of 4 to 16 pups are common. Older embryos eat some of the eggs and smaller embryos while still in the uterus.

FIELD NOTES

- Worldwide
- To 13' (3.95 m)
- Potentially dangerous
- During the day, year-round
- Not uncommon; however, reduced by developing fisheries

The very obvious teeth of the shortfin mako shark.

Salmon Shark

Lamna ditropis

The salmon shark shares its generic name, *Lamna*, with the porbeagle (opposite). To the ancient Greeks, "Lamna" signified "a horrible monster of man-eating tendencies," and it was invoked to scare naughty children. The salmon shark and porbeagle are so similar that they were not recognized as two separate species until 1947. Generally speaking, if it lives in the North Pacific, it is a salmon shark; if in the Atlantic, it is a porbeagle.

The salmon shark shares the frightening appearance of all the mackerel sharks. However, it differs from the great white shark (see p. 158) in having smooth rather than serrated teeth, and from the mako sharks (see p. 159) in having a blue-gray rather than an indigo back. The feature that is found only in the salmon shark and the porbeagle is the secondary keel along the base of the tail.

Salmon sharks are heavy, torpedo-shaped predators. They have large, sharp, pointed teeth, and are well designed for chasing and capturing such fast-swimming oceanic prey as salmon and mackerel. Unlike most other mackerel sharks, they form schools of 20 to 30 individuals when feeding. They are not a threat to humans,

FIELD NOTES

■ Subarctic waters of North Pacific, from Alaska to California, USA, and from the Bering Sea to Japan

■ To 10' (3 m)

■ Potentially dangerous

■ Not seen by divers

■ Abundant within center of range

mainly because they are not encountered by humans: salmon sharks inhabit the more frigid waters of the North Pacific, from the surface to depths of 500' (155 m), and they rarely come close to shore. They will consume the catch in fishing nets and sometimes become entangled in nets and lines.

Salmon sharks are viviparous, without a placental connection. As in related species, the embryos consume eggs and smaller embryos in the uterus. There are typically two to four young in each litter. They are born when they are about 26–28" (65–70 cm) in length.

upper and lower teeth

Porbeagle

Lamna nasus

T he porbeagle and its North Pacific relative, the salmon shark (opposite), are the smallest of the five mackerel sharks. They are still an impressive weight at 350–500 lb (158–225 kg). The porbeagle's stout body is dark blue-gray to brown dorsally and white underneath. It has a patch of white on the trailing edge of the first dorsal fin. The porbeagle and salmon shark are the only sharks with a secondary keel at the base of their crescent-shaped tails. This efficiently cuts the water in its side-to-side swimming movement.

This fast-swimming shark inhabits the continental shelves in cold waters, down to depths of 1,210' (370 m). With its sharp, slender teeth, it feeds on mackerel and squid when it ventures into open waters, and also on cod, hake, flounder, and other bottom-dwelling fish. Like all mackerel sharks, but unlike most sharks that live on the bottom, the porbeagle must swim continuously in order to breathe.

It reproduces viviparously, without a placental connection. As with other mackerel sharks, the older embryos feed on some of the eggs and smaller embryos in the uterus.

The mackerel sharks are unique among sharks for their heat-exchanging circulatory system, which makes them, functionally, warm-blooded. They can capture the heat generated by their swimming muscles and, through a complicated arrangement of microscopic arteries and veins, use it to heat the blood. This blood is directed throughout their body, to the muscles, internal organs, and brain. As a result, their body temperature is higher than that of the surrounding water.

This gives them increased muscle strength and allows more rapid nervous-system activity. The porbeagle has achieved the greatest body temperature elevation. Its body can be 20° F (11° C) warmer than the frigid North Atlantic Ocean that it inhabits.

FIELD NOTES

■ Cold waters of North Atlantic, South Atlantic, and South Pacific

■ To 12' (3.7 m)

■ Potentially dangerous

■ Not seen by divers

■ Common

tail with double keel

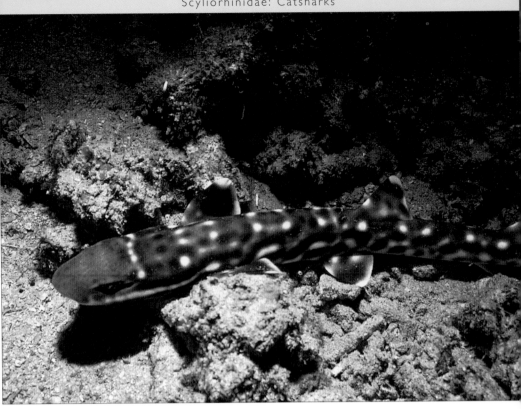

Coral Catshark

Atelomycterus marmoratus

The coral catshark is a rather small species with a striking body coloration of white spots on a dark background grading to a white underbelly. The dorsal fins, almost equal in size, have white spots on their tips. The tail fin is short.

Unique features include the short caudal fin, the long labial furrows at the corners of the mouth, and nasal flaps that extend to the front of the mouth. The eyes are set in front of large spiracles, which are used to move water into the gill chambers when

FIELD NOTES

■ Indo-West Pacific, from Pakistan to Papua New Guinea

■ 2' (60 cm)

■ Harmless

■ Seen mostly at night, almost year-round

■ Common

the shark is at rest or feeding.

The Australian marbled catshark (*Atelomycterus macleayi*), which occurs in northern Australia, is similar in appearance to the coral catshark, but can be distinguished by the gray saddle-like markings along its back and small black spots over most of its body. With more than 100 species, the catshark family is the largest of the shark families. The name comes from the cat-like shape and color of the eyes.

Adult coral catsharks are commonly seen on shallow reefs in temperate and tropical waters. They live among coral branches and in the hole and tight crevices of the reef. With their very slender and flexible bodies, they can also be found swimming with sinuous movements near the bottom. They are more active during the night, when they feed on benthic invertebrates and small fishes.

Females reach sexual maturity when about 20" (50 cm) long. They lay purse-shaped egg cases, usually two at a time, with tendrils to anchor the cases to the bottom. The pups, about 4" (10 cm) long at birth, are rarely encountered. They probably spend their time sequestered within the reef, out of the way of predators.

162 *A coral catshark swimming over a reef in the Philippines.*

Swellshark

Cephaloscyllium ventriosum

The swellshark cannot be mistaken for any other shark. It has a broadly rounded snout and small dorsal [fin]s on the rear half of the body, [an]d is covered in large, spiky [de]nticles. The patterning of dark [br]own blotches and saddle-like [pa]tterns on the yellow to brown [ba]ckground of its back, along with [sm]all dark spots on its belly and [flan]ks, provides good [cam]ouflage for this [sede]ntary shark. It has [a w]ide, grinning [ja]w laden with [sm]all, pointy teeth— [ver]y effective for [cap]turing fish that [care]lessly swim by [wit]hout noticing it. [ ]Divers, too, [fre]quently overlook [swe]llsharks because [of]their camouflage. [Yo]u will see them [fro]m 30' (10 m) to more than 200' (60 m) if you [loo]k carefully in caves and among shallow rocks [an]d crevices around kelp forests. They are not

FIELD NOTES

■ Temperate eastern Pacific, from central California, USA, to southern Mexico, and central Chile

■ To 3⅓' (1 m)

■ Harmless unless handled or provoked

■ Active at night, secretive during the day

■ Not uncommon

dangerous unless handled and provoked. Swellsharks swallow water when distressed. They balloon themselves up in this way when positioned in a rock crevice or other narrow hiding place, until they are wedged tightly inside and are safe from potential predators.

The female swellshark lays large, greenish amber eggs among seaweeds. These purse-shaped eggs hatch after 7 to 10 months, depending on the temperature of the water. The young are about 6" (15 cm) long. The unhatched juveniles use their enlarged dermal denticles to pry themselves free of the egg case.

A small swellshark pup emerging from its purse-shaped egg case.

Striped Catshark

Poroderma africanum

The striped catshark is easily recognized by its pattern of solid horizontal stripes. Like the other two species that belong to the genus *Poroderma*, it has a stout, well-tapered body and a relatively short tail fin. It also has barbels on the middle fold of the nasal flap, which extend back toward the front of the mouth. These barbels are short and usually end before the mouth. In contrast, the barbeled catshark (*Poroderma marleyi*) has relatively long nasal barbels; its body is covered with large, solid black spots. The leopard catshark (*Poroderma pantherinum*) also has relatively long barbels. It has a pattern of broken rings and small dark spots across its body.

The striped catshark inhabits temperate coastal waters, and is common on shallow inshore rocky reefs as well as in deeper waters to about 330' (100 m). This fish will hide in caves or rest in reef crevices during the day. At night, when it is most active, divers will see it moving about the bottom in search of food. Its diet is

quite varied and includes small bottom-dwelling crustaceans, such as shrimp and crabs, small bony fishes, cephalopods, and mollusks.

Females reach sexual maturity when about 27" (70 cm) long. During the mating season, they lay two tendril-bearing egg cases every few days. The young emerge after five to six months and are about 6" (15 cm) long.

FIELD NOTES

- Eastern South Atlantic, western Indian Ocean off South Africa; possibly Madagascar and Mauritius
- 3⅓' (1 m)
- Harmless
- Commonly seen at night
- Common

The tendrils on the egg case of the striped catshark anchor it to the reef or the bottom or, as here, to a convenient piece of kelp.

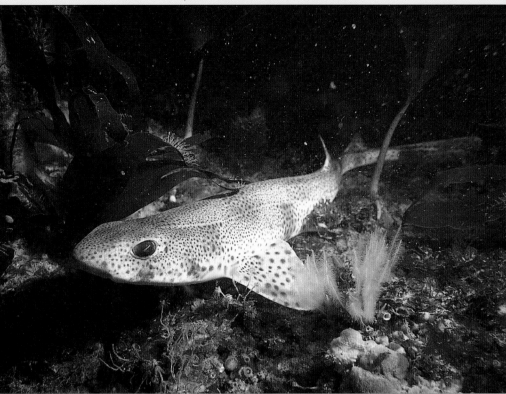

Smallspotted Catshark

Scyliorhinus canicula

The smallspotted catshark has a long, slender body and relatively short tail. Its [he]ad is slightly flattened and has [lar]ge nasal flaps that project back [to] the edge of the mouth. There [are] neither labial furrows at the [edg]e of its mouth, nor barbels at its [no]strils. The catshark's body is [co]vered with small, usually dark, [sp]ots. Some sharks have an additional eight to [ni]ne dark, saddle-like shapes or blotches along [the]ir back. These markings are highly variable [am]ong individuals and in different locations.

This bottom-dwelling shark inhabits temper-[ate] waters. During the day, it can be found [res]ting in open or sheltered areas on rocky reefs, [san]dy bays, and muddy bottoms. [It] also inhabits continental shelves [in] waters as deep as 330' (100 m). [Lik]e most catsharks, it is active at [nig]ht, and divers may see it [fee]ding on a wide variety of small [fish]es, mollusks, and crustaceans [suc]h as shrimp, crab, and lobster. [Ca]tsharks employ a quick biting

FIELD NOTES

■ Eastern North Atlantic

■ 2–3⅓' (60–100 cm); considerably smaller in the Mediterranean

■ Harmless

■ Day and night, almost year-round

■ Abundant

action that sucks water into the mouth along with prey items.

Aggregations of females are found inshore during winter, where they are joined by males in spring. In late summer, the adult population migrates to deeper offshore waters to mate. The male bites the female during courtship, then coils around her to transfer sperm. Females move into shallow water to deposit their egg cases with tendrils for attaching among the rocky reefs or algal patches. After about nine months, the young emerge, measuring about 3½" (9 cm).

This species is commercially important in Europe for meat, fishmeal, and oil.

[Th]e slightly flattened head of the bottom-[dw]elling smallspotted catshark.

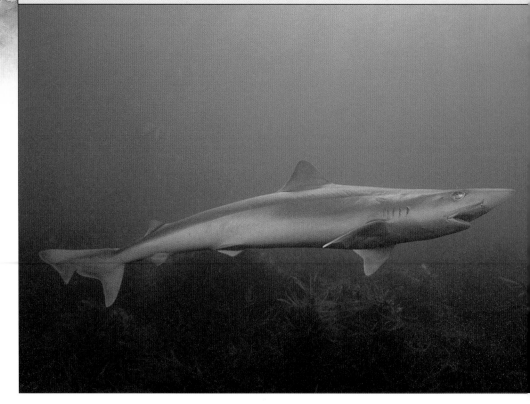

Soupfin Shark

Galeorhinus galeus

The soupfin shark is also known as the school shark or tope. It is a moderately slender shark, bronzy gray on the upper side and pale underneath. It has an unusually large subterminal lobe on the caudal fin. The small second dorsal fin is about the same size as the anal fin.

The soupfin shark is usually found on continental shelves and continental slopes in temperate waters. It feeds mainly on fish, squid, and octopus near the seabed or in the water column. Often preferring to congregate in schools, it lives to be more than 50 years old.

Although considered harmless, it is a very shy creature and encounters are unlikely. It will flee long before a diver arrives in its vicinity. Large numbers of new-born pups are sometimes caught inshore by anglers.

FIELD NOTES

■ Widespread: west coast of North America, east coast of South America, northeast Atlantic, South Africa, southern Australia, New Zealand

■ Varies throughout the world, but up to 6½' (2 m)

■ Not encountered by divers

■ Abundant

This species migrates long distances so pregnant females can give birth in cooler waters. Sharks tagged in England and Ireland have traveled to Iceland (1,530 miles [2,460 km]) and the Canary Islands (1,570 miles [2,525 km]). Sharks from the Californian region have been recaptured off British Columbia (1,000 miles [1,610 km]).

The soupfin shark is ovoviviparous. Litter sizes vary—a litter of 52 pups is the largest known. After a gestation of 12 months, the pups are born, 12–14" (30–35 cm) in length. Discrete, inshore nursery areas have been found in Australia, Argentina, and South Africa. Female sharks reach maturity at 8 to 10 years and breed only every second or third year. This low reproductive rate, combined with the soupfin's longevity, has made it vulnerable to overfishing for its meat, fins, and liver oil.

Close-up of the eye of the soupfin shark, showing the free eyelid.

Gummy Shark

Mustelus antarcticus

FIELD NOTES

- Southern Australia
- Females to 5¾' (1.77 m); males to 4¾' (1.45 m)
- Harmless
- During the day, year-round
- Abundant

The gummy shark takes its name from its teeth. They are flat, and arranged in a pavement-like pattern, ideal for crushing rather than cutting its prey. This includes a wide variety of octopus, squid, crustaceans, and fish found on the sandy and rocky bottoms where it dwells.

The gummy is a slender, bronzy gray shark with numerous white spots and sometimes black spots on its back and sides. A thin ridge runs along its back.

The dusky smoothhound (*Mustelus canis*) of the western Atlantic is another of the 20 or so species of the genus *Mustelus*. It is a slender shark, uniformly gray in color, and similar in biology and diet to the gummy shark.

Both species occur mainly in temperate waters on the continental shelf from the shore down. Some also dwell on the continental slope: the gummy shark to depths of 1,150' (350 m), the dusky smoothhound to 1,900' (580 m). They are abundant, and divers will often see them lying on the seabed in shallow coastal waters. Since they are harmless, they can be approached quite safely.

Tagging has shown that a small number of male gummy sharks make long migrations across the ocean off southern Australia—the longest known journey is about 1,140 miles (1,840 km). Most travel only relatively short distances.

The gummy shark is ovoviviparous. After a gestation of about 12 months, pups 12–14½" (30–36 cm) long are born in coastal areas. There are between 1 and 38 pups in a litter, with 15 being the average. They live for about 16 years. In the past there was concern about declining stocks, but these days they are fished sustainably—for their meat, which is popularly known as "flake."

teeth of the lower jaw

167

Leopard Shark

Triakis semifasciata

L eopard sharks are regular and conspicuous inhabitants of most bays along the coast of northern California, USA.

They have attractive and elongated bodies, with a series of black spots and saddle-shaped markings on a generally gray background. This makes them popular occupants of public aquariums. They possess all the fins typical of a modern shark, but they do not need to swim in order to breathe. In fact, they are usually quite sluggish. They have small, pointed teeth, which they use to capture a wide variety of food,

FIELD NOTES
- Pacific coast from Oregon, USA, to Baja California, Mexico
- To 6' (1.8 m)
- Harmless
- Usually seen during the day, year-round
- Once extremely abundant, now becoming uncommon in places because of intensive sport and commercial fishing

including fish, fish eggs, shrimp, crabs, and clams.

Each year, leopard sharks migrate from the inner bays to the outer coast of the temperate Pacific Northwest. Divers and kayakers will see them there, above the sandy or muddy bottoms of bays and along the outer coast. They are harmless, but because they are social and travel in schools, they are often caught in large numbers.

At maturity, males are smaller than females, but they ultimately grow to be slightly larger. Females produce up to 24 young every spring.

The striking markings (left) of the leopard shark; and its impressive array of small, pointed teeth (below).

168

Silvertip Shark

Carcharhinus albimarginatus

FIELD NOTES

■ Widespread in tropics from East
Africa to Panama; not in the Atlantic

■ 10' (3 m)

■ Aggressive, but not a significant risk

■ During the day, year-round

■ Common

ilvertips are fairly large and slender sharks, dark gray in color. Their common name derived from the distinctive hite tips and margins on all their s. The pectoral fins are narrow d pointed, and the first dorsal is narrowly rounded. Apart om these features, they look like any of the other gray requiem sharks that are mmonly found out beyond the reef edge in arm tropical waters.

The teeth of silvertips are similar to those of her species that belong to the genus archarhinus. They are strongly rated and narrowly pointed in e lower jaw, and sharp, serrated, d oblique in the upper jaw. They are ideal r catching and cutting the fish that they feed on, such as reef wrasses and, in open water, na and flyingfish.

These sharks prefer offshore islands, coral efs, and banks. However, they also enter goons, and it is here that you will encounter em often. Given their size and their aggressive havior, you should always treat them with ution and respect. They have been known harass divers, but reports of them actually acking people are rare.

dorsal fin

Silvertip sharks are viviparous; females usually have 5 or 6 pups to a litter, but there can be as many as 11. The young hatch after 12 months.

Experiments conducted using underwater sound have shown that silvertips are attracted to low-frequency sounds, probably because these frequencies mimic the sound made by an injured fish, potentially an easy meal.

Gray Reef Shark

Carcharhinus amblyrhynchos

The gray reef shark, or longnose blacktail shark, is similar in shape and general appearance to the silvertip shark (see p. 169), although usually smaller. It has a black edge on its tail. Some specimens have a narrow white edging on the first dorsal fin, but they lack the bold white-edged margins of the silvertip's tail and pectoral fins.

The teeth of the gray reef shark are triangular with fine serrations. It feeds on small reef fish. It is one of the most common sharks on Indo-Pacific coral reefs, and is seen in the reef passes. An inquisitive animal, it is attracted to the low-frequency underwater sounds and commotion caused by a speared fish—there are many stories of a gray reef shark taking a fish off the end of an unsuspecting spearfisher's spear.

If you startle one or get too close, it will perform a contorted threat posture. This includes wagging its head from side to side, sweeping its tail, depressing its pectoral fins, and arching its back. That should be ample warning to any diver—such behavior often precedes an attack. Sharks have severely bitten and injured divers, to threaten them, not to eat them.

FIELD NOTES

- Central Pacific to Madagascar
- To 8' (2.5 m); rarely larger than 6' (1.8 m)
- Has attacked if threatened
- During the day, year-round
- Common

The gray reef shark is viviparous. Female sharks give birth to up to six pups after a year's gestation. Pups are about 20–24" (50–60 cm) at birth and reach maturity after about seven years, when they are about 4¼' (1.3 m) long.

tail with black edge

The scars on the female gray reef shark at right are mementos of encounters with males during mating.

170

Bronze Whaler

Carcharhinus brachyurus

The bronze whaler, also known as the copper shark, gets both common names from its brownish red, sometimes grayish red, coloring, which shades to white on the underside. It has a short band of pale pigmentation, like a white stripe, that extends down the side of the body almost to the pelvic fins. Apart from darkened tips on the pectoral fins of some individuals, there are no noticeable markings on the relatively slender body. The narrow snout is rounded at the tip. The upper lobe of its tail fin is broad and used for its powerful swimming motion. While the first dorsal fin is large, the second is far smaller.

The bronze whaler is found in most warm temperate and subtropical waters of the world, except along the eastern coastline of North America and the northern Indian Ocean. It is usually seen close inshore along rocky reefs and shallow bays, as well as in the deeper waters

FIELD NOTES

- Southwest and eastern Atlantic, eastern Pacific, western Indian Ocean
- Up to 10' (3 m)
- Considered dangerous
- Seasonal in higher latitudes; during the day
- Very common

of continental shelves and around islands. This species is considered dangerous when excited by the smell of food, and is known to attack swimmers and bathers, probably attracted, while searching for food, by their splashing.

Like many other requiem sharks, some populations of bronze whalers are known to make spring and summer migrations to waters in higher latitudes, probably to follow prey. Their diet consists of a wide variety of fishes, such as anchovies, sardines, mullet, hake, and jacks. They also feed on small elasmobranchs, such as spiny dogfish, sawfish, stingrays, and electric rays. Sea snakes and squid are also sometimes taken. Their teeth are pointed with many small serrations; those of the upper jaw have a rounded leading edge.

Little is known about the biology of the bronze whaler. Females are mature when about 8' (2.4 m) long. They produce between 13 and 20 young in each litter.

The claspers are visible on this male bronze whaler.

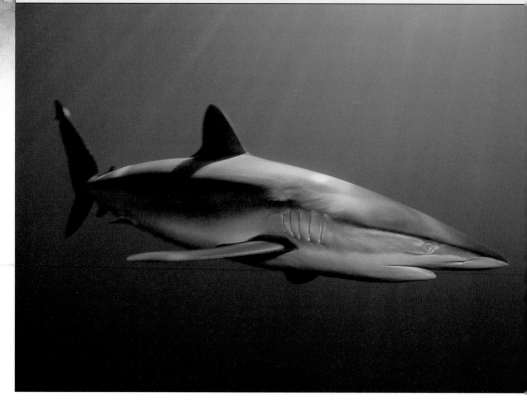

Silky Shark

Carcharhinus falciformis

This large, slender shark gets its name from the smooth, silky texture of its skin. Its body is nearly black to gray above, with no distinctive markings, and whitish underneath. There is a narrow interdorsal ridge on the back. The second dorsal fin is much smaller than the first, and has a trailing tip. The pectoral fins are long and narrow. The smoothly rounded snout is long and the upper teeth are tall, serrated, and nearly triangular in shape, while the lower teeth have a tall, narrow cusp that is only very weakly serrated.

The silky shark is widely distributed in nearly all tropical and warm temperate waters of the world. It is occasionally seen in waters close to shore, but is more common in oceanic waters, especially near large landmasses. A major

FIELD NOTES
- Worldwide
- More than 10' (3 m)
- Potentially dangerous
- Year-round, usually during the day
- Common

pelagic species, it occurs at depths from 60' (18 m) to at least 1,640' (500 m). It is know to form schools segregated by sex—juveniles group in waters relatively close to shore, while adults gather farther out to sea. It is not often encountered by divers, and while it is not responsible for many attacks, it should be treated with respect.

This shark is a fast swimmer and is capable of quick, darting movements. Its diet includes many small fishes, such as mackerel, tuna, mullet, and sea cats, and also invertebrates such as pelagic crabs and squid.

Females reach sexual maturity when nearly 7½' (2.3 m) in length, and give birth to 6 to 14 young per litter. The pups are about 29–31" (75–80 cm) long at birth. These sharks are commercially fished for their fins, meat, and liver.

A silky shark "flying" overhead in tropical Atlantic waters.

172

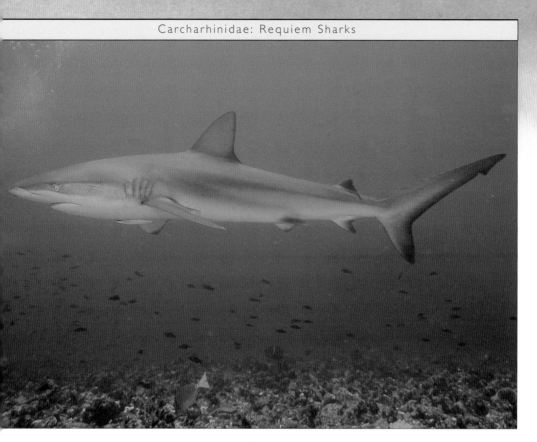

Galapagos Shark

Carcharhinus galapagensis

The Galapagos shark is a large, grayish requiem shark without any distinctive markings. It looks similar to the gray reef shark (see p. 170) and the silvertip shark (see p. 169), except that it lacks their conspicuous white or black coloration on its fins. Its most distinctive feature is a ridge between its dorsal fins, but you would be wise not to get close enough to be able to make it out.

The Galapagos shark is generally not a threat to divers, and prefers to avoid them. However, though it has never attacked a diver, it can be aggressive and divers should always be cautious. Like the gray reef shark, it performs a seemingly awkward threat display before attacking a potential competitor or predator. It has attacked and eaten swimmers.

The shark was named in 1905 after specimens found in the waters of the Galapagos Islands.

FIELD NOTES

- Cosmopolitan in tropical seas, generally near oceanic islands
- To 12' (3.6 m)
- Potentially dangerous
- During the day, year-round
- Not uncommon in Hawaii, USA, and off Galapagos Islands, Ecuador

It has since been found around most tropical oceanic islands, ranging from inshore to well offshore. It prefers clear water, and can be seen beyond the deep reef edge, either near the surface or swimming in groups near the bottom. It feeds primarily on bottom-dwelling fish, squid, and octopus.

There are 6 to 16 young in a litter. They are born alive and remain in nursery areas, where the water is shallower than the area inhabited by the adults of the group. This is a not uncommon adaptation of a number of shark species to avoid cannibalism.

The long, rounded snouts and streamlined bodies of two Galapagos sharks.

173

Bull Shark

Carcharhinus leucas

This large, stout, and sluggish gray shark is widespread along continental coasts. It also enters rivers and lakes, and is therefore known by such names as the Lake Nicaragua shark and the Zambezi shark. It was also thought to be the rare Ganges shark, but this is now known to be a separate, distinct species.

The bull shark can tolerate highly salty sea water and fresh water—it has been recorded as far as 1,750 miles (2,800 km) up the Mississippi River and 2,500 miles (4,000 km) up the Amazon in Peru. It has ample opportunity to encounter, attack, and consume people. Because it has been confused with other similar-looking requiem sharks, it seems likely that it is responsible for even more attacks than those with which it is credited. This makes it more dangerous than the great white or tiger sharks.

In the Americas, it is usually found close to shore in estuaries and shallow marine habitats from 100' (30 m) to just a few feet deep. The famous Matawan Creek incident of 1916, when sharks killed four people and injured one along the New Jersey shore over a 12-day period, was

FIELD NOTES

■ All tropical and subtropical seas; also inland in fresh water

■ To 11½' (3.5 m)

■ Dangerous

■ Not encountered by divers

■ Common

probably the work of bull sharks. It will eat almost anything it can capture, including other sharks, rays, fishes, turtles, birds, dolphins, mollusks, crustaceans, and things that fall overboard, such as cattle, dogs, rats, and people.

The bull shark has a unique appearance. It has a very blunt, rounded snout; small eyes; a pointed first dorsal fin; and dusky fin tips. It is viviparous, and selects estuaries as pupping grounds for litters of 1 to 13 pups, which are born after almost a year's gestation.

Because they live close to shore and in rivers and lakes, bull sharks are vulnerable to fisheries.

The bull shark's blunt, rounded snout is shorter than its mouth width.

Blacktip Shark

Carcharhinus limbatus

The blacktip shark takes its name from the black markings on the tips of the dorsal and pectoral fins and the lower lobe of the tail fin. The spinner shark (*Carcharhinus brevipinna*) has similar markings and a similar range, so the two species can be confused. The blacktip is a much stouter shark, however, and its well-developed first dorsal fin begins at about the middle of the pectoral fin. The spinner shark's first dorsal fin begins much farther back.

The blacktip is a large gray or gray-brown shark, grading along the sides to a white underbelly and a white anal fin. A subtle white band usually runs along the side of the body. The snout is long and parabolic; the eyes are on the side of the head near the mouth's leading edge.

Blacktip sharks are found in all tropical and temperate waters of the world. They live at the surface above continental and island shelves, but will also frequent shallows along sand beaches, bays, and rocky coastlines in warmer months. They migrate along continental coasts in large schools, possibly for food or pupping.

Divers regularly see blacktips inshore. As long as there is no food stimulus present, they do not

FIELD NOTES

■ Western and eastern Atlantic, Indo-West, central, and eastern Pacific

■ 9' (2.8 m)

■ Harmless unless provoked or feeding

■ Day or night; year-round in many areas, seasonal in others

■ Common

Two blacktip sharks in Bahaman waters.

generally present a hazard. The blacktip's diet includes small schooling fishes such as sardines, anchovies, and menhaden, which the sharks feed on in the water column. On the seabed, they also eat bottom-dwelling fishes, crustaceans, and squid. They are often seen near shore jumping out of the water during feeding.

Females reach maturity at about 5' (1.5 m) and produce 4 to 8 pups per litter, about 10" (25 cm) long, after a gestation of 10 to 11 months. South African blacktip populations appear to segregate, with mainly adult males and non-pregnant females grouped together.

Oceanic Whitetip Shark

Carcharhinus longimanus

The oceanic whitetip shark should not be confused with the sluggish, slender, and small-finned whitetip reef shark (see p. 186). The oceanic whitetip's enlarged first dorsal fin and long, paddle-shaped pectoral fins are unmistakable. These fins have conspicuous, mottled white tips; the fins of juveniles may also have black markings.

The oceanic whitetip is a large and stocky gray species, usually found far offshore, from the surface to depths of at least 500' (150 m). It prefers the open ocean, and can sometimes be seen from boats or encountered by divers in open water. Although it is generally slow moving, it is dangerous because it has powerful jaws, large teeth, and it will not hesitate to approach swimmers or small boats. It is probably responsible for many of the open-ocean attacks on people after air or sea disasters. It is most abundant in the tropics, but can also be found from coastal California, USA, to southern Australia, following the warm water masses.

FIELD NOTES

- All tropical and subtropical waters
- To 13' (4 m)
- Potentially dangerous
- Day or night
- Once abundant, now reduced by overfishing

Oceanic whitetips eat just about anything that they can catch in the open sea, including a variety of fishes and squid, whale carcasses, turtles, sea birds and garbage disposed of at sea. They are aggressive and will dominate other shark species that are competing for food. The litter size increases with the size of the mother—as many as 15 live pups are born after a gestation period of about a year.

mottled tail and fin tips

Blacktip Reef Shark

Carcharhinus melanopterus

Blacktip reef sharks are the most common sharks in the shallow lagoons and coral reefs of the tropical Pacific and Indian Oceans, along with whitetip reef sharks (see p. 186) and gray reef sharks (see p. 170). They are different from blacktip sharks (see p. 175), larger sharks with thin black tips on most fins that live mainly in the open ocean.

Blacktip reef sharks are easily recognized by the very distinct black marks on their fins, particularly the first dorsal and caudal fins. They also have a conspicuous white slash along their flanks. They are small to medium in size, with a short, blunt snout. Their teeth are narrow, sharp, and strongly serrated, designed for eating the reef fish that comprise their main food.

Divers and snorkelers commonly see these sharks patrolling in shallow waters from about 1' (30 cm) deep. Divers will find them in reef passes, while waders and snorkelers will see them in lagoons, their dorsal and caudal fins above the surface. On rare occasions, they have bitten waders on the legs and ankles,

FIELD NOTES

■ Indo-Australian Pacific
to central Pacific

■ To 6' (1.8 m)

■ Potentially dangerous to waders;
otherwise, not aggressive

■ During the day, year-round

■ Common

probably attracted by the splashing commotion made by the waders. They will attack speared fish, and are curious, but not aggressive, around divers.

Blacktip reef sharks are viviparous, with the yolk sac being attached by a placenta. Litters number from two to four. The pups are born after a gestation period of about 16 months. They are 13–20" (33–50 cm) long at birth.

In recent years, blacktip reef sharks have entered the eastern Mediterranean via the Suez Canal. Because they are a small, hardy species, a number of them have been captured in the central Pacific, off Christmas Island, and sent to public aquariums worldwide.

Black fin tips, particularly on the first dorsal and caudal fins, make this shark instantly recognizable.

177

Dusky Shark

Carcharhinus obscurus

The long, streamlined body of the dusky shark is brown-gray to gray above and white below. A faint pale stripe extends along the side of the body to the pelvic fins. In juveniles, the tip of the lower caudal fin and the undersides of the pectoral fins are notably dark or dusky, but this is indistinct in adults. The snout is relatively short and broad. The upper lobe of the caudal fin is well developed, indicating that this species is a strong swimmer. Its pectoral fins are long and curved on the trailing edge. Its second dorsal fin is much smaller than the first, and an interdorsal ridge is present.

Although divers occasionally see dusky sharks close inshore, this species occurs primarily above coastal shelves in off-shore waters adjacent to the open ocean. It is widely distributed in warm temperate and tropical waters. While few attacks on humans are attributed to it, this is not a shark to seek out. Like many other large requiem sharks, it migrates into higher latitudes during warm months and more central latitudes during winter. The migratory pattern near South Africa appears to be complex and is at least partly related to pupping and nursery grounds.

The dusky shark has a varied diet that includes small schooling fishes such as sardines and anchovies, larger, fast-moving tuna and mackerel, and bottom-dwelling flatfishes and eels. It is also a significant predator of dogfishes, catsharks, smoothhound sharks, rays, and skates.

Females reach sexual maturity at about 9' (2.8 m). They mate in spring, and give birth after a 16-month gestation to litters of about 10 young that are 8 to 3' (95 cm) long.

Numbers of this species in the western Atlantic have fallen because of overfishing.

FIELD NOTES

- Western and eastern North Atlantic, western Indian Ocean, western and eastern Pacific
- To 13' (4 m); normally about 10' (3 m)
- Considered dangerous
- Day or night; seasonal in many regions
- Numbers dwindling in many areas

Dusky sharks patrolling off the coast of Australia.

178

Caribbean Reef Shark

Carcharhinus perezi

The Caribbean reef shark has a relatively stout body, gray or gray-brown above [sha]ding to white underneath. The [fir]st dorsal fin has a sharp point [an]d a short, trailing tip. The [pe]ctoral fins are relatively long [an]d narrow. It has an interdorsal [ri]dge, and a blunt, rounded snout. [Th]e well-serrated upper teeth [ha]ve broad bases and narrow [cu]sps. The lower teeth also have broad bases [an]d small serrations, but are narrow and straight. [Su]ch teeth are probably designed for a diet of

FIELD NOTES

■ Western Atlantic and Caribbean, from Florida, USA, and Bermuda to southern Brazil, including parts of the Gulf of Mexico

■ Up to 10' (3 m)

■ Potentially dangerous

■ Day and night, year-round

■ Abundant

bony reef fishes, small sharks and rays, and cephalopods.

Large numbers of these sharks occur on island reefs throughout the Caribbean Sea. It is a fast swimmer, but is known to rest in caves and under ledges during the day. It has been called the sleeping shark, although there is no evidence that it is actually asleep when resting.

Divers encounter Caribbean reef sharks in surface waters near shore, cruising over the bottom of coral reefs, or swimming along the reef drop-offs down to depths of 100' (30 m). In the Bahamas, it is possible to dive with them after they have been attracted to "shark feeds" (see pp. 240–1). While they are not particularly aggressive, they have been responsible for attacks on divers, especially in situations involving bait or spearfishing.

Very little is known about the Caribbean reef shark's biology. Females bear four to six pups per litter; these range from 2–2½' (60–75 cm) in length at birth. This shark is targeted by local fisheries for its meat, hide, liver oil, and for fishmeal.

A Caribbean reef shark, with another reef shark behind.

179

Sandbar Shark

Carcharhinus plumbeus

The most notable feature of this shark, also called the thickskin shark, is its strikingly tall first dorsal fin. It can be more than one-tenth of the length of this sizable shark, which usually reaches 6½' (2 m) and weighs 100 lb (45 kg), with some animals to 8' (2.4 m) and twice as heavy.

The broad head is flattened. The streamlined body is gray or brown above, while the belly is white and the dorsal and tail fins both have dusky upper edges. In this strong-swimming

FIELD NOTES

■ Western and eastern Atlantic, western Indian Ocean, western, eastern, and central Pacific

■ 6½–8' (2–2.4 m)

■ Not dangerous

■ Day and night; seasonally abundant in many coastal areas

■ Common, but declining in some regions because of overfishing

species, the upper lobe of the tail fin is well developed. There is a ridge between the first and the far smaller second dorsal fin

With broad, serrated upper teeth to cut up prey, the sandb shark eats many fishes, includin menhaden, eels, flatfish, other sharks, goatfish, skates, octopus squid, and crustaceans.

Sandbar sharks live in tropic and temperate waters around th globe. Large schools range over continental an island shelves, with the schools often being segregated by sex. They can be found behind the surf zone on sandy beaches or at depths as great as 1,310' (400 m). Sometimes, divers see them near sandy beaches or rocky reefs, but they are not particularly aggressive. They prefe to swim near the bottom, often in large bays and estuaries, but do not move into fresh wate

Off the Atlantic coast of north America, females reach maturity at about 16 years of age Mating occurs from spring through early summer, and females carry the developing young for 9 to 12 months. They retreat to shallow nursery grounds to give birth to 8 to 12 young, depending on the size of the mothe Pups are about 8½" (22 cm) long at birth.

The sandbar shark is heavily fished for its meat and fins.

Tiger Shark

Galeocerdo cuvier

This large, dangerous shark is to tropical waters what the great white shark (see 158) is to temperate waters. It is named for the dark stripes on its ay back, which are pronounced juveniles (see above) but beome pale or disappear in large ults. Its wide mouth, broad ose, barrel chest, and the slenderness at the base its tail are distinctive. So, too, are its heavily rrated, cockscomb-shaped teeth. These, mbined with its jaw strength, allow it to cut rough the bodies of large sea turtles, as well as als, sea lions, and cetaceans. It also has a liking r such spicy treats as venomous jellyfish, ngrays, and sea snakes.

ne of the few true shark avengers, it has eaten ttle, pigs, donkeys, eep, and humans that ve fallen overboard.

Adult tiger sharks spend eir days beyond the reef lge to depths of about)0' (150 m), except at

FIELD NOTES

- Worldwide in tropical waters
- To 18' (5.6 m); possibly to 24' (7.4 m)
- Dangerous
- Very rarely seen
- Not common

certain times of the year, when they also come inshore during the day. They are active at night, and enter shallow reefs and lagoons after dusk to feed. In certain areas, they migrate between island groups to take advantage of colonies of young birds learning to fly over water.

Generally, tiger sharks are sluggish, but they can move quickly when feeding, and should be treated carefully on the rare occasions they are sighted. If you see one while diving, calmly leave the water, keeping it in sight at all times.

The tiger shark is the only ovoviviparous requiem shark. It has between 10 and 82 pups after a year-long gestation. The young are 20–30" (50–75 cm) at birth. They mature after about 4 to 6 years, and live for about 12 years.

The shark's powerful body makes it capable of bursts of speed.

upper and lower teeth

Lemon Shark

Negaprion brevirostris

This large, stout-bodied reef shark has a pale yellow-brown body with no obvious markings and a broad, flattened head. It is easily identified by its large dorsal fins, which are about equal in size. The anal fin, immediately below the second dorsal fin, is also large. The pectoral fins are long and curve back on the trailing edge. There is no lateral keel, and unlike many requiem sharks, it has no interdorsal ridge.

The only other species in the genus is the sicklefin lemon shark (*Negaprion acutidens*), found in the Indo-Pacific. The trailing edges of its pectoral fins are more curved than the lemon shark's.

The lemon shark is abundant in tropical reef systems, especially those with seagrass and associated mangrove habitats. It has adapted to be highly tolerant of shallow waters

> **FIELD NOTES**
> ■ Western Atlantic, from New Jersey, USA, to southern Brazil; the Caribbean; possibly the west coast of Africa; eastern Pacific from southern Baja California, Mexico, to Ecuador
> ■ 11' (3.4 m)
> ■ Harmless unless provoked
> ■ Day and night; year-round in tropical regions
> ■ Common

with low oxygen levels, such as warm-water mangrove swamps or bays, places where it is commonly observed. It has attacked humans, but is generally not considered aggressive, unless provoked.

Lemon sharks are active throughout the day and night. Among the Bimini Islands population, in the Bahamas, the level of activity seems to increase at dusk and dawn, possibly due to feeding. The diet consists of bony fishes, rays, crustaceans, guitarfishes, and mollusks. Some populations probably undertake lengthy seasonal migrations in search of food, because they are found in summer along sandy beaches and continental shelves in waters of high latitudes.

Females reach maturity when they are about 8' (2.4 m) long, and mate in spring and summer. About one year later, 4 to 17 live young, about 2' (60 cm) in length, are born.

The eye (above) of the lemon shark is an effective hunting tool.

Blue Shark

Prionace glauca

The blue shark, one of the most attractive sharks, is large and slender. Its upper body is indigo blue, the sides are bright blue, the belly markedly white. With its long, narrow, and pointed pectoral fins, long snout, and large eyes, it is unmistakable.

The blue shark is found in the open ocean throughout the tropics and into cooler seas. In the tropics, it often enters deeper, cooler water, while in temperate coastal waters it comes close to the edge of kelp beds, where divers may see it. It migrates regularly in the Atlantic, following the Gulf Stream to Europe, moving south along the African coast, then returning to the Caribbean.

Open-water divers may see these sharks, particularly if the sharks have been attracted by

FIELD NOTES

- Worldwide in open ocean
- To 12½' (3.8 m)
- Potentially dangerous
- During the day, year-round
- Previously very abundant, now reduced by heavy fishing

chum (berley). Dive operators offer tours using cages off southern California, USA (see p. 230–1), and elsewhere. Although attacks are unlikely, excited sharks have occasionally taken a nip at an unwary diver.

Blue sharks feed ravenously on large schools of squid, but are also very opportunistic and will decimate a floating whale or porpoise carcass. Fisheries consider them a menace because they attack nets and eat fish caught on lines. Once the most plentiful shark in the sea, they are now endangered through overfishing.

Although not yet observed, blue shark courtship is thought to be very lively. Males bite the females' shoulders; fortunately, their skin is three times as thick as that of the males. Females reach maturity when about five. They mate and store sperm for nearly a year, after which fertilization occurs. Litters of from 4 to 135 pups, depending on the size of the mother, are born alive the following year.

A blue shark (left) feeds on a school of northern anchovies off the California coast.

Milk Shark

Rhizoprionodon acutus

One of the most common small requiem species in the western Pacific and Indian oceans is the milk shark, a brownish red to gray shark with a white underbelly. Like the other sharks in this genus, it has a long, slender body, a parabola–like snout when viewed from above, and relatively large eyes near the tip of the mouth. The first dorsal fin is much larger than the second dorsal fin. The pectoral fins are short and stout, and the pelvic fins are small.

Long labial folds at the corners of the mouth distinguish the milk shark from all other requiem sharks in its range. The similar gray sharpnose shark (*Rhizopriono-don oligolinx*) inhabits coastal areas from the west coast of Africa, east to New Guinea and north to Japan. The Australian sharpnose shark (*Rhizoprionodon taylori*) ranges across the northern half of Australia. Both of these closely related species have very short labial furrows at the edge of the mouth.

Milk sharks are found in large numbers in coastal areas and continental shelves to depths of

FIELD NOTES

■ Eastern Atlantic, Indo-West Pacific
■ Up to 6' (1.8 m); smaller individuals about 3⅓' (1 m)
■ Harmless
■ Day and night, year-round
■ Common

upper tooth

lower tooth

655' (200 m). They spend most of their time in small groups or large schools foraging for food near the bottom, where they may be encountered by divers. Their diet consists of small fish (herring, sardines, croaker, mojarra, and flatfish) and invertebrates (squid, octopus, snails, shrimp, and crabs). They are a major food source for large sharks. With barrier nets removing large predator sharks from beaches in South Africa, swimmers and divers are seeing more milk sharks off beaches there. They are no threat to humans, being quite harmless.

Females reach sexual maturity when about two years old and about 2½' (75 cm) long. They produce litters of one to eight live young, about 10" (25 cm) long at birth, after about a year's gestation. This shark is commercially important as a food source in many parts of its range.

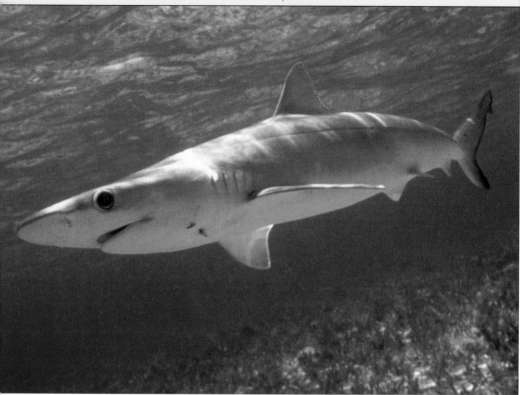

Caribbean Sharpnose Shark

Rhizoprionodon porosus

The Caribbean sharpnose shark has a gray body that grades to white below. Like other *Rhizoprionodon* species, this small shark is slender, with a long, parabolic snout and relatively large eyes adjacent to the tip of the mouth. Its sides are sometimes scattered with white spots and the fins edged in white. The first dorsal fin is much larger than the second, and the pectoral and small pelvic fins are short.

Currently, there are thought to be six or even species in the genus *Rhizoprionodon*. Although the taxonomic relationships among them are still under investigation, most species seem to have non-overlapping distributions in the tropical and subtropical latitudes of the world. The Caribbean sharpnose is similar to the Atlantic sharpnose shark (*Rhizoprionodon terraenovae*), which occurs in the Gulf of Mexico and also along the Atlantic coast of North America, but is distinguished from it by the number of vertebrae.

The Caribbean sharpnose is a common inhabitant of shallow inshore waters along continental and island shelves. It frequents sea-grass beds, coral reefs, and can tolerate the reduced salinity of estuaries. It is also collected at depths greater than 1,640' (500 m). Although common, this shy, harmless shark usually avoids contact with divers.

This species feeds on a variety of small fishes, and invertebrates such as snails and shrimp. It is a common prey for larger sharks. Gestation takes 10 to 11 months, with litters of 2 to 6 pups, about 1' (30 cm) in length, born in spring or early summer. This shark is taken for food and fishmeal by local and commercial fisheries.

FIELD NOTES

- Western Atlantic and Caribbean islands, from Bahamas to Uruguay
- 3⅓' (1 m)
- Harmless
- Day or night; seasonal in some areas
- Usually common

...sharpnose shark swimming ...tropical Bahaman waters.

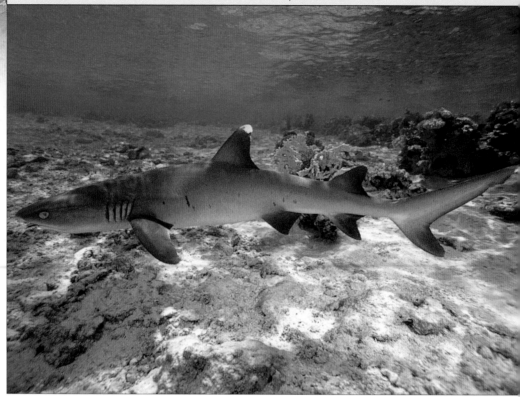

Whitetip Reef Shark

Triaenodon obesus

The whitetip reef shark should not be confused with the larger and more graceful oceanic whitetip shark (see p. 176). It is a sluggish, fairly slender, gray requiem shark with conspicuous white tips on its dorsal and caudal fins.

It has medium-sized, pointed teeth with smooth edges, which are flanked by small cusps. Unlike most requiem sharks, it is not an effective fish hunter in open water. It feeds mostly on the bottom, taking advantage of its tooth structure and its short, broad snout to pursue prey into reef crevices, where they cannot escape. Like most reef sharks, it too falls prey to other, larger sharks and large reef groupers.

Whitetip reef sharks live close to shore, at depths of 26–130' (8–40 m). During the day, divers and snorkelers predictably find them resting in caves, particularly in Hawaii and the Galapagos Islands, or under rock and coral ledges. They are active at night and during slack tides. They can become accustomed to the sounds of boats and to spearfishers, and are

FIELD NOTES

■ Red Sea, Indian Ocean, central Pacific, and tropical eastern Pacific

■ Said to reach 7' (2.2 m), but rarely more than 5¼' (1.6 m)

■ Potentially dangerous

■ Year-round

■ Common

aroused by the presence of divers, approaching them out of curiosity. Although this is not an aggressive species, foolhardy divers have lost a hand when feeding members squid and fish.

Whitetips are viviparous and bear litters of one to five pups. They are born after a short gestation period of at least five months and are 20–24" (50–60 cm) long at birth.

The flesh and liver of whitetips are consumed by humans. It is unique among sharks in having caused ciguateratoxin poisoning, a type of food poisoning with severe gastrointestinal and neurological symptoms.

The whitetip reef shark uses its pointed, cusped teeth to grip and pull fish prey out of their hiding places in reef crevices.

Winghead Shark

Eusphyra blochii

FIELD NOTES
- Indo-West Pacific
- Up to 5' (1.5 m); commonly reaching 3⅓' (1 m)
- Harmless
- Day or night, usually year-round
- Common

The stout-bodied winghead shark is one of the smaller hammerhead sharks. The first dorsal fin is tall, and the second dorsal fin is set behind the anal fin. It is gray to brown above, fading to a white underside, with no conspicuous markings on the fins or body.

The winghead is easily identified by its broad wing-shaped head, the ultimate example of the cephalofoil, measuring about half the shark's total body length. The eyes are set far apart on the extremely broad head; this may have the effect of improving the shark's stereoscopic vision. The nares are located near the middle of the head, but the nasal grooves extend along almost its full width. These wide nasal grooves can sample a very large section of the water column, which may enhance the shark's ability to detect and locate odor sources. The electroreceptive ampullae of Lorenzini and mechanoreceptive lateral line on the wings have an extended distribution across the head. This may be useful for detecting and localizing prey, such as crabs, shrimp, cephalopods, and small fishes, buried in the sediment.

This poorly studied species is widespread along the coast of southern Asia in the Indian Ocean, and around islands of the western Pacific. It is also common in shallow tropical waters on continental and island shelves. It is exploited commercially in Southeast Asia, but because the winghead population has a high natural mercury content, it is not generally marketed elsewhere.

Females reach sexual maturity when about 3⅓' (1 m) in length. They mate in spring and give birth to 6 to 20 young, about 13–18" (32–45 cm) long, after almost a year's gestation.

wing-shaped cephalofoil

187

Scalloped Hammerhead

Sphyrna lewini

The scalloped hammerhead, also known as the kidney-headed shark, belongs to a family of eight sharks with a unique specialization—the front of the skull expands laterally like a hammer to form a head structure called a cephalofoil. This serves many biological functions. Its wide, flattened shape adds lift during swimming, improving hydrodynamic efficiency. The increased surface area allows for the expansion of many sensory systems important for feeding. The eyes and nares are at the tips of the head; the electroreceptors and lateral line are over a wider area. Thus these fast, active sharks can capture large or elusive prey.

FIELD NOTES

- Western and eastern Atlantic, Indo-West, central, and eastern Pacific
- 10–13' (3–4 m)
- Not aggressive, but potentially dangerous
- Day or night; year-round or seasonal, depending on region
- The most abundant and widely distributed of the large hammerheads

Scalloped hammerheads can be distinguished by the broad leading edge on the head, which is arched toward the back. There is a prominent indentation in the center with two smaller lobes on either side, giving a scalloped look. These sharks are found in most warm temperate and tropical waters. They occur in coastal areas above continental and island shelves, and in adjacent offshore waters to depths of nearly 1,000' (300 m). They enter shallow bays and estuaries, and aggregate around seamounts. Here, divers see them interacting, chasing, thrusting, shaking their heads, and biting each other. This behavior needs further study, but may be for social reasons, migration to feeding areas, or reproduction. They are often indifferent to divers, but do make close passes.

Their diet consists of bony fishes and cephalopods. Females bear 15 to 30 pups, 17–22" (43–55 cm) long at birth.

The unmistakable scalloped-looking head.

Great Hammerhead

Sphyrna mokarran

The great hammerhead is easily identified by its thick, broad head, which has an almost flat leading edge, except for an indentation in the center. It is a large, stout shark, gray-brown above, grading to a paler color below. The first dorsal fin is extremely high and pointed, with a curved rear margin. The base of the anal fin is much longer than that of the second dorsal fin.

This species is distributed in nearly all warm temperate and tropical waters. It occurs in coastal areas above continental and island shelves, and in adjacent offshore waters to depths of about 260' (80 m). Divers are likely to see it in shallow waters close to shore, especially near coral reef drop-offs and adjacent sand habitats. It makes long migrations to cooler waters during the summer months.

The great hammerhead has a very keen olfactory sense, and is

The very broad head allows for some unique feeding techniques.

an impressive predator. Its diet consists of many mobile fishes associated with the water column, including sardines, herring, tarpon, and jacks, and benthic species such as grouper, sea cats, flatfish, and croaker. But this shark is best known for its preference for other elasmobranchs, such as stingrays, skates, and other sharks. In its voracious and unique predatory behavior toward stingrays, the great hammerhead uses the side of its head to pin a fleeing ray to the bottom. It then rotates its head to the side and cleanly bites off a large chunk of the ray's wing. It continues to circle and feed on the incapacitated prey until it has been totally consumed.

Females reach sexual maturity when about 10' (3 m) long. They usually produce 20 to 40 young per litter, and the pups are about 2¼' (70 cm) long at birth.

189

Bonnethead Shark

Sphyrna tiburo

The bonnethead shark is a small hammerhead, and can be distinguished by its smooth, rounded, shovel-shaped head. Its body is plain gray-brown above, shading to a light color on the underside. The pectoral fins are short and straight along the rear margin. The anal fin is slightly concave but has no notch.

This shark frequents many different habitats within the temperate and tropical waters of its range. It is abundant in the surf zone, bays and estuaries, on coral and rocky reefs, and over sandy or muddy bottoms. Although harmless, it is timid and not easy to approach. It also inhabits waters of the continental shelf to depths of about 260' (80 m). Large schools migrate to warm latitudes in winter and to cooler latitudes during summer.

Bonnetheads have remarkable dentition, with small sharp teeth at the front of the jaw for grasping either its mate or a soft-bodied prey, and broad molar-like teeth at the back of the jaw for crushing hard-shelled invertebrates. It feeds

FIELD NOTES

- Western Atlantic, eastern Pacific
- About 3⅓' (1 m); individuals 5' (1.5 m) long are known
- Harmless
- Day or night; year-round in many areas
- Common

primarily on invertebrates, crab, shrimp, mantis shrimp, bivalves, snails, and cephalopods, as well as small bony fishes.

The behavior of this species has been well studied. Individual sharks exhibit specific types of behavior toward other individuals, including patrolling, head-shaking, jaw-snapping, hitting, and hunching. The function of such behavior is to establish and maintain dominance hierarchies and other agonistic relationships.

Individual populations are sometimes segregated by sex. Females reach sexual maturity when about 2½' (75 cm) long. They retreat to shallow bays and estuaries to give birth, delivering litters of 8 to 16 pups about 14" (35 cm) long.

The head of the bonnethead looks like a shovel.

Smooth Hammerhead

Sphyrna zygaena

The smooth hammerhead has a cephalofoil that is long and narrow, its leading margin shaped in a smooth arch without a notch in the middle. Its body is olive to gray-brown above, becoming light on the underside. The tips of the pectoral fins are dusky on the bottom. The first dorsal fin is high, with a slightly curved rear margin. The pectoral fins are short and straight along the rear margin, while the anal fin has a prominent notch.

The smooth hammerhead is found in nearly all warm temperate and tropical waters. And while its distribution overlaps that of the scalloped hammerhead (see p. 188) and great hammerhead (see p. 189), the smooth hammerhead is mostly concentrated in temperate waters. It seems to prefer shallow inshore waters less than 65'

FIELD NOTES

■ Western and eastern North Atlantic, western Indian Ocean, western, central, and eastern Pacific

■ 8–13' (2.5–4 m)

■ Possibly dangerous

■ Day or night; year-round in many areas

■ Common

The smoothly arched leading edge of the cephalofoil, or head, of a juvenile.

(20 m) deep, and divers are especially likely to see it around rocky reefs. Divers need to take care, however, especially those who are spearfishing. It also occurs at the surface in the open ocean, and forms enormous schools to make long migrations to cooler latitudes during the summer, then returns to warmer waters for the winter months.

The smooth hammerhead feeds on small schooling bony fishes such as herring and menhaden, as well as porgies and sea bass from the reef, and stingrays, skates, and other small sharks. Large crustaceans and cephalopods round out the diet.

Females reach sexual maturity when about 7½' (2.3 m) long, giving birth to large numbers of live young, between 29 and 37 per litter. The pups are about 22" (55 cm) long at birth.

191

SHARKS *of the* DEEP
MIDWATERS

Below the euphotic zone, at depths of 650' (200 m), the sea is without the sun-driven photosynthesis that supports most life on Earth. Animals depend on dead and decaying plants and animals falling from above, or they venture to the surface to dine. Many small sharks from the dogfish family (Squalidae) ascend at dusk and return at dawn to the safety of the deep midwaters, relying on their large eyes and good vision in low light to detect prey. They also use their ventral bioluminescence to camouflage themselves from potential predators and prey.

BLACKBELLY LANTERNSHARK
Etmopterus lucifer

This small, stocky shark has spines in front of each dorsal fin. Its dorsal side and flanks are brownish, the underbody black, and there is no anal fin. It has blade-like teeth and feeds on squid, lanternfish, and crustaceans. A variety of features distinguish blackbelly lanternsharks from the other lanternsharks. These include the arrangement and number of their denticles, and subtle differences in fin size and coloration. It closely related to *Etmopterus perryi*, the dwarf dogshark, which is a mere 8" (20 cm) long, and probably the smallest living shark.

The blackbelly lanternshark, widespread on outer continental shelves, lives on or near the bottom at depths of 590–2,700' (180–835 m). Its mode of reproduction is presumed to be ovoviviparous, like that of most sharks.

The 17 or more species of lanternsharks have numerous minute, bioluminescent (light-producing) photophores

FIELD NOTES

■ Southern oceans, also the China Sea and off the Philippines

■ Males to 16" (40 cm); females to 13" (33 cm)

■ Harmless

■ Not encountered by divers

■ Not uncommon

ong the underside of their bodies. The light
om the photophores is a means of camouflage
cause it "counter-illuminates" the shark. The
ark produces just enough weak light on the
nderside of its body to equal the amount of
wn-welling light between it and the ocean's
rface. Because of this optical illusion, it
erges with the ocean and cannot be seen by
tential predators, nor by unsuspecting prey.

Lanternsharks produce their own light
mixing a luciferin-like substrate with a
ciferase-like enzyme. This differs from the
ethod many fishes use, which relies on a
mbiotic relationship with certain bacteria.

YGMY SHARK
uprotomicrus bispinatus

lthough it is a member of the dogfish family,
e pygmy shark lacks the spines that normally
ecede the dorsal fins of other dogfishes. Its
orsal fins are quite small and on the rear half
f the body. It has a bulbous head and an
nderslung jaw. It is generally black, with
ontrasting pale fins.

Pygmy sharks live in the open ocean, usually
temperate and tropical waters. They
robably spend their days in deep water and
igrate after sunset to the surface, covering as
uch as 4,900' (1,520 m) in either direction.
his has been compared to a person walking
miles (11 km) every day. They migrate to
llow their food supply, the deep-water
rustaceans, squids, and bony fishes that make
is same journey to feed on surface plankton
night, when there is less risk of being seen.

Pygmy sharks
have lumin-
escent photo-
phores on their
underside.
These help to
camouflage
the shark and
perhaps help it
to find a mate.

Pygmy sharks are ovoviviparous. They
produce about eight young in a litter, and these
are about 2½–4" (6–10 cm) long at birth.

SPINY DOGFISH
Squalus acanthias

The spiny
dogfish is also
known as the
piked dogfish
or whitespotted
spurdog. It is
identified by a
large spiracle
behind each
large eye, the
presence of
spines on the

two dorsal fins, and the lack of an anal fin. It
ranges from gray to brown in color, with small
white spots above a light underside.

Spiny dogfish are cold-water sharks,
preferring temperatures from 45–59° F
(7–15° C). They are caught in waters down to
about 2,600' (800 m) deep, but not exclusively
in deep water. They form extremely large
schools, routinely frequenting the shallow and
coastal waters of higher latitudes in spring and
fall, and migrating into deep waters during the
cooler winter months.

The diet includes small fishes, such as cod,
herring, menhaden, and haddock, as well as
invertebrates such as krill, squid, scallops, and
crustaceans. This species is extremely slow-
growing and lives for up to 70 years. Females
reach sexual maturity when 21 to 25 years old.
They give birth to up to 20 live young, about
8–12" (20–30 cm) long, after a gestation of 18
to 24 months—the longest known for any of
the elasmobranchs.

The spiny dogfish is of high commercial
importance in many parts of the world.
However, with its slow growth rate and low
fecundity, it is very susceptible to overfishing,
and has been overharvested in many regions.

SHARKS *of the* DEEP BOTTOMS

Some shark species live in the abyss, that portion of the ocean that is below the continental slope and covered by 13,000' (4 km) of sea water. This makes up two-thirds of the globe. For sharks such as some of the slow, lumbering sleeper sharks and gulper sharks, it is a cold place, usually 31° to 39° F (−0.6° to +4° C). It is almost completely dark, except for the light made by other animals. Pressure can be a thousand times that at the surface. Adaptation at such depths requires the ability to find and capture food, to avoid being eaten, and to find a mate—in the dark.

GREENLAND SHARK
Somniosus microcephalus

The Greenland shark is also called the sleeper or gurry shark. This gigantic dogfish is the only polar shark of the Atlantic. It lives in deep water to 1,800' (550 m) at temperatures of 36 to 45° F (2 to 7° C), only coming up to shallow water during the colder months. At such temperatures, it will not be encountered by divers, although it may be caught by fishers. It is a sluggish beast, and provides little resistance when captured. Nevertheless, it should always be handled carefully.

There are four or five species of sleeper shark. All have a short and rounded snout, a caudal fin with a well-developed lower lobe, and two small, spineless dorsal fins; they lack an anal fin. They vary in color, some being mottled, while others, such as the Greenland shark, range from pinkish to brown, black, or purplish gray.

The teeth of the Greenland shark's upper jaw are long and pointed, very different from

ose of its lower jaw, which are strongly
blique, sharp, and close set. These teeth allow
to gouge large chunks of flesh from dead
taceans, and probably to remove the heads
seals and sea lions rapidly before dining on
e carcasses. It also eats fish such as salmon,
d a variety of bottom-dwelling fishes.

That this sluggish shark can capture such
ily and fast-moving prey may be because of
all copepods that attach themselves to the
rneas of the shark's eyes. Brightly lumin-
cent, these copepods are thought to attract
rious and hungry prey, which soon end
in the shark's cavernous maw.

Little is known about the Greenland
ark's reproductive behavior. It was
cently discovered to be ovoviviparous,
earing about 10 pups, 15" (38 cm) long,
each litter.

PINED PYGMY SHARK
qualiolus laticaudus

t 8" (20 cm) long, this deep-water dogfish
vals the dwarf dogfish (*Etmopterus perryi*) for
e title of the world's smallest shark. At the
oment, not enough specimens exist to make
final decision. The spined pygmy and its
ustralian relative, the smalleye pygmy shark
Squaliolus aliae), are unique in having a spine in
ont of the first dorsal fin but not the second.
hey are cigar-shaped, with a bulbous snout
d a large spiracle behind the eye. Their upper
w teeth are small and narrow; the lower teeth
e larger and blade-like. Underneath, they
ave many luminous photophores, which serve
camouflage them from predators.

The spined pygmy dogfish lives in temperate
nd tropical waters, offshore near continental
nd island landmasses. Like other deep-water
arks, it makes a daily migration to feed. It
scends at dusk
nd feeds during
e night on
quid, shrimp,
nd midwater
shes, especially
nternfishes,
en descends
gain at dawn.

Unlike other species, it stops within 650'
(200 m) of the surface, before heading down
to ocean depths as great as 6,560' (2,000 m).

Little is known about its reproductive
biology, but it is likely to be ovoviviparous.

PRICKLY DOGFISH
Oxynotus bruniensis

Among the most unusual looking sharks of the
deep ocean bottom are the roughsharks
(Oxynotidae). These small sharks have a stout
body that is laterally compressed and bears a
prominent ridge on the abdomen. Most
notable are the high, spined dorsal fins with
their forward extensions, which give the
appearance of
two sails. There
is no anal fin.
The head is
slightly flattened,
with large eyes,
prominent
spiracles, and
small gill slits.
The nostrils are
placed relatively close together and the fleshy
mouth is small and usually surrounded by
labial furrows.

One of four roughshark species, the prickly
dogfish is distinguished by its forward-pointing
first dorsal spine and its skin, which is covered
with rough, prickly denticles. The body is gray
or brown with whitish margins on the tips of
the dorsal fins and trailing margins on the
pectoral and pelvic fins.

The prickly dogfish occurs in temperate
waters, dwelling at depths of about 165–1,640'
(50–500 m). Very little is known of its biology.
The diet consists of benthic invertebrates, such
as segmented worms.

About seven young hatch from eggs that are
retained inside the mother. The pups are born
live when about 4" (10 cm) long.

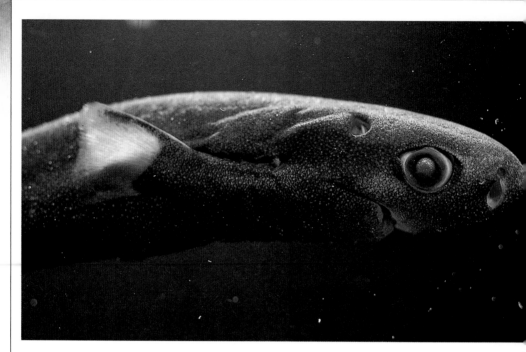

TOOTHY MIDWATER HUNTERS

The deep waters of the open ocean are home to many small predatory sharks. These sharks have developed special features and behaviors that enable them to prey on the many organisms that live in their habitat, and thus survive in the dim to dark waters of the world's oceans.

COOKIECUTTER SHARK
Isistius brasiliensis

Before its feeding behavior was discovered, this species was known as the "cigar shark." It is a small, brown shark with a short snout. Its cigar-like appearance is enhanced by its small dorsal fins being displaced to the rear of its body and by the lack of an anal fin. It also has a black collar around the back of its head.

The cookiecutter shark and its close relative, the largetooth cookiecutter shark

suction mouth and teeth

(*Isistius plutodus*), have specialized suctorial jaws and lips, and razor-sharp, saw-like lower teeth. The shark forms a suction cap with its lips on the skin of its prey, then bites and swivels around to cut out an oval-shaped plug of tissue, just like a cookiecutter in pastry.

The cookiecutter shark's victims include large marlins, tunas, seals, whales, and dolphins, and it has even bitten the rubberized dome of a nuclear submarine. Scientists believe that it uses its bioluminescent light organs, which glow in the dark, to lure fast-swimming prey close, so that they can ambush them.

A tropical shark, it has been caught at the surface at

FIELD NOTES
- Throughout the tropical oceans of the world
- To 20" (50 cm)
- Harmless
- Not seen by divers
- Probably not uncommon in deep oceanic waters

ight, but it normally inhabits depths as great as 1,500' (3,570 m). It is ovoviviparous, but nothing is known about the size of its litters.

CROCODILE SHARK
Pseudocarcharias kamoharai

also sometimes seen offshore. It is probably a fast-swimming predator that chases small prey, either near the surface at night or down to 1,000' (300 m) in the mesopelagic zone during the day. The shark has powerful jaws and long, thin, needle-like teeth, which

he crocodile shark, the only species of the family Pseudocarchariidae, is related to the sand tiger shark (see p. 152). Its muscular and highly streamlined body looks like a mini-torpedo. The first dorsal fin is about midway between the small pectoral and pelvic fins. The second dorsal fin is much smaller.

The body is dark brown above grading to lighter underneath, with dark blotches often scattered over the sides and bottom surfaces. The head is long, the snout conical, and the eyes large. The liver of this species contains squalene, a fine, low-density oil that increases the shark's buoyancy.

The crocodile shark is widespread through-out the open oceans of the world, from the surface to depths of about 1,970' (600 m). It is

are similar in shape to those found in the larger mako sharks (see p. 159). This combination of jaws and teeth is designed for the crocodile shark to grasp its small midwater prey, including shrimp, lanternfishes, and squid.

Although little is known about the shark's reproductive biology, there seem to be four young in each litter (two from each uterus). After exhausting their own yolk supply, the developing embryos apparently eat all but one sibling in each uterus. They continue to develop by feeding on eggs produced by the mother. It is unknown how or why two embryos coexist in this manner.

FIELD NOTES
- Tropical oceans throughout the world
- About 3⅓' (1 m)
- Harmless
- Near the surface at night, probably year-round
- Common

The characteristic wound inflicted by a cookiecutter shark shows clearly on the Pacific spotted dolphin at the top of this photo.

graceful catshark

SOME UNFAMILIAR SHARKS

Sharks are members of marine bottom communities from the sunlit shallows of intertidal pools to the dark abyssal plains thousands of feet deep. While many of the species that live on or near the bottom belong to families that are familiar and well known, there are also species from smaller families about which little is understood. Among these are the finback catsharks, false catsharks, barbeled houndsharks, and weasel sharks.

GRACEFUL CATSHARK
Proscyllium habereri

The graceful catshark is one of the finback catsharks (Proscylliidae), close relatives of the catshark family. Their first dorsal fin is above or in front of the pelvic fins, while in catsharks, it is behind them. These small, bottom-dwelling sharks have very slender, elongated bodies. The large, cat-like eyes have a nictita-ting membrane, usually reduced in size, and there is a prominent spiracle behind the eye, used for ventilation. The labial furrows in the corner of the mouth are small or absent, the teeth in the back of the mouth are comb-like, and there are no nasal barbels.

The graceful catshark is found above island and continental shelves in warm temperate and tropical waters at depths of between 165–330' (50–100 m). This species is distinguished by the pattern of dark spots that covers its fins and small body. The two spineless dorsal fins are of about equal size, with the second positioned above the anal fin.

The diet of the graceful catshark includes small bony fishes, crabs, and cephalopods. Little is known about this animal's biology, but the females are thought to lay eggs.

> **FIELD NOTES**
> ■ Western Atlantic, Indian Ocean, western Pacific
> ■ About 26" (65 cm)
> ■ Harmless
> ■ Not often seen by divers
> ■ Uncommon

FALSE CATSHARK
Pseudotriakis microdon

The false catshark is thought to be the only species of the family Pseudotriakidae, which is closely related to the catshark family. Its body is long and slender, and its distinguishing feature is the long base and low height of the keel-like first dorsal fin. The eye is oval and cat-like, with the nictitating membrane reduced in size. There is a large spiracle. The jaw of the false catshark is large, and the back rows of its numerous rows of teeth are comb-like.

This is a deep-water shark that lives on shelf slopes from 660–4,920' (200–1,500 m). Its body is watery and soft, which may help to give it the neutral buoyancy that suits its some-what sedentary lifestyle on or near the bottom. The false catshark probably feeds on deep-water fishes and invertebrates. Females are thought to reach sexual maturity when about 7¼' (2.2 m) long, and bear two to four live young.

> **FIELD NOTES**
> ■ North Atlantic, western Indian Ocean, central and western Pacific
> ■ Up to about 9½' (2.9 m)
> ■ Harmless
> ■ Not seen by divers
> ■ Common in certain areas

false catshark

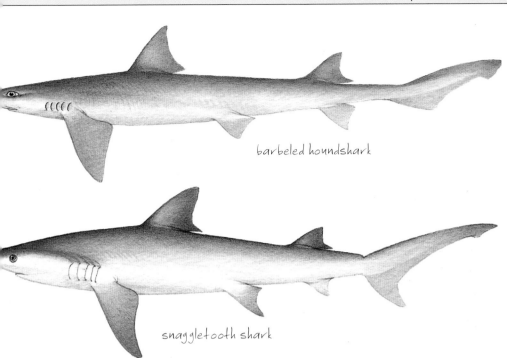

barbeled houndshark

snaggletooth shark

ARBELED HOUNDSHARK
eptocharias smithii

he barbeled houndshark is the only member
of the unusual family Leptochariidae. While
osely related to the requiem sharks and
undsharks, many of its characteristics are
ique. It is a small species, with an elongated
ay or brownish body. The first of two
ineless dorsal fins is between the pectoral and
elvic fins, while the second is positioned
ove the anal fin. The head is small and the
es are large and cat-like. The nasal flaps are
odified into short, slender barbels. The
orners of the mouth have long labial furrows,
d the teeth of both jaws are small, with
rrow cusps and cusplets.

The houndshark is usually found in coastal
eas, both inshore in waters about 30' (10 m)
ep, and also
ove the
jacent shelf at
pths of about
5' (75 m). It
efers muddy
ttom areas,
pecially near
ver mouths,
here it feeds on crustaceans, small fishes, and
phalopods. It can be approached by divers.

Females mature when about 20" (50 cm)
ng. They have a gestation period of at least
ur months and give birth to litters of about
ven live young, probably in October.

This shark is commercially fished by local
heries for its meat and skin.

> **FIELD NOTES**
> ■ Eastern Atlantic coast of Africa
> ■ Up to about 2¼' (84 cm)
> ■ Harmless
> ■ Day or night, most of the year
> ■ Common

SNAGGLETOOTH SHARK
Hemipristis elongatus

This shark takes its name from the long,
conspicuous, serrated teeth that protrude from
the lower jaw. It is the largest of the weasel
sharks (Hemigaleidae), a family of small to
medium groundsharks named for their weasel-
like eyes. The
snaggletooth
shark is usually
gray or brown,
with undulations
on the margins
of its spineless
dorsal fins. The
first dorsal fin
begins above the
rear margin of the pectoral fins. The second
dorsal fin is about two-thirds as high.

The teeth are designed for catching and
consuming prey that includes a wide variety of
bony fishes, such as anchovies, mackerel, and
croakers, as well as other elasmobranchs,
namely butterfly rays and small requiem sharks.

The snaggletooth shark is very common in
some coastal areas of tropical seas. It frequents
waters as shallow as 3⅓' (1 m) and continental
and island shelves to depths of 100' (30 m).
This is a large but harmless shark, commonly
seen by divers close to shore.

Females reach sexual maturity when about
5½' (1.7 m) long. Up to eight embryos are
nourished from a yolk sac placenta and born
live. This species is fished in many parts of the
world for its fins, meat, and liver.

> **FIELD NOTES**
> ■ Eastern Atlantic, western Indian
> Ocean, western Pacific
> ■ Up to 8' (2.4 m)
> ■ Harmless
> ■ Day or night, year-round
> ■ Common

All my life through, the new sights of Nature
made me rejoice like a child.

MARIE CURIE (1867–1934), Polish-born physicist

CHAPTER SEVEN

RAYS FIELD GUIDE

USING *the* RAYS GUIDE

Get to know the rays in all their extraordinary shapes,

sizes, shades, and perfectly adapted behaviors.

This field guide describes and illustrates just a few of the almost 500 species of ray that dwell in the world's oceans, estuaries, and rivers. At least one member of each family is featured here. Some rays are ubiquitous over tropical reefs, drop-offs, and sand flats, and can be curious about, even quite sociable with, snorkelers and divers. Many rays, however, never venture out of the cold, dark depths at the bottom of the ocean. Many more spend most of their days buried up to the eyes and spiracles in mud or sand. Given that they can be hard to find, the biology and behavior of most rays remain something of a mystery. But the next time you're wading in shallow water, watching where you're putting your feet, this guide will give you some insight into the rays you might encounter.

Rajidae: Skates

Rough Skate

Raja nasuta

The *main photograph* shows as much of the species as possible, given the constraints of photographing such wild creatures in circumstances and conditions that can be difficult.

The *common* and *scientific names* of each species. The species are grouped according to taxonomy.

The *text* provides information on the appearance of the ray, its common names, habitat, and where and what to look for when you want to find it. It also gives ideas on how to differentiate between similar species, and supplies information, where known, about the ray's migratory habits and methods of reproduction.

FIELD NOTES
- Southeastern Pacific off New Zealand
- Reaches almost 3½' (1 m)
- Harmless
- Year-round; rarely seen by divers
- Common

The rough skate belongs to a group of skates whose common ancestor lived around the shores of the ancient Gondwana supercontinent more than 80 million years ago. This is indicated by the distribution of the modern-day group of skates, which are all found on the continental shelves off New Zealand, Australia, and South America.

The rough skate has a diamond-shaped disc with a very long, pointed snout. Its slender tail has three rows of thorns along its length, while its back is covered with minute prickles. It is usually grayish or brownish, with white spots and darker marbling. It occurs on soft bottoms to about 490' (150 m), usually beyond diving depths, although divers will occasionally see one.

Few details are known of the rough skate's biology. It lays horny, rectangular egg cases, which it attaches to the bottom by fine,

Port Davey skate

thread-like tendrils. E develop slowly and y after several months. hatched skates can b by a belly scar whe sac was attached. E egg "merm are foun beaches aft A close re rough skate is discovered Port (Raja sp.). Of th skates in the wo one that lives in is confined to tw the remote sou off southern Au stiff snout, mor ocean skates. T used for grubbi the fine silty bottom on w its restricted distribution, this skate left over from t likely to be very specific small, probably no more individuals. This makes to habitat degradation

212

Color illustrations supplement the text by showing basic features of the ray, or a related ray species.

This *illustrated banding* at the top of the page is a visual pointer to indicate that the page is about a ray species.

This *panel* refers to the family of rays that the species belongs to.

Rhinobatidae: Guitarfishes

Platyrhinidae: Thornback Rays

Urolophidae: Stingarees

Thornback

Platyrhinoidis triseriata

FIELD NOTES
- Eastern Pacific from California, USA, to Mexico
- Almost 3' (90 cm)
- Harmless; be wary of sharp thorns
- Year-round
- Once plentiful off southern California

...'s take their ...e from the ...horny spines ...metimes ...ar to ...arfish ...world. ...ps

around the eyes; the thornback's run along the back and tail.

The thornback lives in temperate and subtropical waters, mainly inshore on sandy and muddy bottoms. Divers occasionally see one around kelp beds, where its brownish upper surface blends well with the dark substrate. It rests in small groups for much of the day, remaining partly buried, with only its thorns protruding. These are sharp, and are probably used defensively against its main predators, small sharks. Although it is

...th and nostrils on the underside of the thornback.

harmless, this ray should be treated with caution.

Little is known about the thornback's general biology. It is not a powerful swimmer and so it seems unlikely that it undertakes any long migrations. It seems to be more active at night, feeding on sand worms, sea shells, and small crustaceans, such as crabs and shrimps. Mating occurs at the end of summer.

207

Round Stingray

Urobatis halleri

FIELD NOTES
- Eastern Pacific, from northern California to Panama
- Reaches 22" (56 cm)
- Not aggressive; the stinging spine can cause minor injury
- Year-round
- Very common

...round stingray, a ...ember of the stingaree ...family, is plain brown with ...spots and reticulations. It ...cular disc, the upper ...of which is smooth, ...tubercles. The related ...round stingray (*Urobatis* ...us), from close by in Baja ...rnia and the Sea of Cortez, ...exico, is similar in shape but has large black ...ches over the disc. Stingarees can be ...aken for stingrays because of their similar ...ay shape. However, stingarees have a shorter ..., which ends in a long, leaf-shaped caudal fin.

The round stingray lives mainly on muddy ...d sandy bottoms near the shore, to a depth of ...bout 295' (90 m). In summer, it basks in ...warm shallow inlets, but remains in ...coastal waters during winter, only ...entering inlets to forage. It does ...not range far, rarely moving ...beyond an area of about a

square mile. It seems sensitive to cold, and lives in water warmer than 50° F (10° C).

This ray feeds during the day on small bottom-dwelling crustaceans, bivalves, and sand worms. An efficient predator, it may use a combination of sight, smell, and vibration to detect prey. It uses its disc and mouth to "dig" for food in the substrate, and has also been seen nipping prey off sea-grass fronds. Divers may see a foraging ray in sheltered bays, or notice the outline of one buried in sediment.

Round stingrays mature early. The sexes segregate before the breeding season, and adult females live offshore until June, when they move in to coastal habitats to mate. Sexually aggressive males patrol the sandy strip between the deep sea-grass beds and the shore to select a suitable mate. He nibbles on her disc, then rolls beneath her and inserts a single clasper. Litters of one to six pups are born inshore in September, where they remain until maturity.

The underside of a juvenile round stingray.

213

Quick-reference Field Notes panel
- Distribution range of the ray
- Size
- Possible risks when encountering the ray
- Best time of day or year to observe the species
- Information on population numbers

Secondary photographs show details of particular features or amplify some aspect of the ray's habitat or behavior. In some instances, photographs showing other members of the ray's family are included.

203

Freshwater Sawfish

Pristis microdon

The sawfish family takes its name from its long, blade-like snout, edged with bony teeth, which resembles a crosscut saw. Sawfishes are easily confused with sawsharks (see p. 140) because they have a similar snout. However, the sawfish's gills are underneath its head rather than on the side, and it is much larger. Indeed, sawfishes are among the biggest fish in the sea.

Unlike most other rays, the sawfishes have a small disc and a shark-like tail. Most of them live inshore, in tropical seas. However, the freshwater sawfish usually inhabits tropical estuaries, rivers, and lakes. This slender, powerful sawfish is yellow to gray in color.

It is rare nowadays, so divers are unlikely to encounter it, and given that it is such a timid creature, it would probably flee at the first sign of a human. Anglers occasionally catch one on lines or in nets. It thrashes around wildly, and its saw teeth can cause serious injury. The saw is

FIELD NOTES

■ Tropical Indo-Pacific; possibly Africa and the Americas

■ Up to 21⅓' (6.6 m)

■ Sometimes aggressive in captivity

■ Rarely seen

■ Endangered

thought to be used offensively. The sawfish slashes it from side to side to stun the small fish upon which it feeds. Males also use their saws in battles during the breeding season.

The biology of the freshwater sawfish is not well known. Asian and Australian populations live almost exclusively in fresh water, but in Africa and the Americas, they also live in the sea. They are ovoviviparous. In Central America, they mate during summer in fresh water, where the pregnant females remain until they give birth five months later. Litters number up to 13, with pups being about 2½' (75 cm) at birth.

Sawfish populations have been seriously depleted this century through overfishing and degradation of their habitat. Many species are now rarely seen and their plight is one of the major conservation issues of the sea.

snout from below

Bowmouth Guitarfish

Rhina ancylostoma

This unmistakable creature resembles something from prehistory. It has horny [rid]ges with large thorns above and [be]hind the eyes; a broad, flattened [he]ad; and gills on the underside of [a] small disc. All this is typical of a [ra]y, but its powerful body with [lar]ge, angular fins, and a tail with a [pr]onounced lower lobe, are more shark-like—[he]nce one common name, "shark ray." It is [bl]uish gray to brownish, with large white spots. [Th]e shape of its mouth is also distinctive, [un]dulating like a longbow.

The bowmouth guitarfish lives near the coast [an]d around offshore reefs in tropical waters, down to about 295' (90 m). Scientists once thought it spent most of its time resting on the bottom, but its behavior in aquariums indicates that this ray swims actively for much of the day and night. Its tail is strong, and well adapted to prolonged swimming. It feeds mainly on crabs and large shellfishes by first restraining the prey against the sea bottom using its large head and pectoral fins. Then, with a series of short, sharp thrusts, it directs the prey into its mouth.

Divers sometimes find individual bowmouths resting near wrecks and coral bommies. They will not attack humans. They produce seven to nine live pups in each litter.

Trawl-net fishers occasionally take bowmouth guitarfish as bycatch. Along with the related whitespotted guitarfish (*Rhynchobatus djiddensis*), it is among the most sought-after elasmobranchs for shark fin soup. Consequently, there are concerns about overfishing.

FIELD NOTES

- Tropical Indo-Pacific, from East Africa to Australia and Japan
- Up to 9½' (2.9 m)
- Not aggressive
- Year-round
- Uncommon

The bowmouth guitarfish is likely to avoid humans, and certainly will not attack.

205

Atlantic Guitarfish

Rhinobatos lentiginosus

FIELD NOTES

- Northwestern Atlantic, from North Carolina, USA, to southern Mexico
- Reaches 2½' (75 cm)
- Harmless
- Year-round; most common off Florida, USA
- Reasonably common

Many of the 40 or so guitarfish species have a shovel-like head and a flattened, tapering tail. With a little imagination, their body shape resembles a guitar, hence their common name. The Atlantic guitarfish looks like some of the sharkfin guitarfishes in its general appearance. However, its dorsal fins are located closer to the tip of the tail (behind the pelvic fin tips), and the lower lobe of its caudal fin is much smaller than the upper lobe. It has a grayish to brownish upper surface with hundreds of small white spots. The adult Atlantic guitarfish differs from the related southern guitarfish (*Rhinobatos percellens*), which occurs from the Caribbean to Argentina, in having enlarged tubercles on the tip of its snout.

This is one of the smaller guitarfishes. It lives in warm temperate and tropical waters, mainly in the shallows from the intertidal zone to about 66' (20 m). Soft, sandy or muddy bottoms, or seagrasses, are its preferred habitats. It eats small, sand-dwelling mollusks and crustaceans, such as amphipods and small crabs. Some guitar-fishes are fussy feeders, selectively ingesting only the nutritious parts of their prey. For example, they will crush clams in their mouth and spit out the shell and gritty bits.

The Atlantic guitarfish is most common off Florida. Swimmers and waders see it at low tide on urban beaches, swimming near the water's edge, its dorsal and caudal fins exposed and its snout probing the sand for food. In the Indo-Pacific region, juvenile plain grayish brown giant guitarfish (*Rhinobatos typus*) are also common inshore, as they search for food over sand flats and in mangrove swamps and estuaries.

Larger guitarfish species may have litters of up to 29, but the Atlantic guitarfish only has about 6 pups, each about 8" (20 cm) long. Males are sexually mature at 19" (48 cm) long. The females bear live young.

The shovel-like head and the tapering tail of Atlantic guitar...

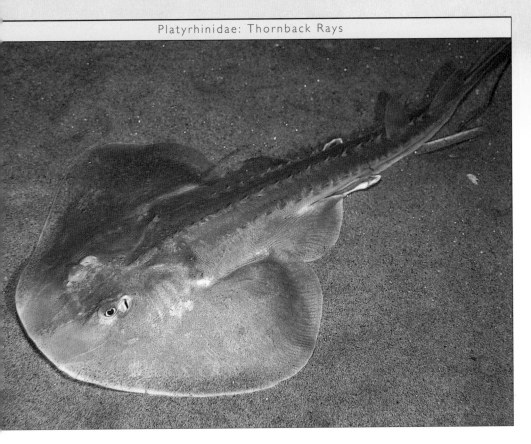

Thornback

Platyrhinoidis triseriata

Thornback rays take their common name from the rows of large thorny spines along their back and sometimes their tail. They are similar to some round-snouted guitarfish found in other parts of the world. These distantly related groups probably evolved similar body forms to adapt to similar lifestyles in different parts of the world. The thornback's disc is short and broad, and the snout is evenly rounded rather than triangular. The fine segmented cartilages that form the skeleton of the outer disc reach

FIELD NOTES

- Eastern Pacific from California, USA, to Mexico
- Almost 3' (90 cm)
- Harmless; be wary of sharp thorns
- Year-round
- Once plentiful off southern California

A close-up of mouth and nostrils on the underside of the thornback.

almost as far as the snout tip. Two narrow cartilages link the snout tip to the skull.

The brownish thornback has three rows of pale thorns. Its dorsal fins, near the tail tip, are of similar size, and the tail is much longer than the disc. It is similar to the Japanese thornback ray (Platyrhina sinensis), although this ray's thorns are confined to the central part of its disc and

around the eyes; the thornback's run along the back and tail.

The thornback lives in temperate and subtropical waters, mainly inshore on sandy and muddy bottoms. Divers occasionally see one around kelp beds, where its brownish upper surface blends well with the dark substrate. It rests in small groups for much of the day, remaining partly buried, with only its thorns protruding. These are sharp, and are probably used defensively against its main predators, small sharks. Although it is harmless, this ray should be treated with caution.

Little is known about the thornback's general biology. It is not a powerful swimmer and so it seems unlikely that it undertakes any long migrations. It seems to be more active at night, feeding on sand worms, sea shells, and small crustaceans, such as crabs and shrimps. Mating occurs at the end of summer.

207

Lesser Electric Ray

Narcine brasiliensis

Possibly the best known of the numbfishes, the lesser electric ray is small and brownish with dusty blotches. It belongs to a family whose taxonomy and biology are not well understood. It has a flattened, oval-shaped disc, and large pelvic fins. Oversized dorsal and caudal fins cover most of the rear of its tapering tail. It eats mainly sand worms, although it also eats small fishes and crustaceans.

The kidney-shaped electric organs of this ray are located in the middle of the pectoral fins. They account for about a sixth of its body weight. Each organ consists of a honeycomb of 280 to 430 columns, containing several hundred electric plates, which deliver a shock of less than 37 volts. This is so weak that it is unlikely to be a means of defense or even of stunning prey. Nevertheless, some fishers claim to have been knocked off their feet after inadvertently stepping on a ray—probably more from surprise than from the intensity of the shock.

In winter, the lesser electric ray moves farther offshore in warm temperate and tropical waters.

FIELD NOTES

■ Central-western Atlantic from North Carolina, USA, to northern Argentina, including the Gulf of Mexico
■ To 1½' (45 cm)
■ Capable of delivering a weak electric shock; otherwise, harmless
■ Summer
■ Reasonably common

The lesser electric ray (below), showing the dusty blotches of its upper surface.

During summer, it usually inhabits very shallow waters near the shore, where it is often caught in beach and trammel nets. Divers may also see it off sandy beaches if they search carefully. Often, only the eyes and parts of the head are visible because it spends long periods concealed under the sand. Barefoot anglers and waders may accidentally step on a buried ray and receive a minor shock. But this is essentially a harmless creature, and you would have to annoy it before it would discharge its organs in response.

Female lesser electric rays venture into the surf zone in summer to bear 2 to 17 live young. Like many sharks and rays, the color pattern of the pups is more intense than in the adult. Pups average about 4¼" (11 cm) at birth.

Spotted Electric Ray

Narke japonica

The spotted electric ray, also known as the Japanese numbfish, is one of the shortnose electric rays. This family of at least 12 species of small rays lives in the temperate and tropical Indo-Pacific, mainly on the outer continental shelf and upper slope, although the spotted electric ray does occur inshore. Like all the shortnose electric rays, its disc is almost oval in shape, with a short, thick tail—the general shape is like the Narcinidae. It has only one dorsal fin.

The spotted electric ray is reddish brown, with black or white spots on the upper surface. Its snout is short, and like other members of the family, its eyes are small. It lives on sandy bottoms, often near rocky reefs, where it remains hidden for long periods of time. For this reason, although it is quite common, divers are unlikely to come across it. It can become aggressive when annoyed, and is capable of delivering a small electric shock (up to

FIELD NOTES

- Northwestern Pacific, from Japan to the South China Sea
- To about 16" (40 cm)
- Capable of delivering a weak electric shock; otherwise, harmless
- Year-round; hard to find
- Not uncommon

80 volts), possibly for defensive reasons or to protect its territory. It feeds on small fish and crustaceans that live in the sand and sediment of its habitat. Its mouth is surrounded by a shallow groove, which allows the mouth to be projected forward to suck up the prey.

The female spotted electric ray gives birth to litters of up to five pups, which are born in early summer.

An unusual New Zealand relative, the blind electric ray (*Typhlonarke aysoni*), lives on the continental slope at depths of 655–2,950' (200–900 m). This little-known ray has minute eyes, concealed beneath a thin covering of skin, making them virtually useless for detecting prey. Instead, it uses electroreceptors. It also has a pelvic fin with a separate anterior lobe, which it can presumably use to prop itself up with when stalking prey.

blind electric ray

209

Shorttailed Electric Ray

Hypnos monopterygium

This ray is unique among the electric rays in having a very large, oval pectoral disc attached to a smaller disc formed from the pelvic fins. The ray takes on a most unusual shape if washed up dead on a beach, swelling in the hot sun to look like a flattened wooden coffin—its other common name is coffin ray. It has a very short tail, with two tiny dorsal fins near the equally small caudal fin. The soft skin lacks spines and denticles, and varies from a rather drab chocolate brown to pinkish or gray.

Shorttailed electric rays live near the coast in warm temperate and subtropical waters. They prefer sheltered habitats, such as muddy bays and estuaries, as well as the continental shelf to 720' (220 m). They are rarely seen because they conceal themselves so well. During the day they remain deeply buried, and they may also change color for camouflage.

This ray's electric organs, located centrally on each pectoral fin, are highly developed. They can deliver a strong shock to stun large prey and may also have a defensive role. Divers who accidentally place a hand on a ray's back will remember the experience for life. Adults feed at night, foraging for fish, worms, and crabs. The

mouth of this ray is capable of taking surprisingly large prey, including flounders up to half the size of its body.

Little is known about the biology of this viviparous ray. Females grow larger than males, and bear pups 3–4½" (8–11 cm) long.

> **FIELD NOTES**
> ■ Only in Australian seas
> ■ Probably 16" (40 cm), but reported up to 2' (60 cm)
> ■ Not aggressive, but capable of delivering a powerful shock if touched
> ■ Year-round; mostly seen at night
> ■ Reasonably common

The underside of a male shorttailed electric ray (above). Only the eyes and spiracles of the ray (left) are visible above the sand.

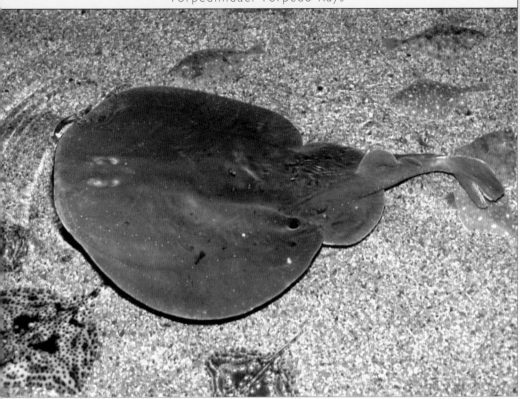

Atlantic Torpedo

Torpedo nobiliana

The Atlantic torpedo is also known as the great or black torpedo ray. It is enormous, and at 200 lb (90 kg), it is certainly the largest of all the electricity-producing rays. It has powerful electric organs in the pectoral disc that can discharge up to 220 volts. The upper surface of its disc is positively charged and the lower surface is negatively charged. During discharge, sea water or an unsuspecting animal creates a path for the current to travel from one side of the "battery" to the other. Without this, the ray could even electrocute itself.

The Atlantic torpedo uses its electric organs in defense and for predation. They may also be used for sensory purposes to detect prey, or as a means of communication. Its back varies in color from dark blue to brown or black, and may be dotted with small white spots and black blotches.

FIELD NOTES

■ Eastern Atlantic, from United Kingdom to South Africa, including Mediterranean; northwestern Atlantic, from Nova Scotia, Canada, to Florida, USA

■ Recorded up to 6' (1.82 m)

■ If surprised or annoyed, produces a powerful electric shock capable of stunning a diver

■ Year-round; rarely seen

■ Not uncommon; more prevalent in temperate seas

mouth and nostrils

All the torpedo rays have a large, flabby disc, broader than it is long, covered in smooth skin. The short tail has two dorsal fins, the first usually much larger than the second. The caudal fin has tall upper and lower lobes.

The Atlantic torpedo occurs inshore in temperate and tropical waters, to depths of about 1,475' (450 m). While it spends much of its time on the bottom, it is also known to migrate in open water. It is rarely encountered by divers.

Adults are efficient predators of bottom fishes such as small ground sharks, eels, flounders, and soles, whereas young torpedoes feed more on crustaceans. This ray prefers to stalk or ambush its prey under the substrate and eat it live (which makes it difficult to keep in aquariums).

For a ray, the Atlantic torpedo is highly fecund. Females are viviparous, delivering up to 60 pups after almost a year's gestation.

211

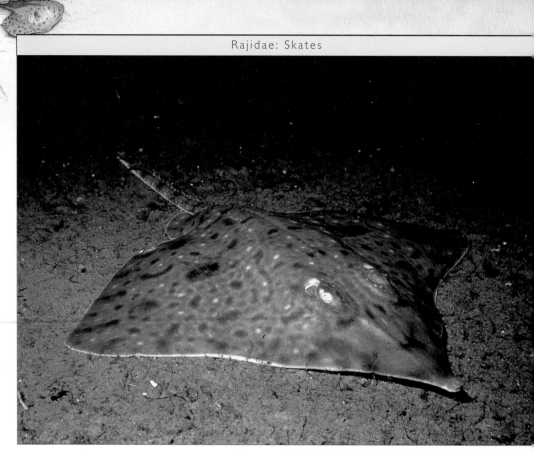

Rough Skate

Raja nasuta

The rough skate belongs to a group of skates whose common ancestor lived around the shores of the ancient Gondwana supercontinent more than 80 million years ago. This is indicated by the distribution of the modern-day group of skates, which are all found on the continental shelves off New Zealand, Australia, and South America.

The rough skate has a diamond-shaped disc with a very long, pointed snout. Its slender tail has three rows of thorns along its length, while its back is covered with minute prickles. It is usually grayish or brownish, with white spots and darker marbling. It occurs on soft bottoms to about 490' (150 m), usually beyond diving depths, although divers will occasionally see one.

Few details are known of the rough skate's biology. It lays horny, rectangular egg cases, which it attaches to the bottom by fine,

FIELD NOTES

- Southeastern Pacific off New Zealand
- Reaches almost 3⅓' (1 m)
- Harmless
- Year-round; rarely seen by divers
- Common

Port Davey skate

thread-like tendrils. Eggs develop slowly and young hatch after several months. Recently hatched skates can be identified by a belly scar where the yolk sac was attached. Empty egg cases, called "mermaid's purses," are found washed up on beaches after storms.

A close relative of the rough skate is the recently discovered Port Davey skate (*Raja* sp.). Of the more than 280 skates in the world, it is the only one that lives in brackish water. It is confined to two estuarine bays in the remote southwest of Tasmania, off southern Australia. It has a long, stiff snout, more typical of deep-ocean skates. This is presumably used for grubbing around for food in the fine silty bottom on which it lives. Given its restricted distribution, the habitat needs of this skate left over from the prehistoric past are likely to be very specific. Its population is small, probably no more than a few thousand individuals. This makes it particularly vulnerable to habitat degradation and overfishing.

Round Stingray

Urobatis halleri

FIELD NOTES

■ *Eastern Pacific, from northern California to Panama*

■ *Reaches 22" (56 cm)*

■ *Not aggressive; the stinging spine can cause minor injury*

■ *Year-round*

■ *Very common*

The round stingray, a member of the stingaree family, is plain brown with yellowish spots and reticulations. It has a circular disc, the upper surface of which is smooth, without tubercles. The related Cortez round stingray (*Urobatis maculatus*), from close by in Baja California and the Sea of Cortez, off Mexico, is similar in shape but has large black blotches over the disc. Stingarees can be mistaken for stingrays because of their similar body shape. However, stingarees have a shorter tail, which ends in a long, leaf-shaped caudal fin.

The round stingray lives mainly on muddy and sandy bottoms near the shore, to a depth of about 295' (90 m). In summer, it basks in warm shallow inlets, but remains in coastal waters during winter, only entering inlets to forage. It does not range far, rarely moving beyond an area of about a

The underside of a juvenile round stingray.

square mile. It seems sensitive to cold, and lives in water warmer than 50° F (10° C).

This ray feeds during the day on small bottom-dwelling crustaceans, bivalves, and sand worms. An efficient predator, it may use a combination of sight, smell, and vibration to detect prey. It uses its disc and mouth to "dig" for food in the substrate, and has also been seen nipping prey off sea-grass fronds. Divers may see a foraging ray in sheltered bays, or notice the outline of one buried in sediment.

Round stingrays mature early. The sexes segregate before the breeding season, and adult females live offshore until June, when they move in to coastal habitats to mate. Sexually aggressive males patrol the sandy strip between the deep sea-grass beds and the shore to select a suitable mate. He nibbles on her disc, then rolls beneath her and inserts a single clasper. Litters of one to six pups are born inshore in September, where they remain until maturity.

213

Banded Stingaree

Urolophus cruciatus

The banded stingaree is a highly distinctive ray, having smooth grayish to yellowish brown skin with a dark, banded pattern on its back, rather like a crucifix. Its tail is very short, fleshy, and highly flexible, usually with a single, large stinging spine on the upper half. If touched or provoked, the ray thrusts its tail toward its head, driving the spine and its venom into a victim. The pain varies from mild to excruciating, depending on the amount of venom and the location of the wound.

Adults are found concentrated in sheltered muddy bays and estuaries, although they are also common on sand patches near reefs and in caves. Divers and swimmers come across them all the time, frequently finding them with the more widely distributed, sparsely spotted stingaree (*Urolophus paucimaculatus*), a plain gray stingaree with a few white

The venomous barb (right) of the banded stingaree, and the view from below of a spotted stingaree (far right).

FIELD NOTES

■ Southwestern Pacific, off southern Australia

■ Reaches 20" (50 cm)

■ Not aggressive; however, the stinging spine can cause injury

■ Year-round

■ Very common

spots on its upper surface. The banded stingaree is quite inactive, and will often lie hidden under the substrate.

This habit of concealment can cause problems for divers and swimmers, as it's very easy to kneel or place a hand on a ray's back accidentally and become the target of its thrusting tail. Net fishers have been stung when sorting through a catch, so gloves should be used for handling.

Stingarees are viviparous; litters of two to four are born after a gestation of about three months. Male banded stingarees mature at about 10" (25 cm). During spring, small groups of females can be found resting on the bottom with their tails raised over their bodies like scorpions. This behavior may be related to courtship; however, the lives of stingarees are not well understood.

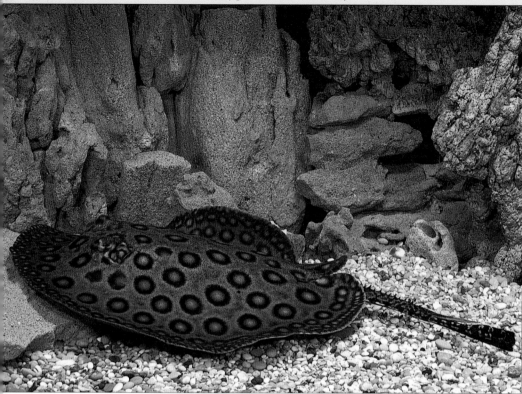

Ocellate River Ray

Potamotrygon motoro

River rays are members of a small stingray family that lives in the large lakes and river systems of tropical South America. They are confined to freshwater habitats and may be found more than 1,000 miles (1,600 km) from the sea. Many species are similar in appearance but inhabit separate waterways. They resemble both stingarees and stingrays in shape. The disc is oval or circular, and the skin is mostly smooth and lacks large thorns. The tail is slender, without dorsal fins but usually with thorns down the middle, and it tapers away beyond a well-developed stinging spine.

The ocellate river ray has a distinctive pattern of dark rings that are biggest on the middle of its back. Smaller, more compact rows of rings are located around the edge. This river ray, from the rivers of Paraguay, lives partly buried in the mud and sand of back eddies and side channels. Once buried, it is very difficult to see, and is therefore easy to step on.

The stinging spine, which is located near the tail tip, can strike well forward, making it a formidable defensive weapon. And despite its small size, the spine can inflict a very nasty wound that produces agonizing pain—it is

Potamotrygon reticulata, *the reticulated freshwater ray (above), another South American river ray, in its natural habitat.*

dreaded by the local fishermen, who catch this ray with nets. Deaths have been reported from stings on the abdomen and from secondary infections that result from unattended wounds.

Ocellate river rays breed between September and October, and the pups are born about five months later. The embryos gain nutrition while inside the mother from the egg yolk and the fluids secreted by her uterine tissues.

Rays that live in the sea need to store high concentrations of urea in the flesh and blood in order to osmoregulate (see p. 122) in their saline environment. However, freshwater river rays use far less urea to osmoregulate.

215

Southern Stingray

Dasyatis americana

The southern stingray has a large, flattened, somewhat angular disc, with a row of small tubercles running down its gray to brown back. The tail has a long skin fold along its under-surface and a low keel on top.

This stingray lives mainly in sandy habitats off beaches, in lagoons, and around sea-grass beds. It eats large invertebrates such as crabs, shrimps, and worms, and small bottom-dwelling fishes. It feeds mainly at night, remaining almost entirely concealed in the sand during the day. To dig into the substrate, it undulates the disc tips, dispersing the sand evenly.

Often, the first sign a diver notices is a pair of holes on the sandy bottom—the ray's spiracles, easily mistaken for its eyes. If approached with care, the ray usually stays still. The southern stingray is known for its social behavior with humans. At places in the Cayman Islands (see pp. 238–9), divers can hand-feed wild stingrays.

It is the long, dagger-like stinging spines on the tail that have given members of the stingray family their name and brought them unjustified infamy. Stingrays have been responsible for some

FIELD NOTES

■ Central-western Atlantic, from New Jersey, USA, to Brazil
■ At least 5' (1.5 m)
■ Not normally aggressive; the stinging spine can cause serious injury
■ Year-round
■ Common in some areas

The eye, with pupil protected from daylight by the lappet shield, and spiracle (above), and the venomous spine (left).

human deaths, but in almost all recorded cases, the attacks resulted from the carelessness or stupidity of the victim. Always treat stingrays with respect, and under no circumstances attempt to ride one. As well as delivering venom, the big stinging spines of the largest stingrays are as sharp as a butcher's knife. Cuts from repeated thrusts can cause more damage than the venom, particularly if a vital organ is struck, but such defensive behavior is used only if the animal is threatened or harassed. Stingrays are typically gentle and inquisitive, easily domesticated, and very popular in aquariums.

Mangrove Whipray

Himantura granulata

This stingray belongs to a group known as the whiprays, which take their name from their very long, thin, flexible tails. Most of the whiprays, including the attractively patterned leopard whipray (*Himantura undulata*) and reticulate whipray (*Himantura uarnak*), live near tropical coasts throughout the Indo-Pacific. Some species, such as the huge and possibly rare freshwater whipray (*Himantura chaophraya*), have adapted to life in rivers and estuaries, and have been seen flapping around in the shallows of muddy rivers as far as several hundred miles from the open sea.

The mangrove whipray is oval in shape, with a thick disc about as wide as it is long. The rough upper surface is dark brown to grayish brown in the center of the disc, merging to brown to slate gray in the outer edges. This is usually scattered with fine white spots. The ray is white underneath, with dark spots along the edges. It has a distinctive white, whip-like tail without skin folds and with one or more stinging spines. When a ray has

lost one of these stinging spines, it is usually possible to see a scar on the tail.

As well as occurring close inshore in tropical waters over sand flats and amongst coral, the mangrove whipray sometimes also dwells in mangrove habitats, as its name suggests. Divers occasionally encounter one in shallow waters. However, not a lot is known about the behavior and biology of this unusual stingray. Its diet includes small fishes and small crustaceans, such as crabs and shrimp. Females give birth to young that are about 11" (28 cm) wide and about 30½" (78 cm) in total length.

The leopard whipray is a large stingray with a distinctive, intricate pattern.

Bluespotted Ribbontail Ray

Taeniura lymma

The vivid ornamentation of the bluespotted ribbontail ray makes it immediately recognizable. It has bright blue spots on top of its flat, oval-shaped disc, and a distinctive blue stripe along each side of the tail. A broad flap of whitish or bluish skin extends along its undersurface to the tail tip.

The bluespotted ribbontail ray is found alone or in small groups, mostly in shallow water over reef flats. It has also been observed around coral rubble and shipwreck debris at depths of 65' (20 m). It moves over tidal flats, usually at high tide, to feed on sand worms, shrimps, hermit crabs, and small fishes. As the tide recedes, it retires to the protective covering of coral cervices. It rarely buries itself completely in the substrate, and divers and snorkelers will often detect this ray by its distinctive ribbon-like tail poking out from a crack or crevice beneath the coral.

FIELD NOTES

- Tropical Indo-Pacific, from southern Africa and the Red Sea to the Solomon Islands
- Up to 2¼' (70 cm) long
- Timid; stinging spines can cause minor injury
- Year-round
- Very common

This is the most abundant of the inshore reef-dwelling rays, and it is often encountered by divers and snorkelers in the Indo-Pacific region. The best viewing sites are over coral reef shallows and on sand patches beneath coral bommies.

Being rather timid, the ribbontail ray will usually swim away frantically if approached or disturbed by divers. The large eyes, which extend above the head on short stalks, give it excellent peripheral vision.

Unlike most other stingrays, its poisonous spines, often two in number, are located closer to the tip than the base of its tail. This enables these rays to strike at potential enemies well forward of their heads.

The bluespotted ribbontail ray produces about seven live young in every litter. Each pup is born with the distinctive blue markings of its parents, in miniature.

The tail of the bluespotted ribbontail ray is well armed, often with two venomous spines, set back near the tip.

Australian Butterfly Ray

Gymnura australis

The characteristic features of this unusual fish are best summed up by several of s common names—Australian utterfly ray, and also diamond ray nd rattail ray. It has a very large nd flat diamond-shaped disc with ectoral "wings" reminiscent of a utterfly. It is ornamented with a elicate greenish gray mosaic overlaid with a eppering of small black spots. The thin, stumpy il, with its alternating black and white rings, as a small dorsal fin but no caudal fin. It also cks a stinging spine, although related ecies may have a short one near e base of the tail.

Little is known about the utterfly rays, but their habits and iet are possibly similar to their latives, the stingrays. They live mostly n the bottom in tropical waters, to epths of about 165' (50 m). They ury themselves deep into the sedients, their wafer-thin bodies needing nly a shallow covering of sand for oncealment. Not surprisingly, divers most never see them. Their main food a variety of crustaceans and small fishes, ch as gobies and dragonets.

FIELD NOTES

- Off northern Australia and New Guinea
- Up to 2⅓' (73 cm) wide
- Harmless; lacks a stinging spine
- Rarely seen by divers
- Reasonably common in some areas

Males mature at about 14–16" (35–40 cm) and are much smaller than the largest females. Females bear live young, which are nourished while in the uterus partly from their yolk sac but mostly from fluid secreted by the uterine wall. An embryo lies in the uterus with its snout tucked in and its pectoral "wings" folded one over the other below its belly. Pairs wrap around each other head to head. The pups are born in this position and unfold soon after emerging from the mother.

The Australian butterfly ray is regularly caught as bycatch by prawn trawlers. Although they are harmless, they tend to flap around vigorously once on deck. One African species is said to grunt loudly by expelling trapped air from its mouth when brought on deck.

upper tooth

219

Spotted Eagle Ray

Aetobatus narinari

The spotted eagle ray is the most common and most widely distributed of the eagle rays. Its distinctive pattern of white spots or rings on its greenish to pinkish back makes it easily recognizable. Its flattened snout, like the beak of a duck, gives rise to its alternative common name, duckbill ray. A small stinging spine is located near the tail base.

The spotted eagle ray occurs near continents, islands, and atolls in tropical waters less than 200' (60 m) deep. It is extremely active, swimming for long periods both in the water column and near the bottom. With its graceful action, it appears to fly and glide along, slowly moving its pectoral fins like the wings of a bird. It is powerfully built and can accelerate rapidly, swerving and twisting away from hungry hammerheads or tiger sharks at extraordinary speeds to find

FIELD NOTES

- Worldwide in tropical and temperate seas
- Reported to attain 11½' (3.5 m) in width but typically smaller, to 6' (1.8 m)
- Timid; the stinging spine can cause injury
- Year-round
- Common

safety in the shallows. Adults will frolic near the surface, at times leaping well clear of the water in a spectacular display. Their pectoral fins, when thus exposed, resemble a thrashing shark—causing more than one quick evacuation of a swimming beach. For a diver, the sight of a school of 100 or more of these rays cruising through clear blue water is an unforgettable experience. They may be wary if approached.

This ray's teeth, a series of flattened bony plates that form the beak, are designed to crush and mill hard-shelled invertebrates like oysters, clams, and snails. Octopuses, shrimp, and fishes are also eaten. The ray digs up food from the bottom with its flattened snout and pectoral fins. The spotted eagle ray bears live young after 12 months' gestation. Copulation is brief and takes place belly to belly. Females may mate with up to four males over about an hour, and produce one to four pups per litter. Sharks often follow birthing females to feed on newborn pups.

A spotted eagle ray in full "flight."

Bat Ray

Myliobatis californicus

The bat ray has a broad, angular disc, from which the head protrudes in a rounded, lobe-like snout. It has a long whip-like tail (sometimes damaged by predators), with no caudal fin and up to five short stinging spines just behind the base. The spines, which are preceded by a small dorsal fin, are used to deter predators. Its heavily built body can be either smooth or have small spines along its midline or around the eyes.

This ray occurs alone or in groups, mainly inshore in temperate waters less than 165' (50 m) deep. It spends most time on the bottom, resting on kelp or in large hollows in the sand and mud when it isn't feeding. If disturbed, it will emerge from its hollow and prop itself up on the tips of its pectoral fins with its back arched in a "starting position." It may swim away with explosive acceleration if divers get too close.

The bat ray feeds on a variety of small animals, including shellfishes, crustaceans, and small bony fishes, which it grubs from the bottom. The diet changes with age. Clams are a

FIELD NOTES
- Eastern Pacific, from the Sea of Cortez to Oregon, USA
- Up to about 6' (1.8 m)
- Harmless to divers; if handled carelessly, the stinging spine can cause a painful wound
- Year-round
- Common

favorite food of juveniles, while worms are eaten more often by adults. The teeth are fused to form grinding plates. Hard-shelled prey are partly ingested, heavily crushed by the jaws, and spat out. The nutritious flesh is then reingested selectively.

The mating behavior of the bat ray is fairly well known. The male swims in synchrony below the belly of a receptive female. Thorns around his eyes poke into the female's undersurface during mating, helping the couple to maintain position while the male twists a single clasper upward and into the cloaca. Up to 10 pups, each about 1' (30 cm) wide, are born a year later.

This school of bat rays, photographed gliding gracefully through Californian waters, is a remarkable sight.

Javanese Cownose Ray

Rhinoptera javanica

The Javanese cownose ray is dark grayish brown on the back. Its head is separate from the broad, diamond-shaped disc, and has a characteristic pugnose snout. This is concave at the front and overlays the rostral lobe, a lobe with such a marked indentation that it looks like two fleshy lobes rather than one.

FIELD NOTES

■ Indo-Pacific, from southern Africa to eastern Indonesia; possibly northern Australia

■ At least 5' (1.5 m) wide

■ One or more small stinging spines on the tail can cause a minor wound

■ Year-round

■ Not uncommon

The Javanese cownose ray flaps its powerful pectoral fins in lazy, lateral undulations to swim almost continuously, rarely ever resting on the bottom. It swims mostly in groups—a related species, the Pacific cownose ray (*Rhinoptera steindachneri*), congregates in schools of more than 1,000. The Javanese cownose is most common along tropical coastlines and in shallow, muddy bays.

This large ray is thought to make daily migrations inshore to feed almost exclusively on bottom-dwelling crustaceans and bivalves. It exposes the buried shellfish by beating its "wings" near the bottom, then grabs it with its rostral lobes. It partly ingests the prey, crushes it between its strong tooth plates, spits it out, then retrieves and swallows the smaller fragments.

Divers sometimes see large schools working their way over shallow sand flats during the day but this ray's timidity makes encounters rare.

Females copulate belly to belly with several males in succession. The young, one to six per litter, are nourished inside the mother, first by the egg yolk and then by uterine secretions.

A school of Pacific cownose rays near the Galapagos Islands.

Manta Ray

Manta birostris

M antas are the largest living rays and among the most majestic of shes. Folklore may have inflated eir width to more than 29½' m), but the reality is still very npressive. A 16½' (5 m) manta und in the Bahamas weighed ore than 3,000 lb (1,360 kg).

The manta is related to the gle and cownose rays, and has a milar diamond-shaped disc. But its tail is short d lacks a stinging spine, and its mouth is ordered by two long, lobe-like extensions of e pectoral fins—cephalic lobes. Mantas differ om smaller devil rays in having a relatively rger mouth, located at the snout tip rather than nder the head. The color is not uniform, but is sually blackish above and pale below, ith light and dark blotches.

Manta rays occur roughout the tropical as of the world, d populations in ch ocean may, fact, be different ecies. They live shore, close to the ast, as well as out in

FIELD NOTES

■ Worldwide in all tropical seas
■ Reported to 29½' (9 m) wide, but probably to about 22' (6.7 m)
■ Harmless unless provoked
■ Year-round; numbers vary according to season and location
■ Moderately common in most areas

the open sea. They are mostly solitary or swim in small groups. Superbly adapted to pelagic life, they are both graceful and powerful movers, probably swimming almost continuously. They are seen along reef fringes near deep water and are also sighted from boats, as they bask or feed near the surface. Unless harassed, they are harmless.

A manta ray funnels microscopic plankton toward its mouth using the extended cephalic lobes, which remain folded spirally when not in use. Then, with a sophisticated filtering system, it sieves the plankton from the same water that it uses to breathe. Large rays also feed on pelagic crustaceans and small fishes and have been seen in feeding frenzies with sharks and other large predators.

Females produce one or two pups at a time, sometimes ejecting their young into the air when breaching.

A feeding manta displays its huge gill arches.

223

THE DEEP-WATER RAYS

Almost half of the world's rays occur only in the cool, deep waters of the outer continental shelves and slopes. They are often caught accidentally during deep-sea fishing operations—this is really the only time they are encountered by people. Many of these species are new to science or are known from only a few specimens, so we understand very little about their biology and lifestyle.

SKATES
Rajidae

Skates are the main group of deep-water rays. While a few true skates (Rajinae), also known as hard-nose skates, live in shallower waters close to shore (see p. 212), most of the 280 or so species live in deeper waters, on soft bottoms down to depths of 9,840' (3,000 m) or more. They are found throughout the world along continental margins, except around coral islands in the Pacific, the only place where they do not occur. Most have rather restricted ranges, and the skates of nearby regions are often quite distinct.

leg skate
Anacanthobatis sp.

The family is divided into two primary groups, the softnose skates (Arhynchobatinae) and the true skates (Rajinae). These groups are essentially similar in appearance. Their discs are very flattened and vary according to sex, ranging from round to almost diamond-shaped. They have a rather short, slender tail that usually has two small dorsal fins and a low caudal fin near its tip.

The main difference between the two groups is the flexibility of their snouts, which is based on the shape and strength of the supporting cartilage. As their name suggests, the softnose skates have a floppy snout, while most true skates have a firm and rigid snout supported by cartilage.

One of the most unusual groups of true skates is the leg skates (*Anacanthobatis*). They are small, evolutionarily advanced rays with a very flattened, leaf-shaped disc and a thin tail without fins. Each pelvic fin is divided into two distinct lobes. The front lobes resemble thin legs and are presumably used for "walking" over the seabed. Mature males of some species have an extended,

blue skate
Notoraja sp.

embryos may take from several months to more than one and a half years to develop and hatch. Young skates are virtually identical to the mother in shape, although their denticles and thorns develop and harden after birth.

Skates are caught for their meat. The wings, or pectoral flaps, fetch high prices and are eaten in some parts of the world. Given the limited distribution of some skates, they are susceptible to overfishing in certain regions.

SIXGILL STINGRAYS
Hexatrygonidae

roboscis-like
out, which they use
r probing around in the sediments for food.
ost of the 18 or so known species of leg skate
ve on continental slopes. They are rarely
ught, even by trawlers.

Skates vary greatly in size. The species of
me genera, such as *Pavoraja*, are less than
5" (40 cm) long, with males maturing at
out 11" (27 cm). Members of the more
biquitous genus *Dipturus* may reach
' (2 m) long and weigh 200 lb
0 kg) or more.

The skin of skates is either smooth or
overed in tiny denticles. Larger denticles,
nown as thorns, are sometimes present
round the eyes and along the back and
e upper surface of the tail. Mature
ales may have additional patches
f very sharp thorns beside the
yes (malars) and also in the
iddle of each pectoral fin
lars), which they use to
rasp females during mating. In many species,
e alar thorns can be retracted into the disc,
aking them difficult to notice. However, they
e well known to those who handle skates
equently, as is the sight of a careless angler
ith a skate dangling from a bloody hand.

Skates feed on bottom-dwelling animals,
ch as soft-shelled mollusks, sand worms,
rustaceans, and small fishes. Some species are
nown to have rudimentary electric organs that
ay be used to locate prey.

Female skates are fertilized internally by the
ale's very well developed claspers, which
ave a series of hooks and spines for grasping
e female during mating. The females lay
orny egg cases and attach them to the ocean
ottom with sticky threads and tendrils. The

The sixgill stingray (*Hexatrygon bickelli*) belongs to the deep-water family of sixgill rays. They live on the midcontinental slopes of the Indo-Pacific, and are more closely related to stingrays than to skates.

The shape of the rear part of the disc and the tail, with one or two stinging spines and a caudal fin, is reminiscent of a stingaree. However, the body is flabby and the features of its head are distinctive and unique.

Unlike all other rays, which have five pairs of gill openings, this ray has six. It has very small eyes and a long, flattened, triangular snout filled with fluid. The snout, which is covered with sensory pores, is highly flexible and is used to detect food. A sixgill ray that had been trawled was observed moving the tip of its snout like a finger.

This ray is likely to bear live young, but like so many of the deep-sea rays, almost nothing is known of its biology.

225

The wonders of the sea are as marvelous as the glories of the heavens.

MATTHEW FONTAINE MAURY (1806–73), American scientist

CHAPTER EIGHT

ENCOUNTERS *with* SHARKS *and* RAYS

USING ENCOUNTERS
with SHARKS *and* RAYS

The challenge of observing sharks and rays can take you from

the Red Sea to the Galapagos via the Great Barrier Reef.

The illustrated banding is a visual point
to indicate that the page is about a site

The following pages feature
21 marine environments where
you have the chance of coming
face to face with a shark or ray in its
own habitat. Some enthusiasts prefer
particular types of encounters, or they
become fascinated with certain aspects
of the behavior of these mysterious
creatures. Whatever your interest,
careful planning is essential if you
are to have the best chance of seeing
sharks and rays in the wild. This
guide will help you to choose the
destination and diving experience
that you seek.

Vivid color plates give a graphic sense of
the principal shark or ray that may be
encountered at the site, or of unique
features and particular types of flora and
fauna that may be of special interest.

The **text** describes the habitat at
the site, the species that can be
seen here, and the behavior
you might witness. It warns of
possible hazards and advises on
equipment that you will need to
dive at the site. It also covers the
other attractions of the region,
the features likely to distract you
from looking for sharks and rays.

Encounters with Sharks and Rays

Ras Muhammad
Egypt

The parched landscape
and rugged moun-
tains of the Sinai
Peninsula in Egypt seem
lifeless. But beneath the
sapphire waters of the Red
Sea dwells a kaleidoscope
of living color. Where the
southern tip of the peninsula plunges into the sea at
Ras Muhammad, incredible
shallow reef flats near the
shoreline give way to sheer
coral walls disappearing into the depths below.
Clouds of Anthias and glassfish shimmer among
the undulating soft corals. And shafts of desert
sunlight penetrate deep into the blue abyss to
reveal patrolling gray reef sharks (see p. 170).
Shark Observatory, one of the best shark sites,
is a stretch of the Ras Muhammad coral wall.
Divers swimming here will see jacks, tuna,
barracuda, and other pelagic marine life
traversing the deep ocean. Only the wall is there
to orientate you, with the seemingly bottomless
sea dropping away beneath you. It is quite
common to turn a corner and come face to face
with several gray reef sharks searching for food or
checking their territory for competitors. It is
hard to decide who gets the bigger surprise, as

*Anthias, famous for their vivid color, dart about the coral
reef (top); and the Red Sea and Sinai Desert (above).*

the sharks veer out into the
limitless blue and the
divers kick toward the
security of the wall.
Gray reef sharks are
curious and territorial, and
pay much attention to
divers, circling constantly,
coming and going, and
sometimes even becoming
slightly aggressive. But
during December and
January, you may have
the rare privilege of witnessing groups of 5 to
10 gray reef sharks that completely ignore you
because they are engrossed in mating behavior.
Females circle in the water off the reef, within 30
feet (10 m) of you. A male will dash into the
group, single out a female and pursue her,
repeatedly biting her flanks. This action is
thought to promote ovulation, and the female's
thick skin has evolved to deal with it. While you
are unlikely to see an actual coupling, these
encounters provide opportunities for unique
observations and rare photos or video footage.
Shark Reef and Jolanda Reef are two small
submerged reefs just below the surface, a short
swim from the tip of the peninsula. On their
ocean side, these reefs again drop away in coral

248

Ras Muhammad

other gray reef large s and also look itetips ed and (see nta rays one of

manner of species could hallows at Jolanda Reef, wreckage from the k in 1981, beautiful rays (see p. 218) cruise

rine Park is considered dive sites. With its w reefs, coral walls, and s a site for both divers the reef is easy. Jeeps,

A reef shark patrols its territory (left); and a handsome yellowbar angelfish (below).

live-aboards, and day boats operate from the nearby resort town of Sharm El Sheikh.

EQUIPMENT

Scuba and snorkeling equipment is available for hire or purchase, but the range is limited and expensive. If possible, bring your own. The Red Sea can be cool for a tropical destination, so 5 mm wetsuits are recommended for the cool season, and 3 mm wetsuits should be worn at other times.

SPECIAL FEATURES

Divers and snorkelers can see a spectacular variety of fish at Ras Muhammad, but two species are worth special attention. Giant Napoleon wrasse are particularly striking and endearing, and are likely to accompany divers in the hope of a handout—a practice discouraged these days. They look at you with big eyes that revolve like ball turrets as they seek out more generous divers. Yellowbar angelfish, unique to Africa and the Red Sea, have markings on their sides in the shape of Africa. **KD**

RAVELER'S NOTES

litions · Dive logistics Day boats, live-
nore seas aboards, and shore-
ks and based diving from jeeps;
g the pre-booking recommended.
Accommodation Excellent range, days, from budget hotels to five-star resorts.
winds **Notes** Very cosmopolitan dive travelers;
d be prepared for many different diving techniques and attitudes. Heed any political advisories for Egypt and neighboring countries.

Traveler's Notes: These provide brief details on when to visit, the weather, water temperature, and possible hazards that might be encountered. They also list the type of diving amenities that are available, live-aboards or day trips, and what level of accommodation to expect.

249

San Diego

United States of America

The California Bight lies between the southern Californian coast and Channel Islands, which dot the temperate Pacific waters off the American West Coast. The warm temperate marine communities of this region make it one of the world's richest oceanographic areas. Inshore is dominated by golden kelp forests. Offshore are the deeps of the blue-water channel. This is the place for diving with blue sharks (see p. 183).

Dive boats transport groups of divers 12 to 15 miles (19 to 24 km) off the coast from San Diego. The Coronados Islands rise in peaks to the south; the long, rounded mountain of San Clemente Island breaks up the western horizon. All around is the vast Pacific, sometimes green, sometimes blue, some days glassy and sunlit, others choppy and covered in fog. April to September is the best time to dive to avoid the strong winds and big seas of winter.

The dive boat sets a sea anchor, then a roomy shark cage with a door at the rear is lowered over the side. This hangs about 10 to

A blue shark (above) eyes a diver in a protective chain-mail suit. Forests of giant kelp (left) thrive close to shore.

15 feet (3 to 4.5 m) below the surface. A divemaster in a protective chain-mail suit (see p. 76) accompanies three divers to the cage. It feels strange to stand in a barred cage suspended in the open ocean, with the clear blue depths falling away, the invisible bottom more than a mile below. You wait, nervously, searching the vast, dimensionless space for a flash of brilliantly blue shark.

As soon as the divemaster, still outside the cage, begins to release bait and chum, they start to arrive—speeding, graceful blues—first 1, then 6, soon as many as 20. The sharks snap at the bait and bump the cage, wanting to test its taste and texture. In the midst of this rush of blue muscle, white teeth, and adrenalin, the practiced (and suit-protected) divemaster allows a small blue shark to bite his chain-mail-clad arm. Photographers, safe inside the cage only inches away, consume film faster

Harbor seals (right) visit the Channel Islands. Hilton's aeolid (below), a local marine snail.

han the sharks do bait. You will soon become accustomed to the excitement, and revel in the spectacle. Elegant juveniles barely 2 feet (60 cm) long jet between adults up to 7 feet (2.1 m) and more, all feeding voraciously. A mako might race past in the distance, while strange, seemingly tailless mola molas (ocean sunfish) swim round at a leisurely pace.

The bait and chum are soon gone, and once the ocean current has dispersed any remaining food scraps, the blues begin to slip away, back into the vast ocean. Divers can now return to the boat, being especially careful as they go.

EQUIPMENT

Only scuba diving is possible in the shark cage. A full ³⁄₁₆ inch (5 mm) wetsuit is recommended, but some divers prefer a dry suit as it can get cool waiting in the cage. Dive guides will help you get your weight right for the stationary cage.

SPECIAL FEATURES

California gray whales migrate through the channel in winter on their way to their calving grounds in Mexico. Blue whales also visit the California Bight, and the second known specimen of the megamouth shark (see p. 154) was caught in the vicinity.

You should explore the kelp forests close to shore. Beneath the canopy of massed fronds there are colorful fish, lobsters, eels, swellsharks (see p. 163), leopard sharks (see p. 168), California hornsharks (see p. 142), and even the occasional stingray. Watch especially for California's state marine fish, the bright golden (and pugnacious) garibaldi.

The Channel Islands, which can be visited by boat, are a refuge for seals, sea lions, whales, and sea birds. Back on the mainland, Sea World, in San Diego, offers one of the world's best introductions to living sharks. The Steven Birch Aquarium, of the famous Scripps Institution of Oceanography, has exhibits on local sea life and international marine research. LT

TRAVELER'S NOTES

When to visit *Best diving conditions Apr–Sept*
Weather *Temperate year-round; summer mornings can be foggy, clearing by midday; rain and rough conditions most likely Dec–Feb*
Water temperature *59–70° F (15–21° C)*

Dive logistics *Cage diving with scuba gear from day boats or live-aboards for trips of three days; pre-booking essential; shore diving and snorkeling around kelp beds and rocky points*
Accommodation *A wide selection is available in San Diego, ranging from budget motels to bed-and-breakfast guesthouses and five-star resorts*

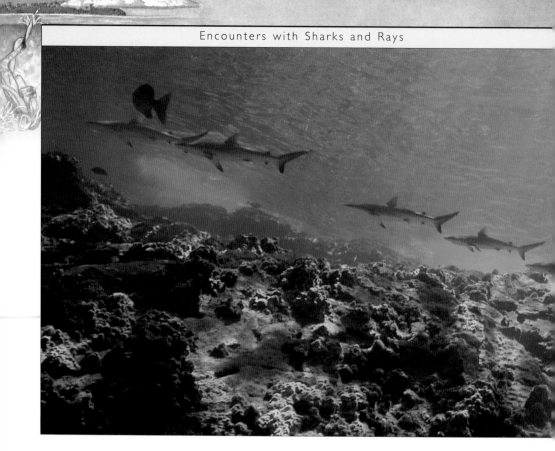

Kona Coast

United States of America

The largest and most diverse of the Hawaiian islands is Hawaii, also called Big Island. Its western coast is known as the Kona Coast, and extends more than 85 miles (135 km). This area is a mecca for divers—calm, clear waters, massive corals, and abundant marine life. Among the many highlights are nightly manta ray "rush hours."

At night, the coastal luxury hotels in the Kona and Kohala districts shine floodlights over nearby rocky points into the shallows below. The powerful beams attract swarms of plankton, the smallest of sea creatures, and the food of choice for giant, filter-feeding manta rays (see p. 223). With the lights and the plankton come the mantas, ready to feed. Undoubtedly, they have been in the area for years, but "Manta Mania," the ad hoc festival of lights, people, and rays, is a recent phenomenon.

While there are no guarantees that the manta rays will show up, they usually do, especially on calm, moonless nights. Those who like to stay dry can watch them from a hotel balcony, or take one of the glass-bottom boats that depart from the harbor at Kailua-Kona. Alternatively, don snorkeling or diving gear and join these huge and graceful creatures in the water. Some snorkelers and divers are dropped off by dive operators' boats, while others simply swim out from shore. Night swims with rays can be enjoyed in many places along the coast. For a more private experience, ask a local diver.

A popular site is the area off Kona Surf Hotel at Keauhou Bay, about 6 miles (9.5 km) south of the town of Kailua-Kona. Here, the water is 15 to 20 feet (4.5 to 6 m) deep, usually with very

The open mouth of a feeding manta ray (left); and (below) the eastern coastline of Hawaii Volcanoes National Park.

A convoy of gray reef sharks (above); and a diver checks out a spotted pufferfish (left).

ittle surge. Floodlights make the water glow a luminous pale green. To a diver looking up from the bottom, the lights seem to blink occasionally. The blink is really huge mantas passing overhead, their 12 foot (3.6 m) wide bodies eclipsing the light.

The water is often so clear that you can see myriad tiny plankton swarming near the surface, and look into the open mouth of a feeding manta. And you can easily distinguish the gray and black spots on the ray's pure white underside as it passes close overhead in slow, balletic flight. It is a great temptation to touch or hold on to a passing manta, but such behavior is strongly discouraged.

EQUIPMENT

Snorkeling is the best way to see the manta rays. A Lycra suit or 3 mm wetsuit affords good protection and warmth. Dive operators are based around the Kona district and the town of Kailua-Kona; most offer rentals and sell a range of equipment.

SPECIAL FEATURES

Hawaii is one of the best served and safest places to dive in the world. Dive boats cover the entire western coast, while excellent snorkeling areas also abound. Among bays, coves, lagoons, lava flows, and undersea lava tubes, an alert diver can find almost 600 species of fish—176 of them are found only in Hawaii.

Good encounters with a number of shark and ray species are possible. At particular sites along the western coast, you are likely to see whitetip and blacktip reef sharks, scalloped hammerheads, and eagle rays. You might also see whale sharks, tiger sharks, Galapagos sharks, gray reef sharks, even the occasional oceanic whitetip.

In winter and early spring, huge humpback whales fill these waters with song, vaulting into the air off Hawaii and the nearby island of Maui. Above ground, there is the spectacle of Hawaii Volcanoes National Park to be explored. LT

TRAVELER'S NOTES

When to visit Fine year-round; best months for mantas May–Nov; humpback whale season Dec–May

Weather Warm days and cool nights; 70–85° F (21–29° C); gentle to brisk northeast trade winds; rainy Dec–Feb

Water temperature 74–82° F (23–28° C)

Hazards Venomous animals include medusae and Portuguese man-of-war

Dive logistics Snorkeling from shore; day boats and live-aboards for week-long trips (pre-booking essential) offer access to sites along the Kona Coast

Accommodation A wide range, from beach camping and budget hotels to five-star resorts

Notes Bernice P. Bishop Museum, the archive of Hawaiian culture in Honolulu, has many artifacts relating to sharks

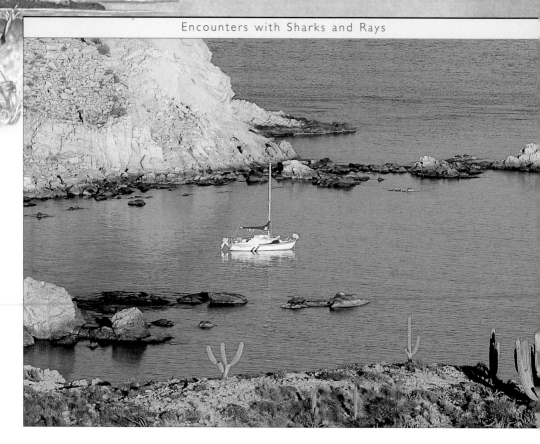

Sea of Cortez

Mexico

The strikingly beautiful Sea of Cortez is formed by the long peninsula of Baja California to the west and the mainland of Mexico to the east. To people who live here or visit, the Gulf is clearly a special place, where stark, rocky desert meets this inland sea's sparkling waters.

A complex system of currents divides the Gulf into a cooler northern half and a warmer southern half. Both offer fine diving, but fans of sharks and rays prefer the warmer waters around the major port of the Baja peninsula, La Paz, and adjacent islands. Divers usually fly to La Paz and join a live-aboard boat.

High on the desired site list is a seamount, El Bajo, just east of Isla Espiritu Santo. In this group of rocky pinnacles, 60 feet (18 m) below the surface, moray eels seem to occupy every crevice. Shoals of fish abound and Pacific manta rays (see p. 223), billfish, and an occasional finback whale or whale shark (see p. 151) may also swim by. But schools of hundreds of scalloped hammerhead sharks (see p. 188), with adults up to 12 feet (3.6 m) long, are the main

Elephant Rock (above), off Isla Santa Catalina; and scalloped hammerheads approaching (left).

attraction. The boat uses sonar to locate the underwater pinnacles and divers drop down to look up at the grand fleet of sharks, all headed in the same direction, schooling around the pinnacles.

Despite continued study and many creative explanations, scientists are still not certain why the hammerheads do this.

Isla Las Animas to the north is one of the most exciting and colorful dive spots in the Sea of Cortez. Rock walls are dominated by sea fans and gorgonians and are dense with invertebrate life. Schooling jacks number in the hundreds and there are underwater caves for the adventurous, plus more opportunities for viewing the hammerheads and other pelagic species.

Isla Los Islotes, just north of Isla Espiritu Santo, hosts a sea lion rookery. The island's east end, with a drop-off into deep water with many detached boulders, is good for sighting big fish.

Although spearfishing is not permitted now, years of overfishing and careless practices have

234

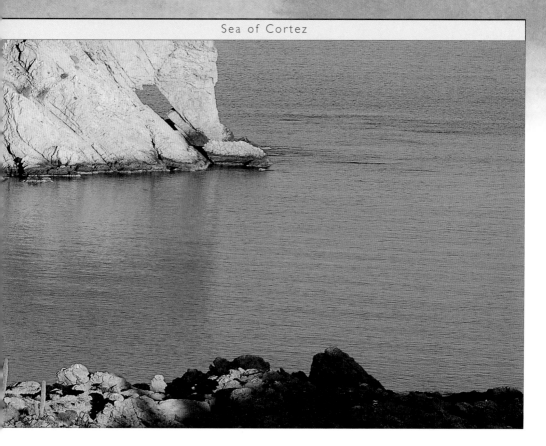

jeopardized the Gulf's ecological health. Baja's dive operators, Mexican and American alike, are dedicated to preserving its fragile beauty. The area is still rich in marine life, although numbers of large groupers and shellfish are declining.

EQUIPMENT

Dive shops in La Paz are well-equipped but it's best to travel with your own gear. Live-aboards provide weights and tanks. Night-diving is popular and worthwhile. Divers often bring good diving lights, batteries, and "cool light" sticks. On the boat deck, a 5 mm wetsuit can become unbearably warm, but it feels good in the water, especially during winter.

SPECIAL FEATURES

Isolated small coral heads occur throughout the southern Gulf, but Cabo Pulmo, south of La Paz, can be said to have the only living coral reef on the Pacific coast of North America. Many

reef fish will be recognized as relatives of central and South Pacific species. Farther offshore, fields of garden eels wave sinuously in the current, half their bodies burrowed into the sand while their big eyes search the water for plankton to snatch into mouths the diameter of a soda straw. Where rocks meet the sand at Cabo Pulmo and farther north toward La Paz, a sharp-eyed diver may see the rough-skinned Mexican hornshark, discovered near here in 1972.

In spring, the Sea of Cortez is a good place for sighting whales, including gray whales, finback whales, and the occasional 80 foot (24 m) blue whale. LT

TRAVELER'S NOTES

When to visit Year-round; preferred diving season June–Dec

Weather Generally temperate to hot; 100° F (38° C) or more June–Sept; strong winds and tropical storms occur infrequently May–Oct

Water temperature 70–80° F (21–27° C) June–Nov; 61–70° F (16–21° C) Dec–May

Hazards Variable weather conditions and occasional strong tidal currents

Dive logistics Day boats operate from La Paz and Cabo San Lucas; live-aboards offer 3–10 day excursions to Gulf Islands; pre-booking advised

Accommodation La Paz has a full range, from pensions, comfortable hotels, to high-rise luxury hotels

Rainbow parrotfish (above left) are a colorful sight; and a rookery of Californian sea lions (above), basking in the Baja sun.

235

Revillagigedo Islands

Mexico

If a friend asks you to dive at "Revillagigedo," you could end up in the cold waters off Revillagigedo Island in Alaska. Or—and this is our recommendation—you could be diving in warm Mexican waters, far south of the tip of Baja California. Whichever island you visit, most people pronounce it "Ree-vee-yah-hee-hey-do."

The Mexican Revillagigedo archipelago is 300 miles (480 km) south-southwest of the tip of Baja and 370 miles (590 km) west-southwest of Cape Corrientes on the Mexican mainland. The islands, uninhabited except for a Mexican naval installation on Socorro Island, are made up of numerous pinnacles and oceanic rocks. The major islands, spread over a large distance, include San Benedicto, Roca Partida, Clarion, and the largest, Socorro, which rises to 3,707 feet (1,130 m) with 110 square miles (285 sq km) of emergent land. Like most Pacific oceanic islands, the Revillagigedos are volcanic—San Benedicto's last eruption took place in the 1950s.

The great attractions for divers are the large pelagic sharks and schooling tuna that share these remote waters with huge manta rays (see p. 223). As well as the scores of giant mantas, a typical visitor's species list includes large scalloped hammerheads (see p. 188), Galapagos sharks (see p. 173), tiger sharks (see p. 181), and schools of jacks, tuna, and wahoo.

Comfortable live-aboard dive vessels depart from Cabo San Lucas, on the tip of the Baja peninsula, and usually spend 7 to 10 days visiting Socorro and San Benedicto. Boiler Rock, a pinnacle at San Benedicto, is home to "the friendliest manta rays in the world," according to renowned underwater photographer and biologist Norbert Wu. Groups of five or six mantas are common, and they are not shy with divers. Part of the reason for their friendliness may be that they associate this area with fishes that provide a "cleaning

A school of scalloped hammerheads (top); a Pacific manta ray (left), with remoras and orange Clarion angelfish.

Roca Monument (left), Clarion Island; sightings of humpback whales (below) are often made in spring.

ervice." Young wrasses, damselfish, and other cleaner fish groom away dead tissue and parasites from the rays' gills, mouths, and body surfaces.

A close pass by a manta with a wingspan of up to 15 feet (4.5 m) may tempt a diver to grab on for a ride, but dive operators discourage this and so does the required permit from the Mexican government. Resist temptation and enjoy the glorious soaring dance of these huge rays as your bubbles caress their pale, muscled undersides.

EQUIPMENT

This is scuba diving for experienced divers only. A 5 mm wetsuit is recommended. Dive vessels provide weights and tanks and all the comforts of home, but bring reliable, well-tested, gear and a body that's in good physical condition. This is very rigorous diving in remote oceanic waters with strong currents.

SPECIAL FEATURES

It's a long trip to the Revillagi- gedo Islands, but worth it, with the adventurous feel of an oceanic expedition. Watch for

sea birds, dolphins, and whales—visitors in May might spot humpback whales.

As well as other large pelagics, keep an eye out for schooling yellowfin tuna, and solitary toothy wahoos, 6 feet (1.8 m) blue-water predators that look like a cross between a tuna and a barracuda. Clarion Island gives its name to the rare and beautiful Clarion angelfish, a species unique to these Mexican waters. LT

TRAVELER'S NOTES

When to visit *Nov–May only, to avoid stormy Pacific waters and seasonal problems caused by offshore location*
Weather *Tropically warm; often windy*
Water temperature *70–80° F (21–27° C)*
Hazards *Strong currents, rough water, and the remoteness of the location*
Dive logistics *Large, comfortable live-aboards only; book well in advance; boats depart from San Diego, USA, or Cabo San Lucas, which is closer*
Accommodation *Cabo San Lucas offers a range of accommodation from lodges to luxury hotels*
Notes *This is a very rigorous outing, but it pays off in large numbers of approachable manta rays*

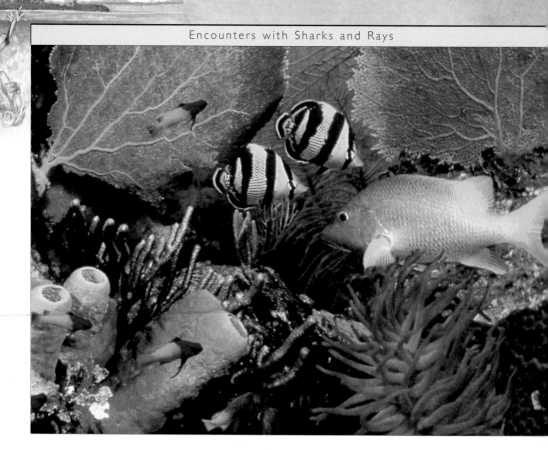

Grand Cayman

Cayman Islands

Three islands make up the Cayman group, islands of dense mangroves and lagoons, powdery beaches set in the Caribbean's aquamarine waters. The steep coral and lime-stone walls of the outer reefs offer grand diving, but the big attraction is inside the barrier reef of Grand Cayman, the opportunity to get close to southern stingrays (see p. 216).

The experience of wading, swimming, snorkeling, or diving with these huge rays is thrilling. They grow to 4 or 5 feet (1.2 or 1.5 m) wide, and have long, whip-like tails, complete with dagger-like stinging spines. They usually spend their days buried in the sand, but Cayman stingrays have overcome their characteristic shyness.

Southern stingrays (above) of the Caymans show off their tails. Vivid orange cup coral (left).

They were originally attracted by scraps from cleaned fish, because fishers and tourists used to clean their catch in the area. People began to feed them regularly, as they came to expect the visits. They are now quite gentle and tame, and seek out interactions with humans, who learn to enjoy the company of these fantastic creatures. Take a deep breath and stretch out on the sandy bottom to watch a ray fly gracefully overhead, its wings and gill slits moving slowly, its extraordinary mouth and

nostrils like something from an unknown world. Or simply watch giggling children frolic with rays as wide across as the children are tall.

Cayman stingrays like to be fed, and have developed the manners of a starved dinner guest. If you don't have a squid or ballyhoo ready, the ray will move on after giving you a firm nudge.

There are two popular sites for "dancing" with rays. The most famous is the original Stingray City, on the west side of the Main Channel, close to Barker's Cay. This site is actually a wide, shallow, sandy channel spotted with coral heads. Visibility is usually excellent

238

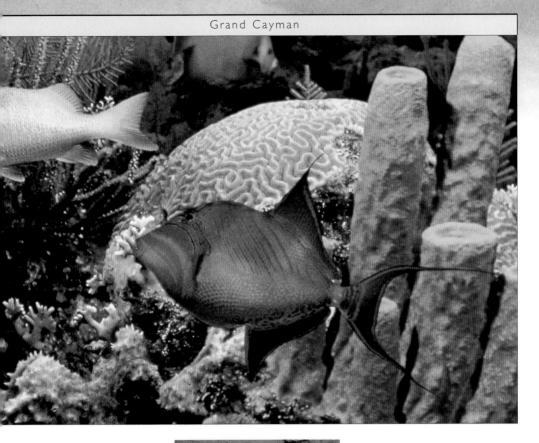

A Caribbean collage (above) of fish, corals, and sea fans. Dancing with the rays (left), an experience unique to the Caymans.

ver the bright white sand. idal currents can cloud the vater, but the rays come so lose you can't miss them. Water depth varies from 6 to feet (1.8 to 2.4 m). Take a oat to Stingray City, then imply drop off into the water nd wade around in sneakers, vith mask and snorkel.

Another good site, known as andbar, lies at the entrance to Rum Point Channel. The water s shallower here, never reaching nore than chest high, and the ea floor is flat and sandy. The onditions are usually ideal.

The main challenge for the photographer is he popularity of the sites. You will have to vie or a prime position with many others. The best vay of ensuring that you get clear views and ood photos of the stingrays is to stay on the

fringe and out of the crowd. The rays will check you out and leave if you offer nothing. By keeping your distance, you will get shots of these friendly rays, with and without people.

EQUIPMENT

You need only a pair of sneakers and a mask to see these southern stingrays. You can also snorkel or dive with them, and well-equipped dive shops rent and sell all kinds of snorkeling and scuba gear.

SPECIAL FEATURES

Not to be missed is diving the Cayman Walls, a system of cliffs, slopes, canyons, and valleys encircling the islands. These are encrusted with massive elkhorn coral, bushy black coral, giant sponges, and delicate soft corals, and are home to vast numbers of fish. Look for small creatures, such as a button-sized flamingo tongue cowrie feeding on a purple sea fan. Eagle and manta rays cruise the outer reef walls in this protected marine park.

TRAVELER'S NOTES

When to visit Year-round; May–Oct offer the best conditions
Weather Influenced by trade winds; cooler Nov–Apr, warmest June–Aug; watch weather patterns for tropical storms July–Sept
Water temperature Summer; 70–80° F (21–27° C); winter, a bit lower
Hazards Clear water and steep walls can tempt divers to dive too deep. Plan your dive and dive your plan.

A recompression chamber is maintained at George Town Hospital, on Grand Cayman Island
Dive logistics Day boats to Stingray City; day boats and live-aboards serve the major Cayman dive spots and other islands; booking essential
Accommodation A full range, from rented houses and condominiums to luxury resorts; booking essential
Notes Holiday periods can be busy

LT **239**

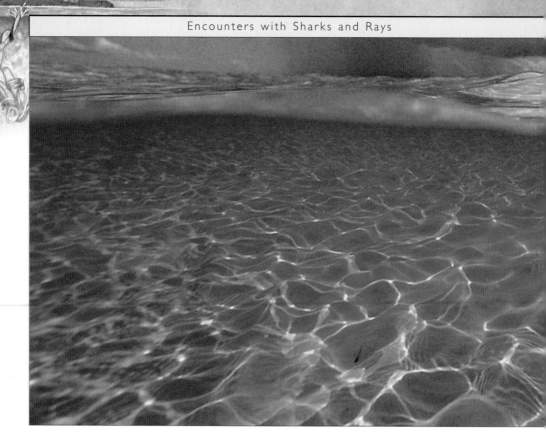

The Bahamas

The Bahamas

The Bahamas consist of about 700 low-lying limestone cays, islands, and islets, only 20 of which are inhabited. Major islands include Grand Bahama, Bimini, Little Abaco, Abaco, Andros, New Providence (Nassau), Eleuthera, the Exumas, Long Island, and Great Inagua. The archipelago extends 600 miles (1,000 km) southeast from Grand Bahama, less than 60 miles (100 km) from the Florida coast of the United States, to Great Inagua Island, within 50 miles (80 km) of Cuba. With such an expanse, the Bahamas offer plenty of variety in dive locations. Every level of diving experience is catered to, and visibility is superb.

Areas that specialize in shark dives are easy to spot from their names: Shark Alley, Shark Arena, Shark Junction, Shark Rodeo. These are open areas to watch free-swimming sharks. Cages are not used. Divers descend 40 to 60 feet (12 to 15 m) to a reef area well known to experienced dive operators. A divemaster joins the group and signals for the boat to lower a bait-filled metal or

A lone sea star in crystalline Bahaman waters (top). Divers look on as Caribbean reef sharks circle in search of food (above).

plastic box. The thawing bait inside soon attracts sharks. Most operators promise from 60 to 100 sharks feeding for an hour.

The old reliables are the graceful but stocky Caribbean reef sharks (see p. 179). These stream in by the dozen, circling the divemaster and bumping each other in their haste and excitement. Sometimes, the bulkier and bossier bull sharks (see p. 174) will move in (these have much larger first dorsal fins set farther forward than the Caribbean reef sharks). Very rarely, a tiger shark (see p. 181) may come by, but big as they are, tiger sharks tend to be shy around bull sharks.

Divemasters are well-trained and careful, but you are in the open with feeding sharks. Follow tips the guides give before the dive; maintain a discreet distance; stay calm and follow instructions

In the excitement of the feeding, speeding sharks, it's easy to get confused and see only the

Divers are guaranteed close-up views of huge stingrays (above) and Caribbean reef sharks (left).

big picture, but it's a pity to miss the details, so here are some ways to slow down the action in your mind and to help you look more closely at this thrilling spectacle. Count the sharks. Can you tell the species apart? Are they all Caribbean reef sharks or are some bulls? How do the smaller sharks react to the larger sharks? Which are males and which females? (Remember to look at the pelvic fins. Adult males have long, paired claspers extending rearward; in immature males the claspers don't yet reach the margins of the pelvic fins.) Look at the gill slits. Are there any parasitic copepods or juvenile shark suckers there? Such careful and disciplined looking will enrich your shark-watching experience, especially in the Bahamas, where dozens of sharks create such a spectacle.

EQUIPMENT

Scuba diving is the only way to see the sharks. Equipment can be purchased or rented in larger centers, such as New Providence. Some gear is available in the more remote areas and on live-aboards, but it's best to bring your own. Weights are always provided. During the winter months, use at least a 3 mm wetsuit as the water cools

considerably. Take your camera. Remember that nothing can be removed from the water.

SPECIAL FEATURES

Bahaman diving is big and superb, with steep walls, blue holes, large sharks. Take time to really look at the small things, too. Inside sponges lurk tiny golden gobies. Green sea grass shelters slender, delicate pipefish. Purple sea fans tolerate elegant flamingo tongue cowries that feed on the sea fans' soft tissue. Reef squid stare into your eyes, flash a colorful neon signal, then dart off. Don't miss these tiny miracles. LT

TRAVELER'S NOTES

When to visit Year-round; summer is hot, but the sea refreshes
Weather Influenced by trade winds; cooler Nov–Apr, warmest June–Sept; watch forecasts for tropical storms
Water temperature From 70–75° F (21–24° C) in Feb to 82–88° F (28–31° C) in Sept

Dive logistics Day trips from Grand Bahamas and New Providence; live-aboards also; booking essential
Accommodation A wide range even on remote cays, from camping and comfortable dive lodges to luxury hotels; Walker Cay on Abaco Island has shore-side accommodation near Shark Rodeo

241

Cocos Island

Costa Rica

Diving Isla del Coco (as the host country of Costa Rica calls it) is a high-seas adventure. A typical dive trip to Cocos begins with a flight to San José, in Costa Rica. An overnight stay in this capital city precedes the morning's three-hour bus trip to the coast, where the dive vessel departs. The 260 mile (420 km) crossing from Puntarenas to Cocos Island, over long, rolling Pacific swells (occasionally shortened to a steep chop), takes 32 to 36 hours. The lush green island, once a favored pirate haunt, is washed by 300 inches (7,620 mm) of rain annually and consequently streams with rivers and waterfalls.

Cocos is famous for what have come to be affectionately called "LLPs" or "Large Legendary Pelagics" ("pelagic" is the oceanographic term for "open sea"). The LLPs of note are silky sharks (see p. 172), scalloped hammerhead sharks (see p. 188), Galapagos sharks (see p. 173), huge manta rays (see p. 223), the occasional whale shark (see p. 151), and schools of tuna and jacks.

Once the vessel arrives, it becomes the mother ship for groups of divers using roving skiffs to reach the diving sites. To justify the long trip to Cocos, most operators stay for a full seven days of diving, with three dives a day. The ship anchors and the skiffs stay mobile to pick up divers surfacing in the strong currents. Deep

diving, fast currents, and plenty of sharks are all thrilling aspects of Cocos diving.

One popular dive spot is a small rock spire on the north side of the island, called Manuelita. This can be a very strenuous and exciting outing. Typically, divers chance the bottom at 140 feet (45 m) to get upward views of schooling scalloped hammerheads shyly aggregating in the murky depths. Currents can be unpredictable, and sometimes flow from different directions at various depths. During your descent to deeper waters, several 12 to 15 foot (3.6 to 4.5 m) manta rays may make lazy barrel rolls close by.

At Punta Ulloa, about 100 whitetip reef sharks are a frequent sight, sharing the area with

Circling sailfish, just some of the large creatures seen at this site.

dozens of large marbled ribbontail rays, 4 to 6 feet (1.2 to 1.8 m) across. Whitetips come in all sizes, alone, in pairs, and in groups. Most divers lose count after the first 50. Dirty Rock and Viking Rock usually offer lots of whitetip reef sharks (see p. 186) and numerous scalloped hammerheads too, congregating in water about 120 feet (35 m) deep. The mix often includes a few large Galapagos sharks.

Scalloped hammerheads are abundant on the deep reefs and spires off Cocos. Scuba divers describe them as generally shy, elusive, and difficult to approach within close range. To get good close-up photographs, divers make use of rebreathers (which produce fewer bubbles and make less noise than other types of breathing apparatus). Hammerheads like to stay in deeper, colder, murkier depths, and you can count on seeing them below 120 feet (35 m), although solitary individuals may wander into shallower depths. Most of the LLPs can be seen while diving no deeper than 100 feet (30 m).

A magnificent manta ray (above) with two remora companions; and countless squirrelfish (left) swimming on a Cocos Island reef.

EQUIPMENT

This is an active dive trip for experienced divers able to handle strong currents and deep diving. At least a 5 mm wetsuit is essential. Bring reliable gear, a good dive computer, and a body in good physical condition. Nitrox and rebreathers are available on some dive boats that serve Cocos, as are weights and tanks.

SPECIAL FEATURES

An attentive diver can find all kinds of interesting fish and invertebrates, but the big fish are the main attraction. If you tire of open-water sharks, drop to a ledge and get close to a whitetip reef shark. There are hundreds in the area. LT

TRAVELER'S NOTES

When to visit *Mar–Sept.*
Weather *Cocos Island can be wet; offshore weather can be windy, with rough seas; trust the skipper to make a safe crossing and find the lee*
Water temperature *Varies with currents; surface can be 80–82° F (27–28° C), with thermoclines dropping to 65–70° F (18–21° C)*
Hazards *Strong currents and deep diving in a remote area*

Dive logistics *Live-aboards for 11-day trips, offering 7 full days of diving; advance bookings with dive charter operators are necessary*
Accommodation *Large, comfortable live-aboard vessels are necessary because of the long ocean passage to Cocos Island; they accommodate between 12 and 22 divers*
Notes *This is a trip for avid and experienced divers only*

Galapagos Islands
Ecuador

Politically part of Ecuador, the Galapagos Islands are a remote evolutionary show-case. This archipelago of volcanic islands only five million years old sits astride the Equator and is washed by three major ocean currents. Many of the species of sharks, rays, and reef fishes that live in Hawaii are also here, but only in the Galapagos can you see marine iguanas and penguins basking on a black lava coastline.

Most visitors to this natural treasury fly first to the Ecuadorean capital of Quito, and then west 600 miles (1,000 km) off the coast of South America to the small Galapagos islet of Baltra. Live-aboard charter vessels pick up visitors and, accompanied by a government-licensed naturalist guide, the adventure begins.

Sharks and rays are seen almost anywhere among the many islands, but the favored spots for shark diving are two remote rock islands, Isla Darwin and Isla Wolf, 100 miles (160 km) north of the main group. Here the water is usually warm and clear, and the under-water fauna is large and abundant. Schools of scalloped hammerheads (see p. 188) number in the hundreds; green sea turtles paddle by in their dozens; eagle rays coast above the bottom; and mantas (see

244 p. 223) barrel-roll in

Crowds of cownose rays (above) gather in sheltered mangrove bays; a marine iguana (below), seen only in the Galapagos Islands.

midwater, then break the surface. Whitetip reef sharks (see p. 186) rest on the bottom beneath overhangs before venturing forth for a meal of reef fish. A large whale shark (see p. 151) may pass through on its way south. The species list is long and thrilling, and includes sea lions, barracudas, fur seals, and false killer whales. Pacific cownose rays, rare in open waters, gather in large numbers in enclosed mangrove bays. Hot spots include Tortuga Negra on Santa Cruz Island and Elizabeth Bay on Isabella Island. Locals call them *raya dorada*, or golden ray, for their rich color.

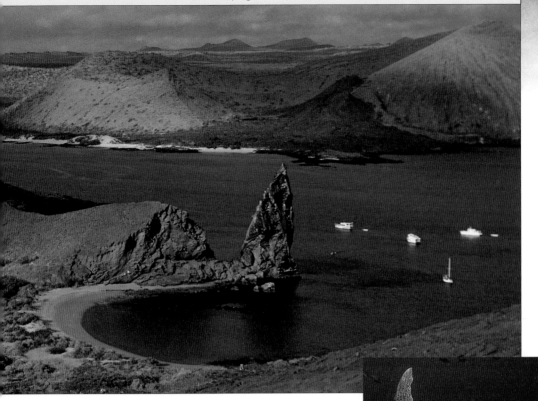

The first Galapagos shark (see p. 173), collected here in 1904, was named in honor of the islands, but they are now known to occur throughout the world's tropical waters. Graceful and strong, they are seen swimming either alone or in small groups, and should be treated with caution. The Galapagos hornshark, unique to the Galapagos and adjacent South American coastline, lives on the bottom or in rocky crevices. Its large black spots contrast with its cream body.

Divers must pay attention to currents and surging swells. Huge boulders on the bottom look stationary but have only recently been moved by the ocean's power. One diver has described the surging swells as leaving divers "feeling like guppies in a washing machine." The shallower rocky reefs are home to fascinating invertebrates and fishes.

EQUIPMENT

You are strongly advised to bring your own dive gear. Booking through a dive-travel operator will ensure that your live-aboard vessel is equipped

Pinnacle Rock (above), Bartolomé Island; a green sea turtle (right).

for scuba diving (many boats here serve only shore excursions, with limited snorkeling). The mix of currents creates a range of surface water temperatures, and there are marked thermoclines. A 5 mm wetsuit with hood is recommended year-round. Galapagos is not recommended for inexperienced divers because of its remoteness and strong currents.

SPECIAL FEATURES

Visiting the Galapagos to see only sharks would be worse than visiting Africa to see only lions. There are thousands of reasons to come here; most of them involve animals and plants, both land and marine. Nowhere else can you see coral reef fishes, penguins, sea lions, marine iguanas, and flightless cormorants all on the same day. At the Charles Darwin Research Station at Puerto Ayora, Santa Cruz Island, conservationists are trying to save the endangered giant tortoise.

Prepare for your visit by reading some good books on Galapagos natural history, including young Charles Darwin's accounts of his adventures. LT 245

TRAVELER'S NOTES

When to visit Year-round, but best in late Feb–May
Weather Equatorial; warm to hot; cooler season from May–Dec; hotter season Jan–May
Water temperature Variable with location and depth; from 65–80° F (18–27° C)
Hazards Blue-water diving with strong currents; this is not for novices
Dive logistics Live-aboards only; book packages through dive operators
Accommodation: Live-aboards only, booking essential; hotels and guesthouses at Puerto Ayora, Santa Cruz Island, but little or no diving support
Notes Be aware of the political climate in Ecuador; check government advisories

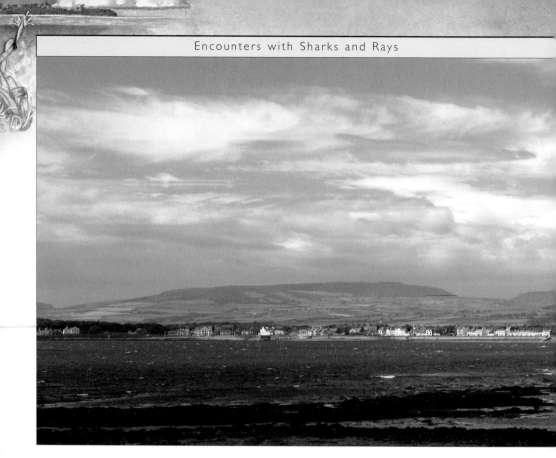

Isle of Man

United Kingdom

A location with good conditions for the reliable sighting of basking sharks (see p. 157) is found at the Isle of Man. In the heart of the Irish Sea, this is a Celtic island of unspoiled beaches, undulating hills, friendly people, and 10,000 years of history. The area is also popular with shark biologists. A research project was begun here during the 1980s, when a sighting and reporting system for basking sharks was organized.

The forbidding walls of Peel Castle (above), on the beachfront. Visitors are offered glimpses of the history of the ancient Celtic race on the island.

The sighting system now extends throughout Britain, and reporters include ferry operators, fishers, divers, charter-boat operators, lighthouse keepers, lifeboat operators, coastguards, and walkers on coastal paths. Information collected over the past 10 years is being used to assess the population and migration patterns of these sharks. They visit British coastal waters from June to early September, but where they go during the winter is as yet unknown.

The basking shark is one of three species known to feed on plankton. Of the other two, the whale shark (see p. 151) is regularly sighted by divers, while the megamouth (see p. 154) is rarely seen by anyone. The basking shark prefers the colder, plankton-rich waters of the temperate zone. Divers can see them in Monterey Bay along the Californian coast of the United States, off the Scottish west coast, and at sites in the Irish Sea. The place to see large gatherings is the Isle of Man.

You can make trips with local dive operators, but a great way to see the "baskers" is to link up with a research group. Biologists welcome volunteers, and organize outings, dedicated to natural history, with Isle of Man travel companies. Headquarters for visitor-volunteers are usually family hotels in the picturesque village of Peel. Venture forth as a volunteer

A small town hugs the coast of the Isle of Man (above). A basking shark (right) feeds in the murky waters of the Irish Sea.

researcher on a scientist's day boat, and listen to the radio crackle with news of shark sightings. Suit up in a warm dry suit as the engine is cut. Slip overboard into the cool blue-green water, sometimes with snorkel gear, sometimes with scuba, and slowly approach the path of a giant plankton feeder.

Perhaps you will be asked to assist in measuring parts of the shark, or to watch for identifying markings or scars. Pause and look into the shark's gaping mouth and see daylight beaming in through the huge gill slits. Visibility is up to 20 feet (6 m), with good opportunities for photographing the sharks.

Basking sharks are still hunted, and researchers estimate that about 5,000 animals are taken each year for their fins. As a result, the species is gradually disappearing from areas in which it was previously common. British biologists are particularly concerned because their observations show that about 95 percent of surface-feeding baskers (the ones killed by hunters) are females. Obviously, the selective removal of this group has severe consequences for a species whose numbers remain unknown.

EQUIPMENT

The water here is cool and sometimes murky, and you will be most comfortable diving in a dry suit. Dives are made from unanchored boats after basking sharks have been encountered.

SPECIAL FEATURES

A local dive operator also offers dive outings to see the rich benthic invertebrate fauna on rocky bottoms off the island. Don't miss the chance to experience the history of the island and its people—few dive vacations offer the Celtic warmth of a local pub. The seals, whales, and fish of these waters are at the heart of many a tale you might coax from your companions after a day in and on the Irish Sea. LT

TRAVELER'S NOTES

When to visit June to early Sept
Weather Cool, maritime climate influenced by the warm Gulf Stream; cool summers, 61–63° F (16–17° C)
Water temperature 61° F (16° C)
Hazards Avoid becoming chilled
Dive logistics Day trips on local dive boats and as volunteers with a

well-organized research project, the Isle of Man Basking Shark Project; look up its website at http://www.isle-of-man. com/interests/shark/index.htm
Accommodation Hotels and guesthouses; special packages can be pre-booked through travel agents and dive operators

Ras Muhammad

Egypt

Anthias, famous for their vivid color, dart about the coral reef (top); and the Red Sea and Sinai Desert (above).

The parched landscape and rugged mountains of the Sinai Peninsula in Egypt seem lifeless. But beneath the sapphire waters of the Red Sea dwells a kaleidoscope of living color. Where the southern tip of the peninsula plunges into the sea at Ras Muhammad, incredible shallow reef flats near the shoreline give way to sheer coral walls disappearing into the depths below. Clouds of Anthias and glassfish shimmer among the undulating soft corals. And shafts of desert sunlight penetrate deep into the blue abyss to reveal patrolling gray reef sharks (see p. 170).

Shark Observatory, one of the best shark sites, is a stretch of the Ras Muhammad coral wall. Divers swimming here will see jacks, tuna, barracuda, and other pelagic marine life traversing the deep ocean. Only the wall is there to orientate you, with the seemingly bottomless sea dropping away beneath you. It is quite common to turn a corner and come face to face with several gray reef sharks searching for food or checking their territory for competitors. It is hard to decide who gets the bigger surprise, as the sharks veer out into the limitless blue and the divers kick toward the security of the wall.

Gray reef sharks are curious and territorial, and pay much attention to divers, circling constantly, coming and going, and sometimes even becoming slightly aggressive. But during December and January, you may have the rare privilege of witnessing groups of 5 to 10 gray reef sharks that completely ignore you because they are engrossed in mating behavior. Females circle in the water off the reef, within 30 feet (10 m) of you. A male will dash into the group, single out a female and pursue her, repeatedly biting her flanks. This action is thought to promote ovulation, and the female's thick skin has evolved to deal with it. While you are unlikely to see an actual coupling, these encounters provide opportunities for unique observations and rare photos or video footage.

Shark Reef and Jolanda Reef are two small submerged reefs just below the surface, a short swim from the tip of the peninsula. On their ocean side, these reefs again drop away in coral

A reef shark patrols its territory (left); and a handsome yellowbar angelfish (below).

walls, and are another favorite area for gray reef sharks and other large pelagic fish. Divers and snorkelers should also look out for oceanic whitetips (see p. 176), scalloped and great hammerheads (see pp. 188–9), and manta rays (see p. 223). This is one of those sites where any manner of species could turn up. And in the shallows at Jolanda Reef, amid the remaining wreckage from the MV *Jolanda*, which sank in 1981, beautiful bluespotted ribbontail rays (see p. 218) cruise among the corals.

Ras Muhammad Marine Park is considered one of the world's best dive sites. With its crystalline waters, shallow reefs, coral walls, and wealth of marine life, it is a site for both divers and snorkelers. Access to the reef is easy. Jeeps, live-aboards, and day boats operate from the nearby resort town of Sharm El Sheikh.

EQUIPMENT

Scuba and snorkeling equipment is available for hire or purchase, but the range is limited and expensive. If possible, bring your own. The Red Sea can be cool for a tropical destination, so 5 mm wetsuits are recommended for the cool season, and 3 mm wetsuits should be worn at other times.

SPECIAL FEATURES

Divers and snorkelers can see a spectacular variety of fish at Ras Muhammad, but two species are worth special attention. Giant Napoleon wrasse are particularly striking and endearing, and are likely to accompany divers in the hope of a handout—a practice discouraged these days. They look at you with big eyes that revolve like ball turrets as they seek out more generous divers. Yellowbar angelfish, unique to Africa and the Red Sea, have markings on their sides in the shape of Africa.

TRAVELER'S NOTES

When to visit Best diving conditions during warm months, June–Oct; more variable visibility and risk of rough seas during cool season, Nov–Feb; sharks and manta rays more in evidence during the mating season, Dec–Feb

Weather Arid desert climate, hot days, cooler at night; very little rain; cool winds during Nov–Feb make days cool and nights quite cold

Water temperature 70–82° F (21–28° C)

Dive logistics Day boats, live-aboards, and shore-based diving from jeeps; pre-booking recommended

Accommodation Excellent range, from budget hotels to five-star resorts

Notes Very cosmopolitan dive travelers; be prepared for many different diving techniques and attitudes. Heed any political advisories for Egypt and neighboring countries

KD **249**

Cape Town
South Africa

To dive with great white sharks is the ultimate thrill for shark watchers. Dyer Island, a two-hour drive east of Cape Town in South Africa, offers the possibility of viewing and cage diving with great whites. This very special area is actually comprised of two islands. The main island, Dyer, is home to a huge marine bird population; the second, Geyser Island, hosts almost 13,000 Cape fur seals. Separating the two islands is a shallow channel, roughly 160 yards (150 m) wide and 550 yards (600 m) long, nicknamed Shark Alley. Great white sharks patrol this protected channel to hunt fur seals, and this area is without doubt one of the great white shark meccas of the world.

Divers are transported the 5 miles (8 km) to the site from nearby Gansbaai by a well-equipped deep-sea cabin cruiser, or in speedboats from Kleinbaai harbor. Once in the channel, most operators deploy a specially designed three-person cage that floats at the surface. Although divers need no fins and don't venture more than 7 feet (2 m) beneath the surface, all are required to have a minimum scuba-diving qualification. Divers can make two to four dives a day, taking

Jackass penguins (above), Dyer Island. Cape fur seals (left) at Geyser Island.

turns in the cage. Non-divers can view the activity from the deck or flying bridge of the boat, as the sharks often break the surface in search of bait. One tour operator uses a shark-viewing capsule, which forms part of the boat and offers a 180 degree view of sharks through thick safety glass.

Although sharks are abundant here (on one occasion, researchers working in the area tagged 18 great whites in 7 hours), chumming assures a good turnout. Sometimes the sharks leap boisterously out of the water, but the typical approach is more subdued. First, there is a slight bulge on the glassy surface caused by the shark's bow wave, then two vortices form behind a large dorsal fin as it breaks the surface and a 15 foot (4.5 m) shark heads straight for the bait.

The Twelve Apostles (above), Cape Town. Note the very pointed nose of the great white shark (left), from around Dyer Island.

regulator, and wetsuit—fins are not needed in the cage. A dry suit is best for these waters, but a 6 mm wetsuit will give minimum protection.

SPECIAL FEATURES

Rocky Dyer Island and the surrounding islands host thousands of Cape fur seals, Cape gannets, jackass penguins, whales, and dolphins. Specially organized dives into the enchanting and balletic world of the Cape fur seal are offered at Seal Island, about 18 miles (30 km) from Cape Town on the Atlantic side of the Cape of Good Hope. Or try whale watching at De Kelders, near Gansbaai, where southern right whales come within 100 feet (30 m) of the rocks. These giant mammals visit this coast to mate and calve from mid June to late December; you can see up to 30 as they come to rub their bodies on the kelp.

The Cape of Good Hope also has more than 50 marked wrecks for divers to explore. **LT**

On deck, watchers are at first mesmerized by the sight, then excited, then eager to jump into the cage and look the creature in the eye. Once in the cool water, the excitement can be elevated by the murky background, out of which the great creatures suddenly emerge. Or, depending on conditions, visibility may permit you to spy a large shark from some distance away.

The high likelihood (claimed to be at least 80 percent) of seeing great white sharks makes Dyer Island and adjacent areas appealing for shark watchers. However, this is also an important research site for the study of the biology and behavior of great whites. Be sure to select a dive operator who cooperates with the ongoing scientific and conservation activities here.

EQUIPMENT

Some dive operators supply all diving equipment but it is always best to provide your own mask,

TRAVELER'S NOTES

When to visit *High season Feb–Sept, almost 100% likelihood of sightings; low season Oct–Jan, about 80% likelihood*
Weather *Usually pleasant, temperate; sometimes stormy and windy, or still and foggy*
Water temperature *58–65° F (14–18° C)*
Dive logistics *Day boats; day trips*

from Cape Town; overnight trips or 10-day excursions based at Gansbaai; book through dive operators
Accommodation *A range of accommodation in Cape Town; guesthouses at Gansbaai, some self-catering*
Notes *During winter (June–Aug), high shark activity, but weather only permits trips to the island one or two days a week*

251

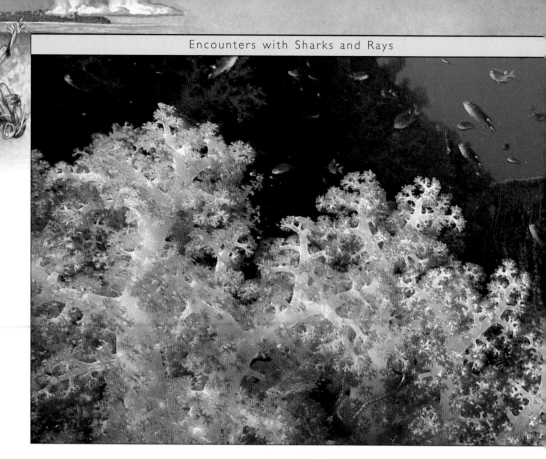

Similan and Surin Islands

Thailand

The Similan and Surin Islands are located in the tropical waters of the Andaman Sea, about 70 miles (110 km) northwest of Phuket, Thailand. Huge granite boulders rise out of the aquamarine water like ancient sentinels. On land, there are quiet bays of talcum-powder sand and groves of palm trees. Underwater, the boulders descend 115 feet (35 m) to the sandy sea floor, with every boulder covered in spectacular soft corals, gorgonians, and sponges. These undersea gardens are home to the zebra, or leopard, shark (see p. 150), one of the most endearing and beautiful of sharks.

Divers descend into the warm, calm waters of the Andaman Sea to discover that visibility is excellent, varying from 40 to 100 feet (12 to 30 m). The gentle currents bring nutrient-rich waters to the area, which help create the spectacular diversity of corals and marine life.

Sooner or later, you will come across a zebra shark resting comfortably on the sand floor among the brilliant reefs. They are gentle and harmless, and will let you come quite close,

occasionally even within a few feet. Scuba divers are more likely than snorkelers to see zebra sharks. It is very pleasant to lie on the sand alongside a shark your own size and feel completely safe. This beautiful creature usually stays quite still and you can see remoras moving about on its skin. Eventually, the shark swims off gracefully through the coral canyons, its long tail moving with an undulating, sensuous, almost hypnotic motion.

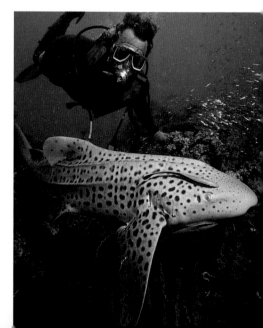

A diver takes a very close look (right) at a zebra shark, also known as a leopard shark. Above, a striking clown triggerfish.

An underwater seascape of soft corals and lionfish (above), and a bay (below), in the Similan Islands.

The islands are visited by live-board dive boats operating out of Phuket. (Day boats also offer tours to reefs and islands just off Phuket, where zebra sharks and plentiful marine life can be viewed.) Today, the nine islands in the Similan group are mostly uninhabited and are designated the Similan Islands National Park, protecting the flora, fauna, and marine life of the area.

EQUIPMENT

Scuba and snorkeling equipment can be hired from local dive centers and resorts in Phuket. Lycra suits will suffice, but divers often find a 2–3 mm wetsuit is better, as sometimes cool water thermoclines occur in this region.

SPECIAL FEATURES

The Similan Islands offer a rare example of differing underwater environments. On the west-facing side, the brilliant colors and unexpected shapes of soft corals and sea fans cover the giant granite boulders. This is in startling contrast to the pastel hues of the hard corals usually populating coral reefs, and which you can find growing prolifically on the eastern side of the islands. Thus, in the same group of islands, you are able to observe the best of both coral worlds.

As well as the tropical fish you'd expect to see—including butterflyfish, angelfish, and orange Anthias—the reefs of the Andaman Sea contain some unique marine life. The Andaman Sea Crown of Thorns sea star, in iridescent red and purple, can be found eating contentedly and blending in perfectly among the soft corals. These sea stars are a necessary part of the reef's delicate ecosystem. The world's most spectacular triggerfish, the clown triggerfish, is also resident, and can be approached.

Between February and May, the lucky visitor may also encounter a whale shark swimming near Richelieu Rock, in the Surin Islands. KD

TRAVELER'S NOTES

When to visit Best during the dry season, Nov–Apr, sunny, calm seas
Weather Tropical climate, 77–89° F (25–31° C)
Water temperature 79–82° F (26–28° C)
Hazards Very wet during the monsoon season in Sept
Dive logistics Snorkeling or scuba diving from live-aboard boats for trips of 2–12 days; pre-booking recommended
Accommodation A wide range of resorts, hotels, and guesthouses is available in Phuket

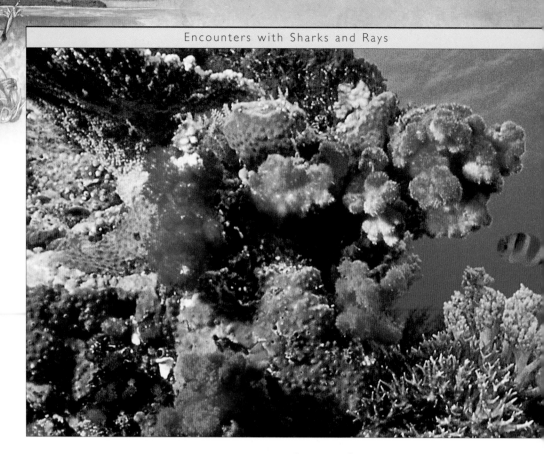

Yap and Palau

Micronesia

The island groups of Yap and Palau in the western-central Pacific, along with the outlying Truk (also known as Chuuk) group 1,000 miles (1,600 km) to the east, offer many dive possibilities. Sharks and rays, the abundant tropical marine life, an extraordinary geography, rich local cultural customs, and arguably the best wreck diving in the world, make Micronesia a favored spot for divers.

Sharks patrol the glorious reef (above). The Seventy Islands National Park (left), Palau.

YAP

Almost unheard of a decade ago, Yap is today renowned for opportunities to get close to manta rays (see p. 223). A combination of tidal barrier-reef channels and favorable weather patterns allows diving with them year-round. Mantas regularly move into two channels for feeding and cleaning. From June through October, locals recommend Goofnuw Channel on the eastern side, where mantas are dispersed over five distinct spots. Milli Channel, on the western side, offers Manta Ridge, where visibility can exceed 100 feet (30 m). Divers cling to the rocks along a ledge about 30 feet (10 m) down while overhead, mantas cruise through the channel.

At both locales, mantas congregate during tidal changes as plankton is funneled out of the lagoon and mangrove areas. Huge volumes of food-rich water are flushed through to the hovering mantas. Some soar directly over your head, close enough to touch, but any such interference with their movements is prohibited.

PALAU

To many divers, Palau is the top tropical dive spot in the world, while to biologists it is a treasury of both land and sea biodiversity. There are more than 100 different dive sites in the vast coral lagoon and adjacent islands, offering diving unlike anywhere else in the world. Thousands of marine species inhabit the region, including manta rays, barracuda, large and small sharks, and an impressive invertebrate fauna ranging from giant clams to the chambered nautilus.

Palau is unusual in having atolls, high volcanic islands, and its famous uplifted limestone rock

islands all in one area.
The edge of the barrier
reef is nearby, with
magnificent wall diving
at such legendary sites
as Blue Corner, a pass
between lagoon and
open sea where sharks
abound. Divers share
swift-flowing tidal waters with gray reef sharks
(see p. 170), blue marlin, manta rays, dogtooth
tuna, and Napoleon wrasse. Nearby Big Dropoff
and New Dropoff are other favorite spots to drift
along in the current, about 30 feet (10 m) down,
with the coral-studded bottom passing below
and gray reef sharks cruising by in search of a meal.

*Longnose hawkfish on a sea fan (left). Some
Palau lakes harbor Mastigias jellyfish (below).*

wetsuits protect divers from
abrasions and stinging plankton,
and on cooler night dives.
Scuba diving is the only way to
see life in the passes, but the
clear waters and glorious reef
development also make for superb snorkeling.

EQUIPMENT

Main centers on all island groups have dive
shops, but it is best to bring your own gear. This
is warm-water diving but Lycra suits and 3 mm

SPECIAL FEATURES

One Micronesian dive experience not to be
missed is the wreck diving at Truk. This cluster
of 12 tiny volcanic islands and many lesser islets,
in a large lagoon girdled by a coral reef, was
heavily bombed during the Second World War.
The great lagoon is now a graveyard for the
wrecks of more than 100 planes and ships, which
provide a dramatic background for diving amid
the richness of Micronesian marine life.

Inland "lakes" on Palau host
large populations of unique
jellyfish. Extensive outer reefs
offer a phenomenal diversity of
invertebrate life, including black
corals, giant sea fans, sponges,
and stony corals, and some
dive operators will
even grant your
wish to swim with
a live chambered
nautilus. LT

255

TRAVELER'S NOTES

When to visit *Year-round; manta
mating season at Yap, Nov–Mar*
Weather *Good year-round; trade winds
May–Nov*
Water temperature *82–86° F
(28–30° C)*
Hazards *Be extra alert when wreck
diving; poisonous spiny trees on Palau*
Dive logistics *Day boats and live-
aboards from all islands; a live-aboard
amphibious airplane based at Palau*

*visits outer islands, including Yap. Pre-
booking before departure essential*
Accommodation *Palau has luxury
hotels; Yap and Truk have comfortable
hotels and lodge accommodation*
Notes *Yap offers best combination
of indigenous culture and dive
sites. Nitrox and rebreathers,
and training in their use,
are available on Yap
and Truk.*

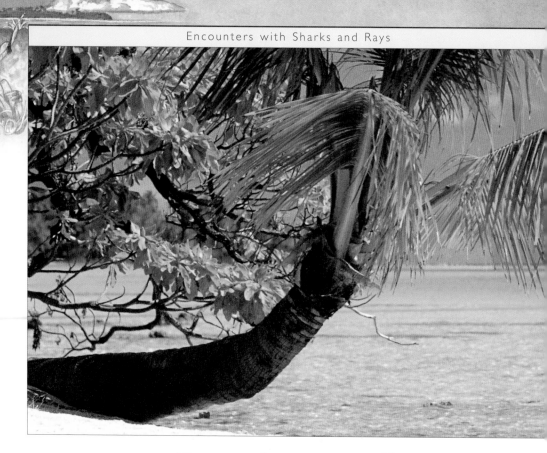

Rangiroa Atoll

French Polynesia

To the northeast and east of Tahiti is a set of low-lying atolls and islands once known as Tuamotu, the Dangerous Archipelago. The largest of the 80 islands is Rangiroa, some 40 miles (65 km) long and 20 miles (32 km) across. In fact, Rangiroa is the second largest atoll in the Pacific Ocean and its lagoon could accommodate the entire island of Tahiti.

Because of its size, Rangiroa offers far more than the usual excitement of a coral atoll. Steep reef faces drop off to almost 1 mile (1,600 m) deep and swift tidal currents rush through the narrow openings in the reef between lagoon and open sea. At full tidal flood, currents can exceed 5 knots, far too fast to swim against. Although tidal extremes are slight (up to 2 feet [60 cm]), the volume of the lagoon and the narrowness of the passes assure fast-flooding currents when the tide turns. It is these passes that offer Rangiroa's most exciting diving, and that includes sharks.

The order for the day is "go with the flow." Dive boats drop divers off inside the lagoon so

The lagoon at Rangiroa Atoll (above) stretches away endlessly. Red brick soldierfish (left) shelter in a pass.

they can swim down 20 to 30 feet (6 to 9 m) and be swept along in the current (to be picked up later out in the open sea by the boat). This is the closest you can get to underwater flying. Imagine soaring from lagoon to open sea while sharing "air space" with a range of sharks, manta rays (see p. 223), and Napoleon fish. Soaring over rich reef growth, you can look down on delicate reef fishes struggling to hold position in the lee of coral heads. You may pass a cave with at least 20 nurse sharks (see p. 149)—perhaps you can return to investigate later.

Outside the reef, where the food-rich and sun-warmed lagoon water meets the water of the open sea, whole food chains are concentrated. Eggs, spawn, larvae, and juveniles born on the reefs of the lagoon meet the predators—sharks, mantas, barracudas, jacks, dogtooth tuna, and mahi-mahi. There is nowhere better to see predation in action than around a flushing pass.

Gray reef sharks (left) wait outside a reef pass for a meal to be served up to them by the tide. A Titan triggerfish (below).

The principal diving spots in Rangiroa include Avatoru Pass, one of the two larger passes at 165 feet (50 m) wide. It is noted for Napoleon fish and manta rays, as well as gray reef sharks (see p. 170), leopard rays, and an impressive fish fauna, especially snappers and jacks.

Tiputa Pass is shorter and not as deep as Avatoru, but it ends with a steep drop-off. Dolphins are often seen in the pass and divers have also reported sailfish and marlin. Drift diving with the current here brings shouts of joy from divers. Photographers are recommended to stay at the end of the group to photograph their buddies in the middle of the action. Gray reef sharks, whitetip reef sharks (see p. 186), and hammerheads guarantee excitement.

Le Failles is a two-hour chartered boat trip across the lagoon. This spectacular dive site on the outer side of the atoll offers rich coral growth and interesting canyons and caves. Shelter in a canyon and see gray reef sharks and perhaps the odd silvertip passing against deep blue space.

EQUIPMENT

Scuba equipment is available for hire, but if possible, bring your own. Lycra bodysuits or 3 mm wetsuits afford protection from scrapes and keep you warm during long exposures.

SPECIAL FEATURES

Every fragment of the land on atolls such as Rangiroa was formed by once-living reef plants and animals. Long ago, volcanic Rangiroa was a high island of black lava, like Hawaii or the Galapagos Islands are now. Slowly, the black rock has sunk into the sea and the living reef has continued to grow. Now, the low-lying atoll is just the tip of a thick limestone cap on a basaltic platform far below. LT

TRAVELER'S NOTES

When to visit *Year-round, but best Nov–Apr*

Weather *Excellent, although trade winds can blow strongly across low-lying atoll; sun protection is always necessary*

Water temperature *Up to 80° F (27° C)*

Dive logistics *Day boats essential to dive the passes; pre-book through local Polynesian dive shops; also live-aboards*

Accommodation *Packages from Tahiti by air include live-aboards or, more frequently, lodge-like shore accommodation; booking essential*

Notes *Pass diving is a challenge for beginning divers, and local guides expect some experience. Plan your trip carefully to permit ample diving between the infrequently scheduled flights*

Mamanuca Islands

Fiji

The gray reef shark (above) can be seen in gangs at some sites on the reefs in Fijian waters. A dazzling male blue ribbon eel (far right).

Fiji consists of more than 300 islands scattered over 42,000 square miles (108,800 sq km) of tropical ocean. The only drawback to visiting the region is selecting a single place to stay. Some visitors choose a live-aboard vessel for 7 to 14 days and visit a number of dive sites. Others settle in a shore-based resort and concentrate on the rich variety at hand.

Closest to the visitor's arrival point at Nadi International Airport is the Mamanuca Group (pronounced Mama-nutha). Within this group, Mana Island is a popular choice. The calm, clear waters surrounding the island are protected by a barrier reef, making it an ideal place to learn how to dive or to refine your skills.

One of the best areas for viewing sharks and rays in the Mamanucas is the Supermarket. With coral walls extending about 100 feet (30 m), it is the home of gray reef sharks (see p. 170) and their calmer relatives, nurse sharks (see p. 149) and whitetip reef sharks (see p. 186). Divers drop to the sandy bottom near the reef wall and watch their Fijian dive guide confer with the sharks. Like a generous host at a social gathering, the guide offers chunks of fish on the end of a pole spear. Sharks are cultural resources in Fiji, and some dive guides belong to Fijian shark clans—their job is to protect sharks from entanglement in fishing gear.

Nearby Gotham City is known for its batfish. This rich reef also has abundant triggerfish, barracuda, surgeonfish, and all manner of schooling basslets and damsels. The underwater ecosystem here is typical of the Mamanucas.

The whole Fiji region is full of sharks, and not only the ubiquitous whitetip. Live-aboard vessels have secret spots to share with visiting divers at locations where local Fijian owners have granted permission for diving adventures. These locales offer large gangs of gray reef sharks, both individual and schooling hammerheads and, near reef drop-offs, large silvertip sharks (see p. 169).

Beds of soft coral (above)—the whole area offers wonderful diving; one of Fiji's many islands (left).

EQUIPMENT

All resorts offer weights and tanks, and many also provide regulators and buoyancy vests. Some resorts rent camera or video gear, but most do not. Lightweight wetsuits, vests, or Lycra dive skins are highly recommended. During warm months, a 3 mm wetsuit is a good idea. For cooler times, a 5 mm wetsuit is better. Scuba diving is necessary to see the sharks, but the reefs can be explored with snorkel gear.

SPECIAL FEATURES

Located far from major population centers, Fiji's reef system has, for the most part, not been over-exploited, overfished, or damaged. A traditional land-tenure system rigorously protects tribal lands and waters from misuse. This system means, too, that divers and dive operators must have the permission of the owner to dive in a specific area, including sites that may seem remote and unused.

The reefs that this system protects and allows divers to enjoy are glorious. Imagine soaring along the top of a vertical wall, blue water below you, passing under black coral trees and colonies of soft corals taller than you are. Or consider returning to the same spot at night to watch the hundreds of glowing firefly-like lights, which are the headlamps of flashlight fish, emerging from their daytime hiding spots to seek a nocturnal meal of plankton. Shallower reef areas are home to hundreds of species of coral and reef fish, including bright blue ribbon eels. The males have elongate yellow nasal tubes that give them a scary, threatening appearance, but they are lovely creatures, and harmless as well. **LT**

TRAVELER'S NOTES

When to visit *Year-round; best weather in dry season (May–Oct)*
Weather *Daytime temperatures 68–86° F (20–30° C); mild, dry May–Oct; wetter, warmer Nov–Apr (wet season); highest rainfall and humidity in Jan–Feb; east–southwest trade wind*
Water temperature *Temperature 80–83° F (27–28° C) from Nov–Apr; 78–80° F (25–26° C) May–Oct*
Hazards *Stonefish and medusae*
Dive logistics *Snorkeling and scuba*
diving from the shore, live-aboards or day boats; booking essential
Accommodation
There is a full range of accommodation, from thatched fales to comfortable lodges and resorts; some resorts cater exclusively to the needs of divers
Notes *Fiji is friendly and hospitable and has a rich culture*

259

Valerie's Reef

Papua New Guinea

The tropical waters and string of islands forming the Bismarck Archipelago lie to the north of the spectacular mountainous mainland of Papua New Guinea. Among the islands of the New Hanover group in the archipelago, hundreds of coral reefs rise to within 30 feet (10 m) of the surface. One of these, Valerie's Reef, is home to a large group of silvertip sharks (see p. 169).

Valerie's Reef had no name until the recent discovery of the silvertips. It was named in honor of Valerie Taylor (see p. 77), renowned shark authority and under-water photographer. Silvertip sharks are the most impressive and largest of the reef shark family, and Valerie's

Reef has become the most famous site in the world for guaranteed silvertip shark encounters.

Between 9 and 12 large, female silvertips, ranging in size from 6½–10 feet (2–3 m), live around the reef area. They congregate on the reef as soon as a dive boat appears—they were once fed regularly from visiting dive boats and still associate the sound of the motor with food. It can be a little daunting at first to look into the water and see several sharks waiting for you. But these large, powerful creatures are well behaved. They are waiting to accompany you on what is, initially, a heart-stopping swim to the reef. Once there, you feel less vulnerable, and are able to watch the sharks patrolling their habitat. They cruise slowly and gracefully through the clear, warm water, circling over the beautiful coral gardens and making occasional inquisitive approaches. The silvertips seem to have a social order, and the smaller sharks respect the larger ones.

Divers (above) admire a gorgonian coral. The lacy scorpionfish (left) can inflict a painful wound with its spines.

These sharks are calm and confident, and do not harass divers. However, silvertip sharks can be dangerous if overstimulated or provoked. Swim beneath the surface to avoid splashing. Always wear dark gloves and keep your hands

A female silvertip shark (above) patrols the reef; and (left) a local fishing canoe.

close to your body to avoid them being mistaken for fish scraps. Dive in buddy teams and give yourself time to get used to the sharks' behavior. Always make your own way back to the live-aboard at the end of a dive rather than signal for a pick-up by the tender. These are small boats with outboards, and the sound of the motor starting excites the sharks, which then dash toward the boat.

The best access to the reef is by live-aboards operating out of Kavieng, on New Ireland, but it is also within range of day boats. The silvertips are accustomed to divers, and photographers will have opportunities for close-ups, wide angles, and even to capture multiple sharks in one shot.

EQUIPMENT
Scuba diving is recommended rather than snorkeling. The sharks perceive scuba divers as just another predator. But with so many sharks competing for food at one reef, a snorkeler might attract the wrong kind of attention. You will need normal scuba equipment. The water is very warm so a 2–3 mm wetsuit will be quite adequate for all dives.

SPECIAL FEATURES
Papua New Guinea is regarded as one of the top 10 dive locations in the world, and it's easy to get distracted from shark and ray encounters. The diversity of corals and fish and the variety of ship and plane wrecks from the Second World War are astounding. The region is also famous for some very rare and bizarre marine species. These include the lacy scorpionfish, an ornately patterned scorpionfish, and the flamboyant cuttlefish, a small, beautiful creature that lays its eggs inside sunken coconuts. *Octopus horridus* is often seen in these waters—no one has yet discovered if it is poisonous or not.

Papua New Guinea also has some of the world's most diverse, unique, and unspoilt indigenous cultures. The people of the Gazelle Peninsula near Kavieng are famous for their fire dancing, so consider a stopover on the way. KD

TRAVELER'S NOTES

When to visit All year round
Weather Very warm, tropical; no distinct wet season
Water temperature 79–82° F (26–28° C)
Hazards Malaria
Dive logistics Scuba diving from day boats or live-aboards; the snorkeling is excellent, but is not recommended where there are sharks
Accommodation Hotels in Kavieng; excellent live-aboards, booking essential
Notes Heed security advisories, particularly in the capital, Port Moresby

Ningaloo Reef

Australia

In the remote far north of Western Australia, 161 miles (260 km) of coral fringing reef are washed by the tropical waters of the Indian Ocean. The reef is protected as Ningaloo Reef Marine Park. Whale sharks (see p. 151), the gentle giants of the oceans, congregate here in large numbers each year from late March to early May.

The higher temperatures of the Indian Ocean in summer and the full moons in March and April trigger a mass explosion of synchronized spawning of the corals of Ningaloo Reef. The coral spawning coincides with the congregation and mass spawning of millions of other marine life forms. This extraordinary phenomenon provides a bountiful food supply, which is what attracts the large numbers of whale sharks to Ningaloo Reef.

The possibility of diving with these huge, slow-moving sharks brings thousands of divers and snorkelers from around the world. Nothing prepares you for the enormous size of one of these creatures, and the feeling of awe as it materializes out of the blue haze, its massive head filling the view, its tiny eye watching. Divers can

A whale shark (above) dwarfs a snorkeler. The vast Ningaloo Reef Marine Park (left).

swim alongside the shark as it moves majestically through the ocean, occasionally opening its cavernous mouth to feed, always accompanied by an entourage of juvenile jacks, pilotfish, cobia, and a mass of remoras. Caution is necessary as the wide sweep of the shark's powerful tail can easily stun or disable a diver.

There are numerous dive tours operating out of Exmouth, the gateway to Ningaloo Reef. A spotter aircraft works with the dive boats to help locate the sharks. Fast and maneuverable, the dive boats repeatedly drop divers off ahead of the shark, picking them up when the shark has moved on, then overtaking the shark to drop them off in front again. Whale sharks may swim slowly, but trying to keep up with them is still tiring. Snorkeling is easier than diving. The sharks spend a great deal of time on the surface, and a snorkeler can swim faster and operate from the dive boat more comfortably than a scuba diver.

Strict rules have been introduced to protect the whale sharks from stress during the season.

There is a total
ban on divers
touching or riding
the sharks, and there
are limits on the number of
divers in the water with a shark at any one time
and on the amount of time they can spend with
it. Strobes (flash units) are not allowed. Tour
operators must have a permit and boats have a
restricted approach zone of 100 feet (30 m).

*Oval butterflyfish (above left) thrive on the reef; and corals
caught in the act of spawning (above right), an annual event.*

EQUIPMENT

Snorkeling is an ideal way to see whale sharks.
Consider using a high-tech snorkel and high-
performance fins, because you will do a lot of
swimming in seas that vary from flat to choppy if
the wind picks up. A full-length Lycra suit is also
a good idea; it will protect you from marine
stingers (nothing deadly) and sunburn.

SPECIAL FEATURES

Ningaloo Reef does not have world-class coral
but it does boast a wealth of marine life. A dive
at the Navy Wharf at Exmouth is also very

rewarding—the rich artificial reef has an
incredible diversity of fish species, including
resident tasselled wobbegong sharks (see p. 146).

CAPE RANGE NATIONAL PARK

Ningaloo Reef Marine Park is parallel to the
rugged landscape of North-West Cape and the
Cape Range National Park. It was formed when
ancient beds of rock were pushed up from the
ocean floor between 1.6 and 5 million years ago.
The rocks contain fossils of the huge teeth of the
prehistoric shark *Carcharodon megalodon*. This
awesome predator, estimated
to measure more than 40 feet
(12 m), is believed to be an
extinct relative of the great
white shark. It could once be
found throughout the oceans
of the world. Local rangers and
guides conduct tours to these
extraordinary fossil sites. KD

TRAVELER'S NOTES

When to visit *Late Mar to early May*
Weather *Warm, tropical, very sunny;
afternoon sea breezes*
Water temperature *73–79° F
(23–26° C)*
Hazards *Occasional cyclones*
Dive logistics *Snorkeling or scuba
diving from day boats; some live-aboard*

boats, but not essential for good access
Accommodation *Hotels, karavans,
and camp sites in Exmouth*
Notes *Avoid operators without spotter
planes. Book your dive tours and
accommodation before departure.
Plan a minimum of five day's diving to
guarantee many encounters*

Neptune Islands

Australia

Neptune Islands are situated in the cold, often inhospitable waters of the Great Australian Bight, off the southern coast of Australia. The remote, rocky islands, accessible only by boat from Port Lincoln, South Australia, are home to thousands of Australian sea lions and New Zealand fur seals. It is the abundance of this important food source that draws the great white sharks (see p. 158).

These islands are regarded as the world's best location for encounters with this awesome predator. And although great whites can be found here year-round, January to May is the best time to visit. This is when the seals and sea lions breed, and you avoid the fierce winter weather.

The logistics of organizing a great white shark trip are considerable. A large live-aboard dive boat is required and excursions of at least one to two weeks are recommended. A crew works day and night to spread chum (a mix of products used to attract sharks) across many miles of ocean in the hope that a great white shark will be lured to the boat.

The first sign of this huge fish is its dark shadow beneath the water, with perhaps a dorsal fin

emerging briefly. Large shark cages made of aluminum are lowered into the water and the divers enter the cages via the wide trapdoor in the roof. Jumping from the safety of the dive boat into the cage is frightening, initially. You feel that the walls are too close and the windows too large, and stare into the steel-blue void trying to locate the shark before it sneaks up on you. It materializes slowly, purposefully, swimming straight up to the cage. It will "taste-test" the bars, boat, and anything else it finds to see if it is edible. Then the animal will disappear into the void, only to startle you by suddenly reappearing from another, unexpected direction, to inspect you again and re-test the cage.

Eventually, you will become more used to the unpredictable nature of its presence, and realize that the shark is simply there for the tuna and other chum. It can be very cautious at times, but bold when it wants to feed. Its extraordinary hunting techniques, streamlined beauty, and power command fascination and respect. And it is possible to take excellent photos

A New Zealand fur seal basks on the rocky shoreline of one of the Neptune Islands.

A great white shark (above) approaches the shark cage. Australian sea lions (left) at play.

or video footage of great whites, both underwater and above water, as it is the only shark that will put its head out of the water and look at you.

If divers are very experienced, some operators will lower the cage to the ocean floor so the great whites can be viewed approaching along the floor or circling overhead. The recent advent of the shark POD (see p. 77) has resulted in successful encounters without a cage, up until now considered out of the question.

Many great white shark trips are undertaken for scientific study and to film educational documentaries. Shark and ray enthusiasts are encouraged to participate to help offset the huge costs and to develop their understanding of and support for the protection of these sharks.

The great white shark is comparatively rare and its numbers are believed to be declining. Sightings cannot be guaranteed. But a trip to the rugged Neptune Islands is a rare opportunity to explore a remote wilderness and to learn more

about this impressive creature. To have good encounters with the sharks is a very lucky bonus.

EQUIPMENT

Either scuba diving or snorkeling in the shark cage is possible. Some operators provide long hoses that are attached to large onboard air cylinders to allow ease of movement. Extra-heavy weight belts are supplied, and because dive fins are not worn inside the cage, good dive boots are essential. Full-length 5 mm wetsuits with hoods are recommended; however, a dry suit might be preferable as you could be spending long hours in cold water.

SPECIAL FEATURES

Dives with the fur seals and Australian sea lions are organized away from the chum area or at other islands. Shore excursions to see the seal colonies, busy with newborn pups, are a delight. And it is impossible not to be entranced by the sea lions, particularly when these rare and beautiful blond creatures play. The lucky diver might also see the bizarre leafy sea dragon, unique to southern Australia. KD

TRAVELER'S NOTES

When to visit Jan–May
Weather Temperate; very changeable from calm and hot to windy and cold; calm to quite rough seas
Water temperature 61–66° F (16–19° C)
Hazards Seals can be aggressive

when ashore; seek local advice
Dive logistics Cage diving with snorkel or scuba gear from live-aboard dive boats, trips from 3–16 days; pre-booking essential
Notes No guarantees; on average, one trip in three is successful

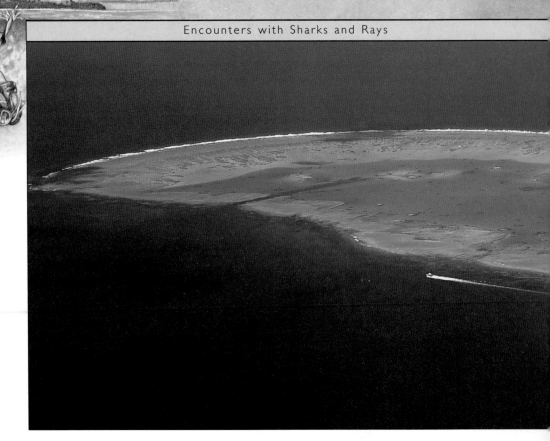

Great Barrier Reef

Australia

The Great Barrier Reef, off Australia's northeast coast, is the only living thing that can be seen from space. Much of the 1,430 miles (2,300 km) of reef is protected as the Great Barrier Reef Marine Park. It is the pristine home to an extraordinary diversity of coral, invertebrates, and fish—including sharks and rays.

The problem for the enthusiast who wants to see sharks and rays is the enormous choice of sites here. Many dive boats also visit the oceanic reefs of the Coral Sea, 115 miles (185 km) offshore. Some sites virtually guarantee encounters.

Lady Elliot Island is a small coral cay at the southern end of the Great Barrier Reef. It has one of the few resorts actually out on the reef. A dive at Lady Elliot is wonderfully simple. Divers or snorkelers

The giant clam (left), with its blue-green mantle, needs strong sunlight to grow. Yellow soft corals (above) put on a show for divers.

wade into the water to explore the fringing coral reef surrounding the island. The reef descends into 65 feet (20 m) of water, where you will find zebra sharks—also known as leopard sharks (see p. 150)—usually resting on the sand near large coral heads. Manta rays (see p. 223) can arrive at any time, flying overhead like huge spaceships. The hardest decision for the diver is whether to look up for mantas, down for zebra sharks, or to be distracted by fish, turtles, and coral gardens.

Another extraordinary site—for scuba divers only—is Scuba Zoo at Flinders Reef, out in the Coral Sea. A giant shark cage has been permanently stationed here at a depth of 65 feet (20 m). As soon as the dive boat moors, up to 40 reef sharks appear, cruising the deep reef slope beyond the cage. Divers can feel very vulnerable as they swim down through open water to the cage, but the sharks keep their distance, moving about on the bottom like gray shadows. They are mostly gray reef sharks (see p. 170), with some whitetip reef sharks (see p. 186) and silvertip sharks (see p. 169).

Once everyone is inside the cage, a dive-master hauls down a container of fish. When the

Looking down over Lady Musgrave Island (above), in the Bunker Group. Gray reef sharks (left).

A 5 mm suit is recommended for southern Queensland. Bring your own equipment if you are planning a live-aboard excursion, as equipment is generally not available for hire on board.

lid of the container is pulled off and the food is released, dozens of sharks descend on the bait, tearing it apart in a feeding frenzy. They are so close to the cage, you can hear their teeth crunching on bone. Within minutes, the baits are entirely consumed and it is all over. The sharks continue to dash about, excited by the odor of blood and the tiny pieces of fish meat floating in the current. Divers remain in the cage until the current has dispersed all food remnants and the sharks have resumed their normal, relaxed behavior. Only then is it safe to leave the cage and move among the sharks, taking photos in less restricted circumstances.

If your air supply is low because of all the excitement, you can head back to the boat. The sharks will patrol the area and make close passes to inspect divers before dispersing into the deep blue void again.

EQUIPMENT

A one-piece, 2–3 mm wetsuit will suffice in the warmer waters of northern Queensland.

SPECIAL FEATURES

The incredible diversity of marine life and the grandeur of the reef are impossible to ignore. Some unique creatures include sea snakes, stonefish, giant clams, and spider shells. During the Australian spring, turtles come ashore to lay eggs, and the mass, synchronized coral-spawning of the Great Barrier Reef occurs for several nights after the October and November full moons. At the Cod Hole off Lizard Island, up to 20 giant potato cod regularly interact with divers. KD

TRAVELER'S NOTES

When to visit Good conditions almost year-round; occasional strong winds; cyclone season late Dec–Apr

Weather Warm to very hot, tropical conditions; consistently dry, except during the cyclone, or wet, season

Water temperature 72° F (22° C) in southern Queensland to 82° F (28° C) in northern Queensland; cooler June–Aug

Hazards Venomous animals include the lionfish, stonefish, sea snakes, box jellyfish (or sea wasp), cone shell, and blue-ring octopus. None is aggressive and accidents are rare, but learn to identify these species and their behavior

Dive logistics Day boats (be prepared for long trips to get out to the reef); live-aboards, trips of 4–8 nights, mostly from Cairns and Townsville, pre-booking recommended

Accommodation From camping to five-star resorts ashore or on coastal islands; also on several islands out on the reef; pre-booking recommended

Notes Shark feeding not permitted inside the Marine Park

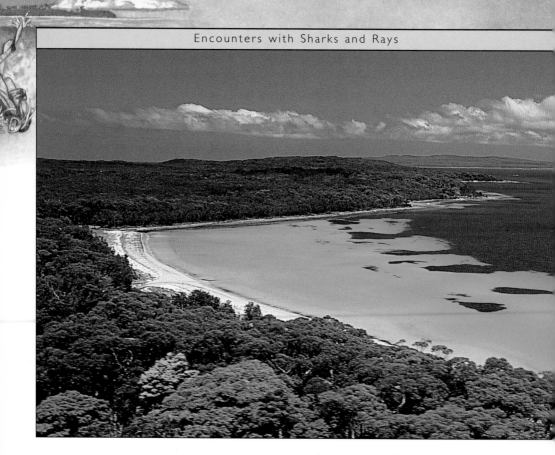

New South Wales

Australia

The coast of New South Wales, on the eastern seaboard of Australia, is dotted with towns and cities, lined by sandstone cliffs and beaches, and edged by the temperate waters of the Tasman Sea. Here, there are underwater worlds to explore with a diverse range of sharks and rays.

SEAL ROCKS

Just over 185 miles (300 km) north of Sydney, Seal Rocks is renowned for its large schools of resident sand tiger sharks (see p. 152), also known as gray nurse or spotted raggedtooth sharks. They congregate in packs of 5 to 20, and occasionally even 40, around the spectacular underwater rock formations, in the large reef gutters and sea caves.

Sand tiger sharks have a fearsome appearance, with their long, hooked teeth perpetually protruding from their mouths. However, these are gentle, fish-eating animals that will not attack. They generally have no fear of small groups of divers, and scuba divers can swim safely among them, observing their characteristic circling pattern and photographing them at very

Jervis Bay (above), on the east coast of Australia. The restless sand tiger shark (left), which feeds only at night.

close range. Sometimes, they make a sudden, determined approach and the diver has to get out of the way fast. It is quite a thrill to lie on the sea floor and watch that mouth and those teeth pass only a few feet above your head. A careful search in the gutters on the sea floor will often reveal sand tiger shark teeth, shed during mating or feeding.

Day trips from Forster are offered year-round by several dive operators. Although larger congregations occur between November and July, there are always sand tiger sharks to be seen.

JERVIS BAY

Jervis Bay, a sheltered bay about 115 miles (180 km) south of Sydney, features a rugged sandstone coastline, pure white beaches, and protected coves. Each year during August and September, thousands of Port Jackson sharks (see p. 143) converge on this area to mate and lay their bizarre, spiral-shaped egg cases. Divers

Swimming in the midst of a mating group of Port Jackson sharks (above); and the extraordinary spiral egg case (left) of the Port Jackson shark.

exploring the bay from boats will come across large groups of exhausted females lying about in gutters, caves, and hollows on the reef. Single males patrol the reef, probably looking for receptive females.

During November and December, most of the adult sharks disperse. But a careful search of the bay's sand flats will reveal newly hatched Port Jackson sharks, each a perfect replica of its parents, except for its fins, which seem too large for its tiny body.

These sand flats are covered with many species of algae, sponges, invertebrates, and sea pens—an ideal habitat for angelsharks, eastern fiddler rays, and shorttailed electric rays (see p. 210). Electric rays can give an unwary diver a severe shock if they are touched or harassed.

Jervis Bay also has huge sea caves and giant boulder reefs covered in vividly colored sponge gardens. Spotted and ornate wobbegongs—most unusual sharks with beautifully decorated skin (see p. 147)—lie perfectly camouflaged among the sponges, waiting for passing prey. Divers

have occasionally been bitten simply because they disturbed a wobbegong they had not seen.

EQUIPMENT
Use snorkeling equipment in the shallow coves and foreshores of Jervis Bay to see mating Port Jacksons and also skates, but scuba diving is recommended at all other sites. In summer, wear a one-piece 5 mm wetsuit; in winter, use a two-piece 5 mm wetsuit.

SPECIAL FEATURES
Around Jervis Bay lives the biggest member of the cuttlefish family, the giant Australian cuttlefish. More than 3⅓ feet (1 m) long, its colors change with its emotions. It will try to bluff by raising its large tentacles if you seem to be a competitor for its territory, but as long as you only observe, encounters are usually spectacular stand-offs. Also look out for the weedy sea dragon, with its delicate coloring. KD

TRAVELER'S NOTES
When to visit Year-round
Weather Warm Oct–Mar, cool Apr–Sept; no distinct rainy season; unpredictable
Water temperature 57–70° F (14–21° C)
Hazards Rough seas during periods of strong offshore winds
Dive logistics Forster: day boats only; Jervis Bay: live-aboards or day boats, both offering equally good access
Accommodation Good-quality hotels, guesthouses, camping, and caravan sites at all locations
Notes An excellent region for self-driving, camping, and exploring a diverse range of dive locations and sighting the plentiful marine species

Lord Howe Island

Australia

Tiny Lord Howe Island stands alone in the Tasman Sea, about 745 miles (1,200 km) north-east of Sydney, Australia. It is an extinct volcano, its peaks rising sheer from sapphire blue subtropical waters that support coral reefs. These corals have formed a beautiful shallow lagoon, home to giant black stingrays and Galapagos sharks (see p. 173), as well as many indigenous species of fish.

At Comet's Hole, groups of giant black sting-rays rest, camouflaged in the sand. When they move, it is an extraordinary sight. They rise languidly off the sea floor, creating a cloud with the sand that was covering them. It streams off their bodies and trails in their wake. Divers and snorkelers can move among the resting rays or follow those that are swimming. Sometimes, you will see a ray pause close to the bottom and use a flapping motion to disturb the sand and uncover prey, which it blankets with its wide body so the prey cannot escape. It then maneuvers itself until its mouth has located the prey.

If you get too close to a ray, it will raise its thick tail high above its back like a lance and make aggressive stabbing movements into the water column. There is no doubt as to the outcome should you venture any closer.

The flamboyant Spanish dancer (left), a nudibranch, or sea slug. The view of Lord Howe Island (below) from Mount Eliza.

Young Galapagos sharks enter the lagoon with the rising tide and leave before it falls. The best place to see them is at Erscott's Hole. Because this area is also full of beautiful fish and coral, divers may be concentrating on something else when the sharks first appear. They are fast, frisky, and a little wary, and usually circle on the edge of visibility before dashing in to take a close look at you. A small, sleek shark speeding toward you is bound to get the adrenalin going, but they are simply curious.

A Galapagos shark (above) circles inside the coral lagoon. The rare Lord Howe Island woodhen (left); and a giant black stingray (far left).

Occasionally, divemasters add a little bait to the water to encourage the sharks to come closer, and up to a dozen usually appear. They will continually come up to investigate divers—several sharks approaching at once can be very exciting. If one gets too insistent, a light tap on the nose will result in its rapid departure, leaving you in awe of its speed and streamlined design.

The lagoon is an excellent site for snorkelers and scuba-diving beginners. Even non-divers can view this pristine world from the glass-bottom boats that make daily excursions into the lagoon. Scuba divers can use a fast day boat for single dives in the lagoon or for offshore dives on the reefs surrounding the island.

EQUIPMENT

Basic snorkeling equipment will suffice and is available for hire, as is scuba equipment. Scuba divers should use either a 3 mm or a 5 mm wetsuit. Be sure to bring a compact waterproof dive light for night dives.

SPECIAL FEATURES

Lord Howe Island is a World Heritage Area. Its isolation and its position at the crossroads of the Tasman and Coral Seas have encouraged the development of many unique and endemic species of animal, bird, and marine life. It is an important bird sanctuary, providing a haven for many nesting seabirds, as well as the Lord Howe Island woodhen, one of the world's rarest birds. This flightless creature was almost extinct, but a rescue breeding program has seen its numbers increase gradually.

Divers and snorkelers should also seek out some of the unique fish species, including the doubleheaded wrasse, the wide-band anemonefish, and the Spanish dancer, a red and white nudibranch that resembles the ruffles on a flamenco dancer's dress. KD

TRAVELER'S NOTES

When to visit *Nov–May*

Weather *Cool, tropical summer, Oct–May; occasional unpredictable strong winds and regular rainfall; no distinct wet season*

Water temperature *68–75° F (20–24° C)*

Hazards *The banded scalyfin, a very aggressive small fish, has a bite that can draw blood; swim away from its territory*

Dive logistics *Glass-bottom boats and day boats for snorkeling or scuba diving; pre-book during peak season, Dec–Jan*

Accommodation *Small resorts and guesthouses, fully catered or self-catering; pre-book Dec–Jan*

Notes *Only 400 tourists are allowed on the island at one time. Pack a waterproof coat for rainy spells and a warm jacket for cool evenings*